Fire from the Mountain

By the same author

Last Resorts: The Cost of Tourism in the Caribbean
The Gardens of Dominica (with Anne Jno Baptiste)
Home Again: Stories of Migration and Return (co-compiled with Celia Sorhaindo)
Introduction to The Ethical Travel Guide

Fire from the Mountain

THE TRAGEDY OF MONSERRAT AND THE BETRAYAL OF ITS PEOPLE

Polly Pattullo

PAPILLOTE PRESS

First published in the UK by Constable & Robinson in 2000
This edition published by Papillote Press in 2012
23 Rozel Road
London SW4 0EY, UK

www.papillotepress.co.uk
www.papillotepress.co.uk/facebook

ISBN 978 0 9571187 0 6

A CIP catalogue record for this book is available from the British Library.

Printed in the UK by Short Run Press Ltd, Exeter, UK

Contents

List of Illustrations

Waiting for the ferry (Mary Walters)
Surviving the ash (Rex Features)
A scientist at work (S. Loughlin, British Geological Survey)
David Brandt (Universal Pictorial)
Frank Savage (Foreign and Commonwealth Office)
A defiant T-shirt (Mary Walters)
New post-volcano housing (Polly Pattullo)

Acknowledgements

I have a small green shamrock in my passport: the stamp for Montserrat, with the day of arrival 23.6.97 written by hand and stamped 'valid until' 26.6.97. Two days later the airport was closed by the most devastating and destructive pyroclastic flow of all: nineteen Montserratians died that day. I had gone to Montserrat from nearby Dominica – another island where the air is full of sulphur and there are occasional rockings in the night, for in the eastern Caribbean one is always close to volcanic life. I left Montserrat not by air but in a rolling boat that took three hours to reach Antigua.

Those disaster days on Montserrat were both shocking and inspiring. Such a contradiction prompted me to try and explore – as an outsider – what had happened to Montserrat and its people during the years of the volcano crisis. The result is this book – it is not a chronological narrative, but I hope it tells a coherent story.

The more I learned about Montserrat's volcano years and the more stories I heard, the more complex the issues became. I felt that what Montserratians had experienced was important not just to the island itself, but to the Caribbean and beyond – especially to the United Kingdom, where many decisions about Montserrat (as an Overseas Territory) are still made and where many Montserratians and those of Montserratian ancestry now live. What I have tried to do is to examine some of the central issues and to allow some of the local voices to be heard. I hope I heard them well.

In Montserrat, on all my visits, and despite the extraordinary circumstances of life under the volcano, my thanks go to many people for their knowledge, help, friendship, large and small kindnesses. In particular, I am indebted to Bennette Roach, Carol and Cedric Osborne, John Ryner, Susan Edgecombe, Clover and David Lee, Don Romeo, Basil Lee, Rose Willock; and to the scientists of the Montserrat Volcano Observatory, especially William Aspinall, Paul Cole, Sue Loughlin, Gill Norton and Richard Robertson. And thanks to Candia Williams in Antigua.

In the United Kingdom, I am grateful to members and friends of the Montserratian community who gave their time, shared their experiences and helped me to understand the volcano crisis. In particular, my thanks to Janice Panton, John Wells and David Taylor who all advised on the manuscript and helped in many other ways; also to Danny Daley of MOPPA, Gabriel Parsons, Jennette Arnold, Esther Wason, Simon Maty, Gertrude Shotte, Glenn Lewis, John and Maeve Kennedy, Jasmine Huggins, Philip Nanton, Gloria and Richard Pope, John and Clodagh Maher-Loughnan. Thanks, too, to Tony Glaser and the Electronic Evergreen.

My appreciation goes to all those who feature in this book, including those who felt unable to give their names, hoping that in quoting you I have not misrepresented your views.

To my excellent copy editor, Ruth Thackeray, and publisher Carol O'Brien, many thanks for your judicious thoughts, helpful suggestions, enthusiasm and goodwill. And also to Annie Davies, Lennox Honychurch and Peter Prince, old friends who pored over all or parts of the manuscript in its early days.

Chronology

The list below outlines the history of Montserrat (focusing on the story of the volcano since 1995) and the main volcanoes and earthquakes in the Lesser Antilles. All events refer to Montserrat unless otherwise stated.

c. 17,000 BC	Major pyroclastic flows from the Soufrière Hills
c. 500 BC–AD300	Settlement by Saladoid Amerindians
1493	Christopher Columbus sights and names the island (known by the Amerindians as Alliouagana) Santa Maria de Monserrate on 11 November during his second voyage
c. 1611–65	Eruption of Castle Peak
1625	Sir Thomas Warner, the first governor of St Kitts, receives a royal patent from Charles I giving him permission to colonise Montserrat
1632	Settlement by dissident Irish Catholics from St Kitts
1660s	African slaves brought to Montserrat in growing numbers
1667	Hurricane

1672	Christmas Day earthquake
1692	Eruption of Mount Misery, St Kitts
1694	Eruption of La Soufrière, Guadeloupe
1766	Eruption in St Lucia
1768	St Patrick's Day slave rebellion
1782	France captures Montserrat
1783	Treaty of Versailles returns Montserrat to Britain
1812	Eruption of La Soufrière, St Vincent
1833	Abolition of Slavery Act
1843	Earthquake in Guadeloupe, 5000 dead. Major earthquakes hit Antigua and Montserrat. Appearance of Gages Upper Soufrière
1866	Britain establishes Crown Colony rule
1880	Phreatic eruption at the Boiling Lake, Dominica
1897–1900	Volcano-seismic crisis
1899	Hurricane kills 100
1902	7 May: eruption of La Soufrière volcano, St Vincent, kills some 1500 people; 8 May: eruption of Mont Pelée, Martinique, kills around 30,000 people
1924	Hurricane kills 30 people; followed by severe drought
1928	Severe hurricane hits Plymouth and the south of the island
1929–1932	Eruption crisis Mont Pelée, Martinique
1933–7	Volcano-seismic crisis
1951	Universal adult suffrage
1958–61	Montserrat joins the short-lived West Indian Federation
1960	Lang's Soufrière 'discovered'
1960	Ministerial form of government adopted
1961	W. H. Bramble becomes first chief minister

1966–7	Volcano-seismic crisis
1976	Phreatic eruption at La Soufrière, Guadeloupe
1978	John Osborne becomes chief minister
1979	Eruption of La Soufrière, St Vincent
1980	Population, 12,073
1982	Montserrat joins Organisation of Eastern Caribbean States (OECS)
1988	Publication of Wadge and Isaacs report
1989	17 September: Hurricane Hugo hits Montserrat
1991	Reuben Meade becomes chief minister
1992	Volcano-seismic crisis begins
1993	Frank Savage appointed governor
1994	Population, approximately 10,400
1995	18 July: steam venting in Soufrière Hills
	21 August: first large phreatic eruption on 'Ash Monday'; first large-scale evacuation of population of Plymouth and the south (ends 7 September)
	5 September: Hurricane Luis
	30 November: confirmation of dome growth in English Crater
	2 December: second evacuation of the south (ends 2 January)
1996	29 March: first pyroclastic flow down the Tar River valley
	3 April: third – and final – evacuation of Plymouth and surrounding areas
	12 May: pyroclastic flows reach the sea for the first time
	17 September: first explosive event of the volcano crisis
	11 November: general elections; Bertrand Osborne forms coalition government
1997	30 March: pyroclastic flows pour over

Galway's Wall and destroy the Great Alps waterfall

29 May: first pyroclastic flow activity in northern ghauts

25 June: nineteen people die when pyroclastic flows destroy villages in the east and parts of central corridor; airport shut down

3 August: pyroclastic flows into Plymouth

5–8 August: volcanic explosions occur at twelve-hour intervals

15 August: Salem and neighbouring areas declared unsafe for night-time occupation

19 August: announcement of Assisted Passages Scheme

21 August: announcement of Assisted Regional Voluntary Relocation Scheme; resignation of Chief Minister Bertrand Osborne

22 August: David Brandt sworn in as chief minister

23 August: Montserrat Building Society suspends operations

24 August: Clare Short's 'golden elephants' comments reported

28 August: insurance companies withdraw cover

29 August: visit of Bernie Grant, MP

31 August: visit of George Foulkes, under-secretary of state at the Department for International Development

5 September: Salem area declared total exclusion zone; 1580 people living in shelters

17 September: Anthony Abbott sworn in as governor

22 September–21 October: seventy–six

volcanic explosions

14 October: International Development Committee, London, begins inquiry into Montserrat

December: population, 3381

26 December: massive pyroclastic flows and surges destroy west coast communities south of Plymouth

1998   14 February: Foreign Secretary Robin Cook visits Montserrat

March: dome stops growing

30 September: reoccupation of Salem and surrounding areas

30 December: verdict on inquest into the deaths of 25 June 1997

1999   13 January: signing of three-year Country Policy Plan

17 March: publication of UK's White Paper on Overseas Territories

26 March: announcement of Evacuees Return Airfare Scheme (introduced on 1 May for evacuees in the Caribbean region and 1 June for those in UK)

April: Isles Bay safe for reoccupation; shelter residents number 372

20 July: large dome collapse down the Tar River

27 August: scientists forecast that dome could become stable within nine months

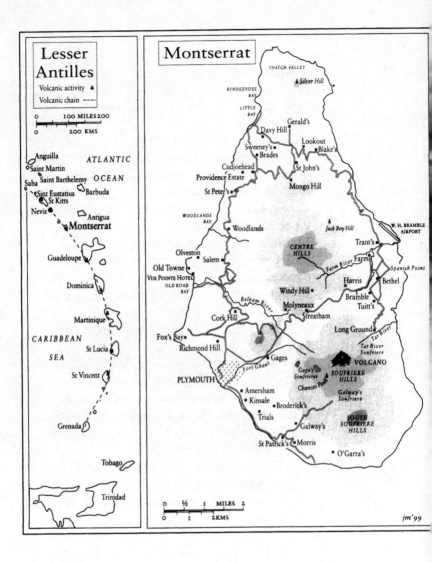

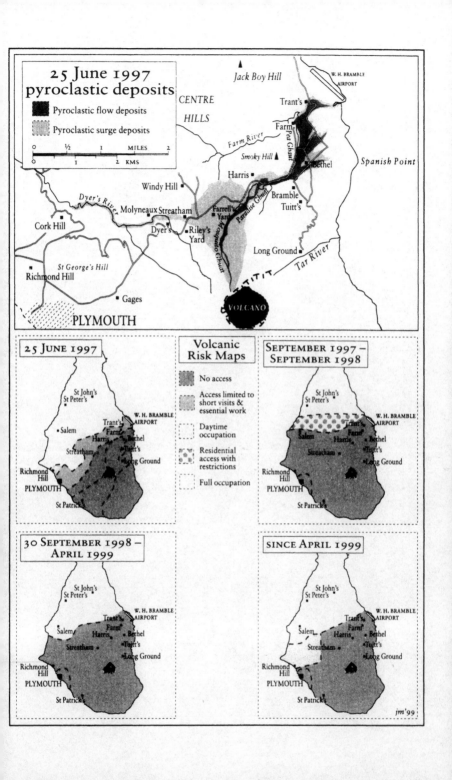

1

....

The Day of Death

'Teacher, the donkey fast,' said the boy from Smoky Hill near the village of Harris. His teacher had pleaded with him that his family should move from their vulnerable home close to the Soufrière Hills volcano. But the boy was convinced that he and his donkey could gallop away if the rushing, boiling-hot, tumbleweed cloud of ash, gases and rock that sometimes spewed down the steep sides of the volcano were to threaten his community. Every Montserratian schoolchild knew that this was a pyroclastic flow, that it could immerse everything in its path and that with it would come a plume of ashes that could rise as high as a cruising jumbo jet and blot out the sun. Even so, it was hard for the boy to believe that the gentle green hillsides around him could really be at risk from the turbulent volcano.

The day that the volcano reached Harris, the boy and his donkey were safe, but nineteen other Montserratians were to die within minutes, killed by a force hotter than the inside of a kiln. No person, no animal, could outrun the Soufrière Hills volcano. It was 25 June 1997.

It was not in global or even in Caribbean terms a lot of deaths. A few months later the international media stirred only briefly when 172 people died in Haiti after an overloaded ferry sank near Port-au-Prince. However, in the British Overseas (then Dependent) Territory of Montserrat, an island of roughly 17 by 8 kilometres, less than half the size of the Isle of Wight and so small that it is sometimes left off maps, everyone knew the dead or at least knew people who knew them or called them family. Where they were and what they were doing at the time of their deaths was common knowledge: in Montserrat, everyone knows where everyone is and what everyone is doing. That knowledge made the deaths more immediate and more shocking. But there was more to it than intimate, personal sorrow: the deaths were to become a focus for the anger many felt – and continue to feel – about the wrongs endured by Montserratians during the frightening and wearisome years of the volcano crisis.

Those nineteen people, aged from three months to seventy-three years old, died in ordinary places, in fields, in their homes or vehicles, but in extraordinary circumstances. For two years the people of Montserrat had lived with the Soufrière Hills volcano since its eruption, on 18 July 1995, for the first time in recorded history. But this was the day of death.

The setting for the events of Wednesday 25 June stretched across what was once one of the loveliest corners of the 'Emerald Isle', so named for its greenness and its seventeenth-century settlement by Irish Catholics. The northern flanks of the Soufrière Hills were formerly cut by deep green, forested gullies called ghauts. Paradise Ghaut, south of the village of Harris, and the nearby Paradise estate were particularly bountiful with guava, soursop, plum rose and mango ripe for the picking. Between the ghauts, on the lower slopes, were neat fields – once dedicated to sugar and later cotton – where farmers grazed animals and cultivated vegetables. The soil was relatively rich. It was, after all, volcanic. Every visitor to Montserrat would pass through this area – known as the central corridor – on the way from the W. H. Bramble airport in the east to Plymouth, the island's capital, in the west and be charmed.

Harris, with a population of some 500 people, was the largest community in the east. Among its hilly contours, running parallel to the road and north of Paradise Ghaut, were houses, two schools, seven churches, a police station, a sub-post office, one cricket pitch (home to some of the island's finest players) and two netball courts. Its people were farmers, taxi drivers, teachers, nurses, pastors, clerks. Some commuted to Plymouth, driving to work along the road that straddled the low-lying slopes of the Soufrière Hills to the south and the Centre Hills to the north. Their homes were of breezeblock or stone, spacious, comfortably furnished and fitted with the familiar fixtures of a global consumer society. Some homes were smaller, humbler, their owners living a simple life still largely connected to the land, village rhythms and a sense of continuity with the past. The poet Archie Markham, who comes from Harris, claims – with some justification – that Montserrat had the best housing in the Caribbean.

Close by were other villages named after former estates, such as Trant's, Farm, Bethel. These communities – on flatter land where Pea Ghaut and Farm River converged to flow to the sea – were formed when slaves became share-croppers living on or close to the estates. While agriculture had long been in decline – 'they finish with the hoe', as a taxi driver from Farm put it – many people continued to cultivate the land, if only in a modest way. They owned land or leased it, either around their house or on 'mountain grounds'. There was, too, grazing land for cattle, goats and sheep. Cattle, in particular, were an investment, 'the poor man's bank'. And everyone had a yard with breadfruit or mango and space for 'short crops', such as cucumbers, peppers and tomatoes.

In contrast, Spanish Point, not far from the villages of Bethel and Farm, had become an expression of a different Montserrat. Once part of the Bethel estate, this chunk of coastal land had become an expatriates' colony in the 1960s when it was sold to Canadians for villa development. Now it had its 'snowbirds', mainly retired North Americans, who would spend winters in their villas. This long-stay, low-key style of tourism, although rather a curious phenomenon, seemed to work reasonably well, and enhanced Montserrat's desired image to be a neighbourly place where foreigners were welcome and where you could safely leave your doors unlocked.

That normality ended on 18 July 1995 with the first signs of volcanic activity in the Soufrière Hills. Since then, the communities of the south, the east and the central corridor had been evacuated to the north of the island. Those who did not leave the island – and by June 1997 the population was reduced by a half, down to some 5000 people – had had to find makeshift accommodation in shelters or move in with family, friends and strangers. So officially, the evacuation zone was empty of people, empty of human activity. What became clear, however, was that on 25 June 1997 some people were still living, and many more still farming, working, visiting or just 'cooling-out' in the so-called exclusion zone; perhaps eighty people in the villages of the east, the central corridor and near the airport.

Some thought that those who died had only themselves to blame. They had known the risks and had taken them. They had been caught in an evacuated area having ignored the government's decree and the advice of the scientists, the experts at the Montserrat Volcano Observatory (MVO), who produced a twice-daily report about the volcano's behaviour and the known dangers. On 24 June, for example, the report had emphasised that the most vulnerable communities, which included Tuitt's, Bethel, Spanish Point, Farm, Harris and Trant's, were 'extremely dangerous and nobody should go into this area'. Some said the dead had been presumptuous to imagine they could defy the volcano; they had been disobedient because they had been in the forbidden exclusion zone. In the end God had punished them.

There were others, however, who blamed the authorities – the British government, the British governor, the local Montserratian government, the scientists. The deaths, it was argued, were essentially a consequence of British neglect of the citizens of one of its few remaining colonies. The United Kingdom and its servants had been indifferent to the sufferings of 10,500 or so black people on a small 'rock' in the Caribbean – in contrast to its robust and unstinting support of the Falklands when that even smaller community, also a Dependent Territory, had been threatened. The locally elected Montserratian government was also called to account: it had failed to plan for adequate alternative shelter and land in the safe zones of the island. Because no one cared enough, because the official priorities were of expediency rather than principle, nineteen people had died.

A kind of mythic quality began to surround these deaths. In many ways, the dead came to represent all that was virtuous about Montserrat and its people. They became symbols of an old-fashioned, God-fearing society in which the values of an emancipated peasantry – individualism, independence, devotion to land and home – triumphed over the circumstances of death. They had refused to accept dependency, and by inference, a colonial status; they had rejected the inadequate conditions in the shelters in the north. Some were reaping their crops in the fields (the biblical echoes are strong here) to feed the island; others were tending livestock, and others had stayed resolutely at home. In a sense, they became the heroic dead, the victims of a colonial war.

The awakening of the volcano in 1995 had centred on the horseshoe-shaped English Crater deep within the Soufrière Hills. It was there that a dome had first begun to grow, pumping out an ever-accumulating volume of viscous lava from the magma chamber. As it grew, it piled its sharp-edged blocks of rubble higher and higher, hotter than a hundred nuclear power stations, shifting, threatening and unstable. By late May 1997, nearly two years into the crisis, its volume was 65 million cubic metres, the equivalent of a bonfire piled with 65 million sacks of coal. By this time, the dome had outgrown English Crater. Pyroclastic flows caused by the collapse of part of the dome had already swirled like broccoli clouds down the eastern side of the crater and had reached the sea at the mouth of the Tar River. They were now poised to spill in other directions, possibly towards the north and the north-west. If that happened, the scientists warned, it would cause those racing flows to hurtle down the ghauts on the northern flanks of the Soufrière Hills towards the central corridor villages and the W. H. Bramble airport.

This began to happen at the end of May, mainly into the upper stretches of Mosquito Ghaut and its neighbour Tuitt's Ghaut. Both these ghauts fed directly down to the airport and the villages in between. On 17 June pyroclastic flows travelled 4 kilometres down Mosquito Ghaut. The next day, one reached an area only some 180 metres short of the road at Harris village, where vegetation on the sides of the ghaut was singed orange by the heat. The ghauts – now grey, shallow cleavages – were fast filling up with material, their sides scoured. Each flow made a smoother route for the subsequent one so that it could travel even faster. The danger was intensifying, although for those who had become used to life under the volcano, conditions perhaps seemed no worse than before.

After all, the airport – some 3 kilometres from Harris – was still open. The little airport with its runway parallel to the shoreline was the island's one point of entry and exit and, as such, was its lifeline. The government of Montserrat had fought to keep the airport open. The daily reports from the MVO stated that the airport remained open 'only for essential travel purposes' although what this meant was ambiguous. Certainly, tourists were not turned away. The regional airline, LIAT, continued, with some reservation, to fly into Montserrat. To arrive at the modest little terminal (where a poster proclaimed 'The Caribbean As It Used to Be') remained routine unless you knew that the man or woman sitting on a bench and clutching a walkie-talkie was a scientist, posted there in case of an emergency. Since early June, LIAT had insisted on the presence of a scientist at the airport as a condition of continuing its flights.

At the beginning of the crisis a map had been drawn up to divide the island into zones of greater or lesser danger. The map changed as the volcano's behaviour changed and by the beginning of June 1997, it had seven zones, from A, the area of greatest risk, to G, the safest. By then, the airport was in zone C. The adjacent village of Trant's, less than 1 kilometre closer to the volcano, was in the more dangerous zone B; both zones B and A meant 'no access'. By early June, the scientists reckoned that material from a large dome collapse could reach the sea near Spanish Point and that some material could be diverted into Pea Ghaut. If that happened, Trant's would be vulnerable while the airport, it was argued, would be slightly sheltered by the river bank. Given the special monitoring arrangements at the airport and the fact that no one lived there, the scientists judged that the exposure at the airport was therefore somewhat lower than at Trant's. The acting airport manager Norman Cassell later told the scientists that his staff had been concerned about the zoning. 'We always maintained,' he said, 'that the level of danger [for the airport] as put forward by the authorities was too low.'[1] There were people who felt that the continued operation of the airport gave mixed messages, and, indeed, that it was not in the exclusion zone only because of its strategic importance.

The scientists, headed at that point by William Aspinall, a British seismologist who had spent many years working in the eastern Caribbean, were also becoming increasingly concerned and felt an uneasy burden of responsibility. In a worst-case scenario there might barely be enough time to evacuate the airport. On 10 June Aspinall handed a statement to Frank Savage, the British governor, at that day's volcano management meeting. It pointed out that 'the possibility of a rapidly growing pyroclastic flow being initiated without obvious precursory activity, big enough to reach the sea in the vicinity of Bramble Airport, cannot be precluded'. The scientific team's statement continued, partly emphasised by capital letters, that in the event of an alert at Bramble, the notice could be 'AS SHORT AS 1 AND A HALF MINUTES BEFORE THE FLOW OR ACCOMPANYING SURGES REACH THE LINE OF THE COAST'. The sentence ended with the warning that 'ABSOLUTELY NO ASSURANCE CAN BE GIVEN THAT EVEN THIS SHORT WARNING TIME WILL BE POSSIBLE IN ALL CIRCUMSTANCES'.

This important statement was not, however, released to the islanders. What was, however, available to the public were the twice-daily MVO reports. For the most part these presented scientific information in a formulaic style. Only occasionally did the flat tone alter to express a sense of urgency. As early as 4–5 June, for example, the MVO report said: 'We repeat our plea to residents in the no-go area to leave immediately, rather than face the possibility of an agonising death which cannot be out-run.' The reports for the days leading up to 25 June described increased activity at the volcano, then some respite, then renewed activity. Studying them in hindsight, however, one finds little sense of new, imminent danger to the northern ghauts. Indeed, that was because there was no 'new' danger and therefore no substantial scientific grounds for emphasising the risk. Indeed, the scientists considered the Tar River and Fort Ghaut (leading down to Plymouth) as being more likely to experience further flows. Aspinall said that they had, for example, been particularly concerned about the 'essential workers' in Plymouth, who would have had a 'long run' to get out safely if a big flow had gone down the western slopes of the volcano.

For some time, police officers and members of the Royal Montserrat Defence Force had been going from house to house urging anyone remaining in the evacuated zone to leave. It had been easier to persuade people in the west to move. There the conditions were unpleasant: the prevailing winds deposited ash everywhere, cattle were dying and the fields were burned. But in the east, there was no ash and everything looked green and normal. There, it was far more difficult to get the message across. Governor Frank Savage, his Montserratian deputy Howard Fergus, a poet and historian, and David Brandt, then the ambitious independent MP for Windward, also visited the villages, appealing to the remaining residents to go. Both Fergus and Brandt are from the east – an area traditionally known as 'behind God's back' on account of its remoteness. Brandt is from Windy Hill on the central corridor, and Fergus, a man 'rooted in Montserrat', is from Long Ground, high up on the eastern slopes of the Soufrière Hills and the first village to have been evacuated.

For the airport workers, many of whom had lived in the nearby communities, it was tempting to go back home – inside the exclusion zone – after a working shift. Even if you could no longer officially live in your own house, it was an opportunity, if only for a few hours, to live a normal life again, to cook a meal, have a sleep, wash clothes, tend animals. It was a chance to forget the communal discomforts and intrusions of shelter life.

Meanwhile, farmers continued to work with scythe and cutlass in the fields of the exclusion zone beneath the dome, cultivating carrots, corn and potatoes even as the flows puffed down the ghauts behind them. Some were even seen, on 24 June, preparing for planting at Farrell's on ground which had been badly scorched by a pyroclastic flow a week earlier. A few people also remained in Harris – and at Streatham, Windy Hill, Tuitt's, Trant's and Farm. The gas station, west of Harris at Margie Ghaut, was still open, as was a shop or two in Harris.

As the airport workers and farmers proved, it was not impossible to enter the exclusion zone. Although there were manned checkpoints at the boundaries of the zone, there were strategies to get through. You told the policeman at the checkpoint that you only wanted to go in for a couple of minutes – and then you didn't come out. Or you would leave your transport on one side of the checkpoint, walk through – and use the pick-up truck you had left on the other side. In any case, if the policeman was your cousin, he might bend the rules; or, if you had more social or political clout, he might feel obliged to let you in. There was even still a rudimentary bus service to Harris from the safe zone. If all else failed, there were trails through the bush. With an understaffed and overstressed police force, a 'cordon sanitaire' was never possible. No one was prepared to remove people by force or to impose fines or any other form of punishment on those found in the exclusion zone.

God, too, was to play a part in the events of 25 June. Montserrat is a deeply religious society in that the church plays a central role in most people's lives and that God is constantly evoked in daily decision-making. Especially among the older people, there is a grand fatalism. Tomorrow depends on God's will, not the will of the self. The view was that either God would choose to send the volcano in anger or that God would 'spare'. As ninety-year-old Ellen Thomas, who refused to move from her home in Harris, said: 'I was on my knees . . . I wait on God.'[2]

Not everyone understood about any increased danger from the volcano: some did not have radios; others had stopped listening to the monotonous MVO reports; yet others were ill or infirm. Don Romeo, who became a one-man campaigner on behalf of the dispossessed of Montserrat during the crisis and videoed many of its key moments, had visited the exclusion zone ten days before 25 June. One of the people whom he filmed was Joseph Browne, a seventy-one-year-old farmer from Streatham in his brown Sunday suit, collecting water from a stand-pipe. He had had one brief stay in a shelter but had hated it and returned home. Romeo asked him: 'Has anyone offered you anything? Has anyone come to your house to say it's dangerous? Has anyone suggested that you should leave?' Browne replied 'no' and continued to collect his water. He would die somewhere 'in the central area of Montserrat'.

By June, all but three of the Spanish Point residents had also moved. The scientists had met them around Easter and had shown them a video about pyroclastic flows and had explained that Spanish Point itself sits on thick deposits from earlier flows. That telling piece of information had not, however, changed the mind of Louis Chloupek, a Christian fundamentalist from Nebraska who had come to Montserrat to escape the communists in the White House, the US military and the United Nations. With his wife, Sandy, and their four-year-old daughter, Mary, he had decided to stay put. The Chloupeks had bought their house just one month before the volcano had begun to erupt.

Unlike many of the other Spanish Point expatriates, the Chloupeks were working-class people. They had little money, and nowhere else to go. So they decided to stay on at Spanish Point for a few weeks more before returning to the States. Louis Chloupek was sceptical about the scientists' analysis. He thought that they had earlier exaggerated the danger and so lulled people into a false security. At another meeting of Spanish Point residents, perhaps six weeks before 25 June, the scientists had produced a 'danger map', according to Chloupek. This showed that 'it was not safe to stay in our house . . . but if we had gone over the road to the north closer to the valley we could have slept overnight in a little bus station on the corner. It said that it was safe to be in the valley but not on the level ground at Spanish Point.'[3] A stubbornness, combined with religious fatalism, provided a rationale to remain at Spanish Point. The Chloupeks were still there on 25 June.

On the night of 24 June, David Lea, an American missionary turned video chronicler of the volcano, was doing his weekly shift as a volunteer at the MVO, watching the seismographs. At that time the Observatory occupied a converted villa in the then safe zone of Old Towne on the west coast. The villa had an excellent view towards the central corridor and the volcano, and the scientists could dash out from the operations' room to watch the floor show: to see the vertical ash plumes and pyroclastic flows with their own eyes from the veranda. Lea, who had lived in Montserrat with his family for many years, remembered that that night the seismographs at the MVO had started 'to cook'. Although the scientific records indicated that there had been equally strong episodes before, Lea said it now 'looked as if this thing was having babies'. In a sense, this was an appropriate simile. Since 22 June the volcano had developed an eight-hour cycle in which regular volcanic 'breathing' patterns signified certain events. This inflation/deflation cycle consisted of hybrid earthquake swarms, which coincided with the inflation of the crater area, followed by a sharp deflation and the onset of pyroclastic flows.

That Wednesday morning, the volcano had started to deflate at about 6.10 a.m. At 7.00 a.m. Chief Scientist Aspinall and

Keith Rowley, a Trinidadian colleague, had gone to Windy Hill, a village which runs in part parallel with the lower reaches of Mosquito Ghaut, and watched pyroclastic flows going down the ghaut. By then, the airport was already open. The scientist on early-morning watch was Paul Cole, a British explosive volcanologist. He had been told about the pyroclastic flows through his radio contact with the MVO, but he had not been able to see anything. Harris Hill obscured part of his view and, furthermore, the visibility was poor that morning. 'I had felt very uncomfortable. I was going to refuse to do the airport shift again. I was just not prepared to accept the responsibility,' he said. Aspinall had also become increasingly exercised about the situation at the airport. 'We began to have real anxieties about the safety of the MVO scientist,' he explained.

The scientists had already drafted a statement to be presented to the governor at the next volcano management meeting indicating that the operation of the airport was no longer satisfactory. That morning they had also prepared a letter indicating that the hazards were such that the scientist at the airport was now 'put at unacceptable risk'. As Aspinall explained: 'With such a limited lead time, one could not really take one's eye off the mountain for a moment, let alone go for a pee. That level of watch was unsustainable hour after hour.'

On the other side of the island, 'essential services', such as the port, the petrol station, the rice mill and Monlec, the island's electricity provider, were all still operating in Plymouth. Ram's, the island's largest supermarket, was also unofficially open, and still being visited by customers, including, it was rumoured, the governor's wife.

Simon Maty went to work in Plymouth every day. He was the manager of Wakel Investments, agents for Texaco, and that morning an oil tanker was due in port. Although Maty was going into Plymouth, an area of high volcanic hazard, in a professional capacity, he was working 'at his own risk', according to his security pass. Conditions with the ash, which blew on the prevailing winds from east to west, were often terrible.

He described himself as often being 'blind from the ash from head to foot'. On 25 June, he was at the port at 6.00 a.m. Maty rang the Observatory to get clearance for the tanker to start discharging. He was told to wait because of the increased volcanic activity, but by 8.00 a.m. he was given the all clear. And at 10.00 a.m., the tanker began to pump out 300,000 litres of diesel.

That was about the time that Thomas 'Scientist' Willock left his home in Tuitt's, inside the exclusion zone. At eighty-three, he was fit, cheerful, and still doing a little farming, having spent much of his working life in a sugar factory in neighbouring St Kitts. Since the onset of the volcano Willock had lived in the Church of God of Prophecy shelter in the northern village of St John's, but he would often return home to check his things, cook and wash his clothes. Early on 25 June he went there on account of a dream. 'I dream the volcano blow,' he said, so early that morning he decided to go and collect some possessions from his house. Sometimes the police at the checkpoint at Jack Boy Hill, on the road high above the airport, gave him trouble, but not that morning, and he passed quickly into the exclusion zone, down past the airport, across the bridge over Farm River at Trant's, through Bethel and into Tuitt's. He did not stay long and as he was going back north, he met a man who worked at the airport. 'The man tell me: "Why you going home already?" I said, "I believe something will happen today".' Willock said that when he got to the north, he told them: 'I report, "the volcano is up there mad. Let us pray".'

Two scientists were still out in the field. Rob Watts of Bristol University and Amanda Clarke, a research student from Pennsylvania State University, had planned to carry out a global positioning survey at Long Ground. This involved setting up field equipment, leaving it to run to collect data, dismantling it and moving on to the next site. The survey measures any changes in what is known as 'ground deformation', in effect, the inflation and deflation of the volcano as the magma moves around beneath the surface. Before leaving, Watts and Clarke had had permission from the Observatory to drive back across the central corridor.

Their route took them close to the villages of Streatham and Windy Hill, where four people were later to die: Hezekiah Riley, a mentally disturbed man, Philip Robinson and Joseph Greenaway, both elderly farmers, and sixty-nine-year-old Edith Greenaway (no relation to Joseph). As the scientists drove through the central corridor, they also noticed a number of farmers working in the fields. Among them was Harry Lewis and his wife Isolyn, Felina Celestine, Isolyn's older sister, and Melville Cuffy. All four had been allowed through the checkpoint at St George's Hill that morning to work at Farrell's Yard, where Lewis rented some land. He had spent a substantial amount of money to clear the land and prepare the plots. The loans had to be repaid, there was no crop insurance programme for any losses. The land was their livelihood and there was no alternative work. 'I'm not scared,' said Felina to a friend who had tried to persuade her not to go back there. She told the doctor, 'The volcano will do its thing and me have to do my thing.' In any case, the farmers felt that continuing to supply fresh vegetables to the people was helping Montserrat.

Felina and Isolyn were originally from Dominica, and had settled in Montserrat. Felina had spent some time in New York since the volcano started, but had returned to Montserrat to visit Isolyn. They were both Seventh-Day Adventists so they would 'reap' early in the week in order to go to church on Saturday, the Adventist sabbath. Cuffy, a Guyanese-born carpenter who worked for Lewis as a labourer, was an elder in the church. Wednesday was their reaping day. Farmer Keithly Ponde was also at Farrell's that morning with his father James, who had showed him where to get some potato vine which he said he would take up to his land. James Ponde left when he saw that the activity at the volcano was escalating. That was the last time he saw his son.

By noon, the two scientists Watts and Clarke had reached the mountainous village of Long Ground. 'The MVO was warning us to hurry up,' said Watts, 'because another cycle of hybrid earthquakes was occurring.' At the Observatory, the seismographs were registering intense swarms of some six events per minute. At noon, faithful to the established pattern, the inflation peaked. Watts and Clarke moved on to the next site, just short of Tuitt's at a place called White's Yard, a little further away from the volcano and 2 kilometres north-east of the dome.

By 12.45 p.m., Watts and Clarke radioed the Observatory again and asked permission to carry on to Windy Hill, in the middle of the central corridor. They could hear rockfalls down the east side, but they could not see what was happening on the northern flanks. Nor could they see much of the volcano itself; it had been masked for much of the morning with cloud dropping low down its flanks. Earlier it had been raining. At the mvo, the instruments were clearly showing a repeat pattern. Aspinall refused Watts and Clarke permission to go to Windy Hill. 'It wasn't the volcano that caused the scientists to get out, it was the weather. The cloud came down and our lead time was cut off,' he explained, instructing them to go to the airport and wait there. Aspinall saved their lives. 'We have a lot to thank the chief scientist for with this judgement call,' said Watts. 'Otherwise we would have driven straight into the main path of the pyroclastic flow.' On the way to the airport, the two scientists drove through Bethel and Trant's, villages that – a few minutes later – were buried under boiling-hot rock, ash and rubble.

At 12.50 p.m. what was to be the last flight to land at W. H. Bramble arrived from Antigua. Out of the small charter plane came Governor Frank Savage and his wife Veronica. As governor, he was the Queen's representative in Montserrat and in charge of the safety of the island's people. A craggy, bushy-browed, kindly-looking man with a mop of grey hair and the face of an Irish priest, Savage had been in Barbados trying to extract more money for Montserrat from the uk's regional aid office.

Eight minutes after Savage's plane landed, a phased evacuation of the airport was ordered by the mvo, and then two minutes later, at 1.00 p.m., an immediate evacuation. The Observatory's seismometers had detected a huge pyroclastic flow at the head of Mosquito Ghaut. The Carib Aviation plane took off fast while the scientists at the airport initiated the evacuation; the scientist on duty was Lutchman Pollard, now joined by Watts and Clarke. When Norman Cassell, the airport manager, heard the siren he grabbed some documents from his office and got out. 'By the time I reached from the control tower to the manager's office everyone was actually out of the main building and only the security officer was waiting for me downstairs.'[4]

Savage described what happened then. 'We came through the door of the terminal lounge to see this enormous pyroclastic flow rolling down the hillside. I had spent two years in the path of ash clouds in the danger zone and there was no mistaking that this was the real thing.' The 'real thing' consisted of three 'pulses', three pyroclastic flows, which, within twenty-five minutes, all raced down Mosquito Ghaut before following the course of Paradise River down Pea Ghaut almost to the sea. Accompanying the flows were lighter surge clouds of ash and gases, which spread out from the flows defying gravity, climbing and burning with an intense heat, like a 'hot hurricane'. Witnesses said they heard no warning sound from the flows. They came in a silent swiftness, like a pouncing animal.

The first flow, which left the summit of the volcano at 12.57 p.m., travelled the 3.9 kilometres to the sharp bend at Harris in 230 seconds. It eventually stopped in Paradise River at Bramble village, 4.7 kilometres from the dome. It had travelled at an average speed of 54 k.p.h. Nearly three minutes later, at 12.59:55, came a second, faster flow. This reached Farm and then Trant's, 6.7 kilometres from the dome in less than seven minutes. With it came a pyroclastic surge, which spilled out of the upper reaches of Mosquito Ghaut pouring over Riley's Yard, in the western part of Farrell's plain, and reaching the main road of the central corridor.

The third and fastest flow started down Mosquito Ghaut at

around 1.08 p.m. It covered 5.8 kilometres in 265 seconds, an average speed of 79 k.p.h., before stopping at Trant's just beyond the airport runway. Unlike the second flow, which remained within Pea Ghaut, the third flow burst out of Paradise River and fanned out over the plain around Bethel and between Spanish Point and Trant's. To the west, a surge had also left Mosquito Ghaut and had inundated Farrell's plain, reaching Streatham and climbing perhaps 70 metres up Windy Hill. In what was to be observed as a completely new phenomenon, this surge then somehow recharged itself to become a new flow, and kept going towards the small village of Dyers before heading west down the Belham River valley towards the populated community of Cork Hill.

After leaving the airport, Norman Cassell drove fast along the dirt track and then on to the main road going north. Looking through his rear-view mirror, he could see that the flows had already gone through Trant's. He was following the governor's car, which, as it raced north, had passed a car going in the other direction. This belonged to police officer Kelvin White. The governor told him to turn back, but White, who had just delivered lunch to the fire and immigration officers at the airport and the police at the checkpoint on the north road, was going to rescue his mother. She was at Trant's, where White was still living at the family home, not far from the airport.

Linda White had been at home in Trant's all morning. A teacher, she had moved north and rarely returned, but that day she needed to prepare some schoolwork in peace and quiet. She had heard the siren but assumed that it was being tested early – the test siren usually went off at 3.30 p.m. on Wednesday. She checked the mountain but the cloud was low and she could see nothing. Then she tried to tune into ZJB, the local radio station, for the daily lunchtime volcano update, but she couldn't get the relevant frequency. At that point, her son arrived and within a minute had picked her up and driven her to safety. Later, White told the scientists who interviewed her about her experiences that she had got up late that morning and had forgotten to pray. So she went to her bedroom to pray: 'I prayed to God to save me from pyroclastic flows and surges – and he did.'[5] The house was lost in the burning.

From the safety of a high spot, at a sharp bend on the road above the airport at Jack Boy Hill, the governor, airport staff, scientists and, soon, many onlookers had seen the flow stop within 50 metres of the sea, at the southern end of the airstrip. Houses at Farm and Trant's burned as gas bottles exploded. A continuous huge black ash cloud swung above their heads blowing north-west across the island.

Back at the MVO, Aspinall had ordered that the sirens also be sounded in Plymouth to alert the port workers; the Texaco fuel tanker immediately cut its fuel lines and left. Simon Maty, who by then was back in his office at Lover's Lane on the outskirts of Plymouth, had heard what he thought was an explosion. He got into his car and drove north – just as an ash cloud ballooned over 9000 metres up into the air and, in less than a minute, covered Plymouth and the west in darkness.

That same cloud could be seen from Providence House, in the north-west of the island, close to the village of St Peter's. The ash did not fall so far north, but a great triangle of sea turned black to the south and two small yachts, their sails curiously illuminated in the darkness that shrouded them, battled to escape from its shadow. Providence is a prettily restored estate house, which at the time was open as a guest-house and served lunch, mainly to expatriates, on Wednesdays. Those enjoying tortillas and guacamole on the veranda that day included Carol Osborne of the Vue Pointe, the island's one functioning hotel. Looking down from Providence to the road, they saw an increasingly long line of trucks, cars and buses climb the steep hill out of St Peter's, trekking north in a sad convoy, away from the ash.

All Carol Osborne wanted to do, however, was to go south, to check what was happening at the Vue Pointe. The hotel, which overlooked Old Road bay, had kept going despite the crisis and had become, among other things, a congenial gathering-place for the scientists from the nearby MVO. That lunch-

[18]

time, Dr Peter Baxter of Cambridge University and in charge of the health aspects of the volcano, and Canadian helicopter pilot Jim McMahon, were at the Vue Pointe. They saw the cloud rising from the east. 'We had got used to seeing the ash clouds, but this was definitely a big one. It was a massive hunk of cloud,' said McMahon, who had spent many months skilfully ferrying the scientists around – and on to – the volcano for reconnaissance and research.

McMahon took off with Paul Cole as a passenger at about 1.10 p.m. He would normally have gone across the central corridor, but this time he went round the top of the island landing close to the airport. What he saw in the east he had never seen before. It was a 'wall of rolling ash, dark grey and super thick', 'as solid as a freight-train' and 'like an atomic bomb'. Then through the wall emerged fingers of ash, which came leapfrogging one after another down the mountain. It was these flows that consumed the villages of the east.

Nine people died in Farm. The pyroclastic flow down Pea Ghaut had buried the village. Among the dead were Virginia and Anthony Sutton, the elderly parents of eleven children. Now retired, they had a five-bedroom house and some land; Sutton did a little fishing and raised pigs. Since the beginning of the volcano crisis, the couple had been living with one of their sons, John Robinson, in St John's, in the safe zone. He had taken them back home the previous Saturday. 'They went back because they want a little privacy for a few days,' said Robinson. 'I know it's dangerous, but it's my mother. She'd rather stay by herself. If I didn't take her down, she still say she take taxi to take she down. They would rather die in the house than go to the shelter.' Robinson said that he had spoken to his father that morning and that they had planned that his brother who worked in the nearby quarry would take them out later that day.

Baby Allister Joseph and his twenty-three-year-old Antiguan mother, Alicia Joseph, also died in Farm. They had flown back to Montserrat from Antigua the day before with the baby's father, Devon Sutton, the Suttons' grandson. After leaving the airport, they had turned left and reached Devon's house at Farm in minutes. There was no barrier to stop them or sign to warn them of the dangers. The checkpoint at Farm's Bridge had already been moved north, to the foot of Jack Boy Hill, so that the duty police officer would not be exposed to unacceptable danger.

Bernadine Harris was a friend of the Suttons. Her husband, a builder, had not wanted to move from his home. So Mrs Harris stayed with him. 'She usually went down to visit my parents. The only company she could find,' said John Robinson. Her own house was to be spared, the only one in the village to survive. But she wasn't there.

Alwin Allen and his brother Winston were also neighbours of the Suttons. They had been living in a shelter in the north, while their mother had reluctantly gone to the shelter for the elderly at Cavalla Hill. The brothers would go back to Farm to look after their animals and cook food to take back to their mother. No police officer reported that the Allens had been through the checkpoint that day, but somehow they returned to feed and water their animals – sheep, goats, cattle and a dog. It was thought they tried to escape by car but were caught by the volcano near the river where two unidentifiable skeletal bodies were later found.

Chana Boatswaine and Joseph Tuitt were both from Farm and both worked at the airport. The two men left the airport together at the end of their shift to go home at mid-day. Boatswaine had relocated to a shelter in St John's, but had gone to Farm to look out for his animals. He had tried to reach the river on foot but 'never reach up'. Tuitt, who was known as a 'very nice fellow', had gone, said a neighbour, to Farm to shift his goat. Another story was that he had borrowed a car that mid-day to go back to his house to collect some money. Whatever the case, he, too, 'never reach'.

The only person to die in Harris was Beryl Grant, an elderly farmer and huckster, who used to sell her vegetables from a stall outside Ram's in Plymouth. During the crisis, she would visit the scientists and urge them to buy her fresh fruit. Rose Willock, manager of radio ZJB, remembered Grant coming into the radio station looking jaunty in a yellow dress with a flared skirt. Willock said: 'I told her not to go, but she said it would be all right. "The bus takes us from Salem and brings us back," she told me. She didn't think it was dangerous.' That day, she was getting ready to go to Canada to visit her daughter so she had gone to bake cassava bread with a neighbour in Farm and make jams to take with her. She had then left Farm to go to Harris to cut bananas.

By 1.20 p.m., when the pyroclastic flows stopped, some of the scientists went down to the quarry, west of the Amerindian burial site close to the airport. 'We wanted to get to the top of the hill above the quarry,' said Paul Cole. 'We could see Farm from there, and most of Spanish Point. By then we realised that the people working at Farrell's must have been killed too.'

Delia Ponde had seen Harry Lewis, Melville Cuffy and the two Dominican sisters early that morning in the fields at Farrell's. Ponde, her husband and daughter had been picking carrots close by. As the Pondes finished loading the carrots into their van at Farrell's gate, Delia Ponde glanced back at the mountain and saw a huge pyroclastic flow go down a ghaut and then part of it spill over the road. She shouted to her husband and daughter to get in the van, and told her husband: 'Give it all you got.' The family escaped by driving neither up nor down the central corridor but by taking the turning opposite Farrell's Yard to the top of Windy Hill. There they looked back to where they had been a few minutes before. They saw the gas station explode at the bend in the road at Margie Ghaut and the ash pouring down over the fields. 'You know how if you throw baking powder into water. You know how it puffs up before it expands? You watch it just start rising from the level of the road and getting into the air and just spread out like. It moved very, very fast, very, very fast.'[6] They could see houses burning below them and 'boiling ash like big clumps' at Farrell's.

They felt no heat but a strong wind and hid under a border of ginger lilies. By then the high wind was accompanied by thunder and lightning.

At Windy Hill, Delia Ponde met Harry Lewis, who had last seen his wife, sister-in-law and Cuffy as they started to run from the fields at Farrell's down towards the road. Lewis had got into his pick-up truck and driven down to meet them at the road. But by then he could see the flow coming down Mosquito Ghaut. He started to drive west towards Plymouth but then he noticed the Pondes' vehicle going up Windy Hill. Lewis had reversed back and gone up Windy Hill, too, then back down, looking for the other three, and then up again to rejoin the Ponde family. 'Where are the others?' Delia Ponde asked him. He told her that they had run down the hill and crossed the road. They were 'running like hell,' said Ponde.[7] It was the third pulse that had caught them as it spread, not just into Farrell's Yard, but across the central corridor road and up into Windy Hill. It was that silent, burning surge of hot ash and gases that had felled the running figures.

Jim McMahon's helicopter was the only means of rescue. Going in by land was impossible: the ground was too hot. McMahon wanted to see who had survived and who needed to be rescued. The helicopter managed to reach the outskirts of the disaster area. It picked up a couple of people at Spanish Point and another person at the school, north-east of Bramble. This man, remembered Paul Cole, asked if he could be taken back because he had left some money under the seat of his car.

Gradually, parts of Harris Hill became visible. Everyone knew there had been people there. The helicopter, this time with Dr Peter Baxter on board, landed at the crossroads above the steep hill, where some twenty survivors had gathered. All around, it was ashy, dusty and smelled of burning, the colour scorched out of the landscape into a monochrome of blackened trees. Many houses lower down were still on fire. Despite the fury of the volcano, some people were reluctant to leave. Some of the elderly feared the helicopter, but the fear of loss was perhaps greater. There was poignancy in the departures. Baxter remembered an old man with a bent spine who had sought to secure his door with a rock, while a neighbour struggled to carry a bedridden old lady through her doorway. Some even asked if the helicopter could come back later.

They were rescued two at a time and taken to the checkpoint north of the airport. There, David Lea filmed some of the rescued as they emerged from the helicopter. Some carried bags, some had nothing. There was Leroy 'Slim' Daley, dashing from the helicopter, smiling and commenting, 'The thing came down the mountain like a bullet.'[8] Later, he told the *Montserrat Reporter*: 'I saw the surges coming back up the hill from the pyroclastic flow, which moved at an incredible speed towards Farm and Trant's, breaking over the walls at Bramble and rushing down towards Spanish Point through Bethel.'[9]

Governor Savage was also taken in the helicopter to see what could be seen before he returned to the Emergency Operations Centre in Olveston, on the other side of the island. Meanwhile, the staff at the makeshift relocated hospital in St John's in the north, had been alerted. The casualty department was used as an advanced medical post. Knowing that the hospital had only intravenous fluids to treat serious burns cases, Dr Baxter had devised an emergency plan. (The Foreign Office had asked him incredulously why such a plan was necessary, given that there would be no one in the danger area.) Baxter had planned for an emergency medical team to arrive from the neighbouring French island of Guadeloupe. In the event, the Guadeloupeans did not arrive in Montserrat until noon the next day. 'This would have been problematic if there had been more seriously injured people. We were lucky that so few people were hurt,' said Baxter.

Eleven people were admitted to casualty, mostly with burns to their feet and forearms. Five were flown to Guadeloupe and Martinique. Charles Farrell, a farmer and retired chauffeur from Harris, was the most seriously injured. He had stopped breathing in the helicopter on his way to Martinique. He had third-degree burns to both his forearms and face and had inhaled a lot of hot ash. A year afterwards, the skin on his lower arms and hands had become keloidal, bloated like bubble-wrap.

Describing the pyroclastic surge that seemed at one point to surround him on all sides, Farrell said that the heat 'came and went like a breath'. He had left Harris to gather pigeon peas at Windy Hill. 'There was no sound, but the fire came out of the sky and the place got a little dark. And I went under the house and the house catch fire. I bend down and protect my head with my hands and they did burn.' Despite his injuries, Farrell walked a kilometre down the road towards Harris, but the way was blocked so he returned to Windy Hill. He saw the bodies of Lewis, Celestine and Cuffy – they had been less than 140 metres from safety. Next day, Farrell was found by the search and rescue squad. Later, he said: 'I cannot stifle my conscience. I only stopped on in Harris because I wanted to stop. I knew I was taking a chance.'[10]

One child was injured. This was four-year-old Mary Chloupek from Spanish Point, who received serious burns to her forearms and toes. Her father, Louis Chloupek, was on the roof of his house when he saw the flow coming 'like rushing water' with the front of the flow about 5 metres high. He ran downstairs and closed the back door. His wife said she wanted to take some photographs and so they went back up on the roof. Downstairs again, he felt that they should leave. 'I didn't close the side door, and if I had Mary wouldn't have got burned.' It went from light to pitch black in a second. Although Chloupek was less than 3 metres away from his daughter, he said he didn't feel anything. 'There was no fire, just intense heat that seemed to slip through the door. I was in the hallway, Mary was behind my wife and round the corner.'

All around them, houses and trees were burning, but somehow the Chloupeks' house, sandwiched between the lobes of two flows, was spared. 'We were about as close as you could get and still live,' said Chloupek. The family escaped by walking to the beach, then north to the airport, and back on to the road from where they were rescued. Mary was taken the next day to Guadeloupe where she spent three months in hospital. 'God provided,' said her father, who was severely criticised in some quarters, both for staying in Spanish Point with a child and for not protecting her from the flows.

Governor Savage went on the radio that evening. Seventeen people, he said, were missing but as yet no deaths had been confirmed. Twenty people had been rescued from Harris and the search would continue in daylight. William Aspinall warned that the volcanic activity was continuing and that the activity could become 'more energetic' still. People should be prepared, he said.

Jim McMahon's rescue work in the one helicopter – ferrying two people at a time to safety – was augmented the next day by the arrival of Dutch frigate *Pieter Florisz*, with a winch helicopter from nearby St Maarten. Britain's naval support in the Caribbean had gone in the opposite direction. The HMS *Sheffield*, the on-duty West Indies guardship, had just arrived in Belize, some seventy-two hours' sailing time away from Montserrat. Commander Laurence Smallman of the Ministry of Defence later explained that his Ministry had asked the Foreign and Commonwealth Office in London if HMS *Sheffield* could leave the eastern Caribbean. They were told, said Smallman, that 'All indications were that there was a downward trend [of activity] in early June.' Smallman stressed that the Ministry had sought advice carefully. In the event, its information had been wide of the mark. As the Observatory reported on 26 June, after collating, measuring, observing and analysing, the 'event' of 25 June had 'generated the largest seismic signal seen yet during this eruption'.

By then, members of the police and the search and rescue teams had found some of the bodies. Most were lying on their backs, the palms of their hands open with their fingers slightly curled, their limbs bloated, partly contracted and splayed out in immodest display like discarded shop-window dummies. Like the casts of the bodies at Pompeii, nearly 2000 years earlier, the curling of the limbs was not a protective gesture but the result of a literal roasting. In temperatures as high as 500°C, in a flash of heat clothes and hair ignite and bodies start to burn. A couple of breaths will burn your throat and lungs, and consciousness is lost.

The two sisters, Felina and Isolyn, lay side by side on their backs, beside a road, close to the side of a building which had not been able to protect them from the surge. They lay in ash, their clothes burned away but still wearing shoes. Their skin looked pale and smooth from a coating of ash. Melville Cuffy lay in front of a strong wooden door, its Yale lock still shiny, the timber now burned dark. The lower part of one leg was part twisted and part disintegrated. He, too, looked pale and bloated.

As the search and rescue teams continued to search for bodies, other Montserratians were returning to the exclusion zone on their own pilgrimages. On the sun-baked, bleak road that twists its way down the east coast, but before it drops to the eastern plain and the airport, a pick-up truck filled with young men jolted its way back north. They had been to search for relatives in Farm. They had taken the truck along trails, the familiar back routes in the bush. It was the way you took to avoid the police checks, the way you went if you wanted to get on with your life and forget the petty restrictions in the shelters. The way to return to 'free up'.

Now there was nothing. 'You don't see them?' asked a taxi driver whose own home in Harris had been destroyed, his cattle dead but his family long evacuated. The men shook their heads. They were silent and their eyes brimmed with tears. One of them was Devon Sutton, the grandson of Anthony and Virginia Sutton, the boyfriend of Alicia Joseph and the father of baby Allister.

Above the police checkpoint, at the elbow in the road, was a 'view point'. A group of people scuffed the ground with their shoes, and looked south to a flat grey slice of still-steaming ash deposits where a day earlier had existed the scattered community of Trant's. At the end of the airport runway was a deathly pale spit where the pyroclastic flow had come to rest close to the sea. The land smoked, gently. The smoke was the only thing that moved except for a Lynx helicopter turning south towards the mountain and the grey plain. Everyone stared. The silence was occasionally interrupted by staccato conversation. 'He take everything. A whole village wipe out,' said someone. 'The place tear up,' said a young policeman. Wipe out, tear up, mash up, everyone knew someone who had lived there. 'He there?' ... 'Yes, but he get out' ... 'He live a second life.' Of another: 'The fire take him?' ... 'Yes. He gone.'

On the west side of the island, ash lay everywhere as in the aftermath of a polluted snowstorm. But the 'ashflakes' were like powdered cement and they did not melt, but would remain, an oppressive reminder of the volcano, until the rain fell. The bougainvillaea and hibiscus of the villa gardens were smothered in grey ash. The crowns of the coconut palms were laden with it. Cattle and donkeys, their backs sprinkled with it, stood like statues unable to find grazing. Moving vehicles threw up wild billows of ash, blinding pedestrians in their wake. Most people wore basic ash masks – the ones bought in a pharmacist for use against builders' dust – and struggled to hose down yards or get their children to school. The local radio continued to announce routine activities, such as a youth camp and a flea market. But the only thing the islanders could really think about was the volcano: everyone had a story to tell. Those who had escaped talked biblically of 'rushing winds', 'sweet oil' and 'burning bushes', 'a quiet river of fire making its way to the sea' and of 'the darkness that cover me'.

The official position was outlined at a press conference early on the afternoon of Thursday 26 June. Governor Savage looked sombre. He reported that the first surveillance flight that morning had revealed 'a very considerable devastation over large parts of central and southern Montserrat'. His information was piecemeal: the Anglican church at Harris had 'gone'; Streatham village had been 'completely obliterated'; houses were under some 3 metres of hot ash; there was 'hot material' in the Belham River, near the primary school at Cork Hill. By then, four deaths had been officially confirmed – one in Streatham and three in Windy Hill – but no names were released. Five people had been admitted to hospital and one was in a serious condition. There had been 'carnage and devastation', but up to forty people had been plucked from the area. Savage confirmed that twenty people had been rescued the day before, eleven that morning; others had come out on foot.

Chief Minister Bertrand Osborne, the elected head of the government of Montserrat, sat beside Savage. Osborne, a wealthy businessman who had led a weak coalition since the election of November 1996, was even more subdued and hesitant than usual. There was no life, he said, in Farrell's and Farm. He spoke of what had happened as 'the worst event' and hoped, somewhat unconvincingly, that the 'volcano will go back to sleep'. This was not enough for the local journalists. Their concerns were not, at that moment, focused on the future. They were politely exasperated. They had been down that road before. So how did the authorities explain the deaths? Frank Savage, looking tired and under strain, said: 'We will tackle it honestly. We went to very considerable lengths to educate people, to get the message across. In the case of Harris, we provided transportation [to take people out]. No one will be satisfied with the answers and I will have a difficult time in coming weeks.'

Savage announced that Plymouth and the airport would remain closed for at least twenty-four hours. That meant that apart from two helicopters, the island was cut off. Would there be an off-island evacuation? Savage was cautious. He didn't think it was imminent but it was for 'consideration'. The scientists, he said, 'were not saying that we have a volcanic situation that would necessitate evacuation'.

There was also the crucial question of Cork Hill. This was a densely populated community of some 1500 people strung out south of the Belham River. The third pyroclastic flow, which had unexpectedly regathered, had reached the school at Cork Hill. There were rumours that two roasted dogs had been found near the river. The evacuation of Cork Hill was put on hold, but Governor Savage said people should move away from low-lying areas and keep indoors. It was eerie in Cork Hill that night with men, women and children, struggling along ash-laden roads. There was a sense that no one knew what would happen next or what to do next.

A few days after the death of his parents, John Robinson walked south from St John's through the bush to see for himself what had become of Farm, his home village. Pea Ghaut – once as deep as a four-storey building – was now filled in, white and stripped of vegetation. 'It was terrible,' he said. 'It was just one level. I couldn't face that again. The whole village finish . . . I don't believe I watch Montserrat like that again.'

The natural order of things had disintegrated. The known landscapes, so green and glittering, had been subverted. But the great and terrible sight that Delia Ponde witnessed that day was, for her, something to tell her great-great-grandchildren. 'We all take chances, life is full of chances. I don't regret I was there . . . It was a new experience, a new lease of life.'[11]

Others had their own means of memorial. Howard Fergus, poet, historian, deputy governor and speaker of the Legislative Council, was later to write a poem about Melville Cuffy, the dead carpenter, farmer, Adventist elder and, as Fergus described him, 'a model husband'. Fergus said he wanted to express how he felt about the deaths – 'to counteract the impression that they had it coming to them. I wanted to be more generous to this man.'

The poem, *Post Mortem*,[12] begins and ends with the stanza:

> We can be wise after the event,
> For you there is no afterwards
> just a post mortem on a bed of ash
> unless what you believed has chanced
> and you've lighted on joy.

The day after the disaster, a young man stood outside the hospital in St John's. He had been visiting his stepfather, who had been injured. He was selling bunches of herbs from the back of his car. His thoughts were both for the character of the island – a place where you can sleep with your doors open – and fear for the loss of all that. 'This is such a small place. It will take courage to continue,' he said. It had been nearly two years since the volcano crisis had begun. If the deaths were a watershed in the crisis, the need for housing and land, like an insistent drumbeat, was to echo down the years of the crisis as the fire from the mountain continued to overwhelm the island.

2

....

A Fateful Arc

When the pyroclastic flows swept over the flat lands of Trant's close to the airport and hard by the sea on 25 June 1997, they buried for ever the remains of an Amerindian settlement. It was the Amerindians, the pioneering pre-Columbian settlers of the Caribbean, who were the first to enshrine the island volcanoes in their imagination. They had, no doubt, chosen that site for its gentle contours, its access to fresh water and for its fertility – the product, of course, of earlier pyroclastic flows from the Soufrière Hills.

The first wave of Amerindians probably began to move from South America, migrating from the valleys of the Orinoco up in to the eastern Caribbean, around 3000 BC. The last group, the Caribs, who christened Montserrat 'Alliouagana', the 'land of the prickly bush', arrived perhaps only a century or so before Christopher Columbus sailed along the west coast of the island in 1493. It was, however, the remains of a Saladoid village dating from between 500 BC and AD 300 that was found at Trant's. There had been finds of pottery shards at Trant's at the beginning of the twentieth century, but it was not until 1995 that an archaeological dig – undertaken before a planned reorientation of the airport runway – encountered ceramics, stone tools, shells and human skeletons. It was an exciting discovery and Trant's has come to be considered a key site for the under-standing of Amerindian culture not just in Montserrat but in the whole of the Lesser Antilles. To learn more about the settlement at Trant's, samples of excavated materials, including skeletons, were taken for laboratory analysis supervised by the Smithsonian Institution of Washington, DC (to be returned in due course to the Montserrat National Trust). Three weeks later the volcano erupted.

So perhaps there was a link between the Amerindians of Trant's and the volcano crisis. Perhaps, so the story went, the spirits of Montserrat's indigenous peoples had not liked this upheaval of their bones, this uncalled-for diaspora, and so had sent the fire from the mountain, from their god's ancient seat of power, tumbling into the valleys below. The Amerindians, like all peoples who live near volcanoes, personified the extreme forces of the capricious natural world around them. The little that is known of an Amerindian spiritual life suggests that their internal landscape connected to those unstable, sometimes shud-dering, mountains that define the shapes of much of the eastern Caribbean. The mountains with their 'high forests' were more than just a source of timber or a place to hunt.

In the ancient (and not so ancient) world, volcanoes have been depicted as giants hurling rocks, giants breathing heavily, dragons, battling serpents, and, in the classical Roman world, the smoking forge of the blacksmith god Vulcan, the child of Jupiter and Juno. Vulcan lived on the tiny island of Vulcano, in Italy's Aeolian Islands, from which the English-language word volcano is derived. Volcanoes were also seen as gateways to hell and could evoke images of warfare and disruption, of fire and brimstone. These mythical images are potent. For volcanoes bear powers of destruction that far exceed any force created by man; they 'sleep' only to become startlingly awake. Their energy remains as unforgiving for us at the beginning of the twenty-first century as it must have been for the pre-Columbian Amer-indians. And it is part of a universal irony that some of the most physically alluring parts of the world are also the most dangerous. So it is for Montserrat.

Montserrat lies on that graceful, if sometimes fateful, volcanic arc of Caribbean islands that stretches from the tiny Dutch territory of Saba in the north down to Grenada in the south. These small islands look, on the map, like stepping-stones or, as they are often described, a necklace, a slender protector of the Caribbean Sea from the forces of the Atlantic. They are close enough, one to another, that from the extremities of one can be seen the shores of another. Indeed, such proximity perhaps impelled the Amerindians to move from one island to the next. From Montserrat, for example, you can see Antigua to the north-east, Guadeloupe to the south-east, St Kitts and Nevis to the north-west, and even closer and more starkly, the uninhabited volcanic rock of Redonda.

One of the first people to speculate about the relationship between the Amerindians and the region's volcanoes was an American scientist called Fred Olsen, who spent many years in the 1950s studying 'three-pointer' zemis, the small conical-shaped images made out of conch shell or stone found throughout the Lesser Antilles. Deliberating on their significance, Olsen concluded that they represented the volcanoes that the Amerindians saw – first as tiny cones on the horizon – as they paddled northwards through the islands. It was natural, speculated Olsen, who had himself spent time sailing through the Lesser Antilles, for the Amerindians to associate those shapes with a deity who had guided them to land, and thus 'to have created their principal god in the form of a volcanic cone'.[1] The mountainous topography of the islands, in such contrast to the flat river basins of South America, would have been another explanation for their devotion. So by creating the zemi in the shape of a deity, their shamans would have captured some of its power.

The Amerindian god of gods was Yocahú, the provider of manioc. Yocahú, known as the god of thunder and lightning (elements also associated with volcanoes), was said to live in volcanoes, and his power was somehow vested there. In St Lucia, for example, south along the island chain from Montserrat, Yocahú was thought to live in the Pitons, the dramatic twin volcanic domes on the south-west coast. Close to the Pitons is St Lucia's Soufrière, a scarred area of yellow and grey earth, pitted with bubbling black pools and hot springs drenched in rising steam. Its contemporary name is the 'drive-in volcano', but it was known to the Amerindians as Qualibou, a 'place of death'.

A soufrière is a sign of volcanic life and the word, which can sound as delicate as the brushing of butterfly wings, comes from *soufre*, French for sulphur. It describes a vent, an opening in the earth's crust, with hot springs and sulphurous gases. In Guadeloupe and St Vincent, soufrière is the name of a volcano; in Dominica and St Lucia it is the name of a village close to a soufrière. And in Montserrat it is a complex of hills that bears the name, a witness to the fumaroles that festered high above the once peaceful green hems of the mountains. Wherever you are on the islands, the soufrières are reminders of what has been and what might be; they represent unhealed surface wounds with the potential for deeper change.

The islands of the Lesser Antilles are related in many ways, not least in their geological history. The island arc lies at the point where two tectonic plates, rigid blocks of the earth's crust that float on semi-molten rock, converge. To live on the margin of a converging plate, also known as a subduction zone, is to live with geological instability. In the case of the Lesser Antilles, the Atlantic plate is being forced westward, while the Caribbean plate is moving in the opposite direction. Imagine then a series of events: millions of years ago the Atlantic plate is pushed beneath the Caribbean plate, the squashed Atlantic plate heats up and breaks up. This molten matter, being less dense than its surroundings, rises, penetrates areas of weakness in the Caribbean plate and explodes on to the surface. Out of this sequence the oceanic islands of the eastern Caribbean were born.

Not all of the Lesser Antilles islands, however, are of the

same age. There is an outer, older span of islands composed of long-extinct submerged volcanoes. This arc, which includes, for example, Antigua, Montserrat's close neighbour, has been eroded and worn down and covered in limestone deposits. But for those islands of the inner, younger arc like Montserrat, time has yet to wither them. They are, for the most part, mountainous, with central massifs, broken down and eroded, reshaped by further volcanic activity, covered in volcanic ash and lava, and sculpted into new and glorious shapes by wind, rain and sea. In most cases, these lovely islands have relatively fertile soil, courtesy of those volcanic deposits.

The eastern Caribbean has at least seventeen live volcanoes, of which ten are on Dominica. R. T. Hill, a scientist from the United States Geological Survey who visited the Caribbean in the early twentieth century, described the islands as 'smouldering furnaces, with fires banked up, ever ready to break forth at some unexpected and inopportune moment'.[2] Since European settlement began in the seventeenth century, there have been hundreds of thousands of felt earthquakes but fewer than twenty volcanic events. Some have been fully fledged eruptions, causing massive destruction; others have been minor displays of ash and steam. Although some eruptions have occurred within the same year, and, on one occasion, in Montserrat and St Vincent, only twenty-four hours apart, scientists know that although the volcanoes have 'the same parentage, they have different plumbing'. That is to say that although there is an ancestral geological link, there is no direct physical link between activity on one island and that on another.

A classic volcano shape is that of a cone with steep, concave slopes formed by layers of viscous lava squeezed up over a vent to create a lava dome. The sides of these composite volcanoes are characterised by those deposits of ash and rock fragments that have poured down the valleys in the form of pyroclastic flows. The first-known recorded volcanic events in the Caribbean occurred in St Kitts, Montserrat's close neighbour, in 1692. St Lucia (1766) and Dominica (an 'ash eruption' at the Boiling

Lake in 1880) have also exhibited signs of volcanic activity, but the three islands with the most 'active' volcanic history – before the 1995 crisis in Montserrat – were Martinique, Guadeloupe and St Vincent.

Guadeloupe's Soufrière volcano was active in 1694, 1798, 1838 and, most recently, in 1976. St Vincent's Soufrière has erupted seven times in recorded history, the first in 1718 and the latest in 1979. Its eruption on 7 May 1902 killed around 1500 people when debris poured down the north-eastern slopes. Less than twenty-four hours later, Martinique's Mont Pelée erupted, destroying the glittering town of St Pierre, the 'Paris of the Antilles', killing 30,000 of its inhabitants within minutes. The ash plume reached Montserrat, where lights had to be lit at mid-day. (Only two people survived. One was a prisoner, Auguste Ciparis, who was found in his semi-underground stone cell, badly burned; he spent the rest of his life as a circus 'attraction' in the United States.) The destruction of St Pierre in 1902 remains the Caribbean's most devastating volcano story.

Volcanology was in its infancy at the start of the twentieth century. There was little knowledge of pyroclastic flows and surges such as the ones that have imperilled Montserrat. If there had been, the people of St Pierre might well have been evacuated in time. As it was, it was thought that the eruptions from Mont Pelée could not reach the town because the topography of ridges and valleys would get between the volcano and the city.

The eruption of Mont Pelée remains a landmark, not just for the numbers of its dead. Its eruption stimulated the world study of volcanoes, generating the interest of the leading volcanologists of the time who flocked to the ruined city in the days following the eruption. The French geologist Alfred Lacroix, for example, was one of the first people to describe pyroclastic flows, which he called *nuées ardentes* (glowing clouds), writing of their power to move along the ground like hot hurricanes. It is from the work of such pioneers that a picture of what happened at the mountain – and to St Pierre – emerged. In many ways, the sequence of events at Mont Pelée – a volcano not so different from the one which would emerge in the Soufrière Hills – would be replicated (but without the massive human death toll) nearly a century later in Montserrat.

The first signs of activity at Mont Pelée, a single peak some 8 kilometres north-east of the coastal town of St Pierre, came at the beginning of April 1902 with the steaming of soufrières. Three weeks later came a slight ashfall and minor earthquakes. Further ashfalls and columns of steam followed. In the week before the massive eruption, the local newspaper reported: 'The rain of ashes never ceases . . . The passing of carriages in the streets is no longer heard. The wheels are muffled.'[3] By then, eruptions were almost continuous and mudflows poured down the mountain slopes. When St Vincent's Soufrière erupted, the people of Martinique were pleased. It was believed that the eruption on that island would 'relieve the pressure on Mount Pelée and thus prevent a serious outbreak'.[4] It was not to be.

The eruption was described by assistant purser Thompson of the ship *Roraima*, which had tied up in the port of St Pierre on the morning of 8 May. He was one of twenty-five out of the sixty-eight on board to survive the decimation of the city. Unaware of the danger, the ship's crew were all on deck to 'see the show', which Thompson likened to 'the biggest oil refinery in the world burning up on the mountain top'. Then, at 7.42 a.m., there was a tremendous explosion:

The mountain was blown to pieces. There was no warning. The side of the volcano was ripped out, and there hurled straight towards us a solid wall of flame. It sounded like a thousand cannon. The wave of fire was on us and over us like a lightning flash. It was like a hurricane of fire . . . The blast of fire from the volcano lasted only for a few minutes. It shrivelled and set fire to everything it touched.[5]

The death toll of St Pierre represents the majority of the some 47,000 people in the region who have been killed by volcanoes and earthquakes since records began.[6] The figure well exceeds those killed by hurricanes. Yet, for the most part and for most of the time, and despite the catastrophes in St Vincent and Martinique, the perception of danger from 'occasional' volcanic activity has been put to one side. Erased from collective memories and absent from folk stories, volcanic activity is often poorly documented in official island records. In the case of Montserrat, this was certainly true. Perhaps, understandably, for since the beginning of recorded history – until 1995 – Montserrat's volcano had been virtually silent.

Sitting on the inner, younger arc of the Lesser Antilles, Montserrat consists of four main mountain massifs running roughly north–south and decreasing in size from the south. It forges a profile that prompted Columbus to christen the island after the abbey of Santa Maria de Monserrate in the mountains outside Barcelona. The north-eastern approach from the sea throws up a less sharp profile, of rounded massifs whose summits are often sliced off by cloud. The island is surrounded by cliffs, only rarely interrupted by a beach, its volcanic sand black and shiny. In the north, a long shallow shelf extends far out to sea. Frank Perret, an American volcanologist from the Carnegie Institute in Washington, DC, described Montserrat as 'a mountain standing in the sea . . . we land from a boat somewhere about its flanks'.[7]

All the Montserrat massifs represent volcanoes of varying ages. Very recent research, which shows that the whole island was formed by processes similar to the present eruption, has used new dating techniques to establish revised ages for the main volcanic centres.[8] In the hot, dry north is the oldest such centre, the Silver Hills (403.25 metres), between 1.2 million and 1.6 million years old. In the middle is the younger, much larger, higher – and greener – Centre Hills (731.52 metres), dating from between 550,000 and 950,000 years old. Both these ridges are slashed with ghauts, the gullies that characterise the lower slopes of Montserrat's hills. But the Silver Hills are severely eroded while the Centre Hills are dominated by lava domes and flanked by gentler slopes of pyroclastic deposits. In the south are the South Soufrière Hills and the Soufrière Hills, which have erupted intermittently from at least 223,000 years ago to the present.

The Soufrière Hills complex stretches from one side of the island to the other, on a roughly south–east/north–west axis. But its centrepiece is a cluster of five central lava domes. Here, before the earth started to move again in 1995 – and thus change the contours and topography for ever – the highest dome of all was Chances Peak (915 metres). Close by it, to the north-east, was English Crater, 1 kilometre in diameter, and named after an amateur geologist called T. Savage English who 'discovered' it in the 1920s. Within the grey rubble of English Crater, with its ragged horseshoe shape broken and open to the east, lay rugged Castle Peak, by far the youngest dome of all.

But there was unfinished business in the Soufrière Hills. Signalling this were the soufrières. To the west was Gages Lower and Gages Upper Soufrières, to the south Galway's Soufrière and in the north-east the Tar River Soufrière. On a ridge north-east of English Crater, there was also Lang's Soufrière, which is thought to have first appeared in 1960. In that year David Lang, a soil scientist, had come across a patch of land some 22 metres across where there was a smell of hydrogen sulphide, a steam vent and young bushes dying at the edges. The soufrières broke up the natural forest of cabbage palms and tree ferns with a scarred landscape of sulphur springs and bubbling, hot pools; rivulets of water, sometimes as black as petrol, sometimes cloudy, sometimes blue, yellow or grey reflected the mineral-streaked rocks. Steam rose in random puffs and jets; sulphur and hydrogen sulphide filled the air. Underfoot, the land was soft and crumbly, edged by broken and scalded vegetation.

This was the dominant landscape of Montserrat: ancient – and not so ancient – massifs topped by domes, interspersed by soufrières, and surrounded by gentler flanks, all products of volcanic activity. But knowing this geological history did not mean that the people of Montserrat had any concept of living under a live volcano. They did not. According to widespread belief, with no known volcanic activity within recorded history, the Soufrière Hills were, in popular belief, dormant if not dead.

But recorded history is a mere blink of an eye in the study of volcanoes. (And for Montserrat, written history is barely 500 years old.) For evidence of pre-Columbian volcanic activity, radio carbon dating can establish a chronology of events up to 40,000 years ago. In the case of Montserrat, carbonised logs taken from ancient pyroclastic flow deposits at Fort Ghaut, above Plymouth, first put the last major series of pyroclastic flows at some 19,000 years ago.[9] Further research reached broadly similar conclusions establishing that a series of major eruptions took place between 17,000 and 24,000 years ago, with more modest activity perhaps producing the Castle Peak dome inside English Crater within the last few thousand years.

However, an even more recent burst of activity was suggested in 1959, when scientists at the Seismic Research Unit (SRU), based at the University of the West Indies in Trinidad, obtained a charcoal sample from 'a thin pyroclast flow' in the Tar River area below Castle Peak; it showed an age of '320 years plus or minus 54'. Peter Baker, a British scientist from the University of Nottingham, writing in 1985, called this 'isolated data' and reported that attempts to find the site again had been unsuccessful. He concluded that the lack of historical records and a date so different from others found on Montserrat meant that the evidence 'must be treated with some reservation'.[10]

Two other scientists, however, were less sceptical. Geoffrey Wadge of the University of Reading and Michael Isaacs from the Seismic Research Unit placed the eruption as coming from the Castle Peak dome area and concluded that despite reservations, 'our judgement is that this age date does represent an eruption',[11] albeit a small-scale one. Since the crisis began in 1995, scientists have taken more samples from the Tar River area which have confirmed the more recent date, doubted by Baker, for the Castle Peak activity. The earliest date, 1611, places it before European settlement, but the latest, 1665, brings it well into recorded history, for by then the encounter between Montserrat and the old world was already well under way.

By that time the Caribs had almost certainly departed Montserrat (indeed, Columbus had been told that the island was uninhabited), leaving behind only their cone-shaped zemis, their dead and their middens. Those who came next to Montserrat were Europeans, with settlement and profit on their minds. Their interest in volcanoes would only begin to be articulated in the eighteenth century, with the Enlightenment notions of rational thought and scientific understanding. They would, however, make use of the legacy of past volcanic activity – clearing and cultivating the fertile slopes of the Soufrière Hills. Some of the first sugar plantations, such as that at Galway's, had been established on the leeward coast on the gentle hems of the volcano.

The seventeenth-century settlers were concerned with establishing their rights to the island and laying down a political and economic system. Montserrat's colonial history was not unlike that of the other Caribbean islands, although always on a much more modest scale and reaping a fraction of the benefits of the plantation systems in neighbouring Antigua or Barbados. But the pattern was the same: small-scale settlement, followed by a plantocracy when sugar and slave labour became the economic dynamic. For two centuries, until the abolition of slavery (and, in effect, well beyond), a small white élite ruled by force a large black population. The rights of that élite, however, were also circumscribed – by a tussle with the British Crown to control the exercise of that power. The planters of Montserrat, like their fellow colonists all over the Caribbean, were keen to retain authority over their own often chaotic and corrupt institutions, often to the distaste and disadvantage of the colonial powers in London.

Montserrat's first post-Columbian settlers were Irish Catholics who arrived from St Kitts in 1632, ousted from the neighbouring island by Sir Thomas Warner, its first governor. Other Catholics followed. They grew tobacco, cotton and indigo.

When, like the larger and richer Caribbean islands, Montserrat turned to sugar, African slaves were brought to the island, the first ones probably arriving in Montserrat in the 1640s. The islanders – by the end of the seventeenth century consisting largely of Anglo-Irish planters, poorer Irish servants, and a growing number of slaves – struggled against frequent French (and Carib) raids, occasionally retreating to 'the Garden', a redoubt between Galway's Soufrière and the South Soufrière Hills, at times of attack.

During the eighteenth century African slaves continued to be imported, the sugar industry waxed and waned, and there were intermittent military encounters with the French who carried on attacking or threatening Montserrat until after the Napoleonic Wars (indeed, the island was French between 1782 and the Treaty of Versailles in 1783). In 1768 there had been a famous uprising in which slaves planned to take Government House by force while the plantocracy celebrated St Patrick's Day. In the event, the rebellion never took place: the slaves were betrayed, martial law was declared and the leaders executed. There were also, as there always would be, natural disasters such as earthquakes and hurricanes, which brought a different kind of devastation to Montserrat.

The black population, who would begin to establish their own independent, hard-won peasant culture after the abolition of slavery in 1834, remained impoverished in part in thrall to a share-cropping system, and, as always, short of land. Politically, control remained with the whites through a largely moribund elected assembly and a more powerful, nominated legislative council. Britain tightened its power in 1866 by establishing the more direct Crown Colony rule, abolishing the assembly and ruling through the legislative council, headed by the governor with six members appointed by him. This system remained in place until 1936.

Meanwhile, the soufrières had become tourist sites for curious European travellers. Nicholas Nugent, an honorary member of the Geological Society of London, visited Galway's Soufrière in the first decade of the nineteenth century and noticed the grey igneous rock with its black and white crystals. He rode to the soufrière and was somewhat disappointed 'as there was nothing like a crater to be seen, or anything else that could lead me to suppose the place had any connection with a volcano'. However, he was aware that 'very strong sulphureous exhalations arise, . . . so powerful as to impede respiration, and near any of the fissures are quite intolerable and suffocating. The buttons in my pockets were instantaneously discoloured.'[12] The soufrières were part of the dramatic charm of the island. Visitors would climb the forest-clad sides of the Soufrière Hills to reach the otherworldly landscape that the living earth had created among the peaks and craters. Such natural features appealed to the English barrister Henry Coleridge, who wrote: 'But if you ever visit Montserrat, good reader, go even if you have only one day, to the Soufrière.'

Coleridge, a nephew of the poet Samuel Taylor Coleridge, had made a trip to Gages Soufrière – 'a wild and romantic scene' – in 1825. He compared the gentle landscape up to Gages, almost due east of Plymouth, with his 'native Devonshire lanes'. But once there, the atmosphere was different. 'The whole of the bottom of the valley,' he wrote, 'is broken into vast irregular masses of clay and limestone which are scattered about in the utmost confusion, and render it a laborious task to scramble and leap from one to another. The surface of the ground is hot everywhere, and so much so near the streams of water which ran between the fragments, that I could not keep my foot half a minute upon it . . . A thick vapour slowly rises upwards till it meets the wind which cuts it off at a straight line and drives it down to the coast.' Looking back on his 'morning ramble' to the soufrière, he realised that he could not think of it 'without feeling my heart swell with love and sorrow that I shall never see it again'.[13] Another visitor, John Davy, the inspector general of army hospitals, wrote (quoting Byron on Italy) of Montserrat's 'fatal gift of beauty'. He said of his visit to Gages: 'I will not call it horror in the lap of beauty; and yet in some particulars it calls up the idea.'[14] Other European and North American visitors of the time made similar observations, typically, for their time, mingling science and sentiment.

A major earthquake in the Leeward Islands occurred in 1843. Six people died in Montserrat and many were injured. Cliffs collapsed on to roads and buildings, and all the churches and thirty-three out of thirty-six sugar works were damaged. A pall of dust hung over the island. However, it was not until 1897 that the first known sustained period of heightened local seismic activity occurred in Montserrat. This lasted until 1900, and at one time felt earth tremors totalled one hundred a day, according to Montserrat's Commissioner Baynes in his reports to the colonial authorities.[15] Gages Lower Soufrière was thought to have appeared at this time. In October 1900 the *Montserrat Herald* reported that 'People fled from their houses, cattle bellowed, and dogs yelled'[16] during a night of two heavy shocks when damage to property was judged similar to that caused by the earthquakes of two years earlier. An increase in sulphurous smells was also noticeable in those years, and on one occasion a white-painted liner lying off Plymouth was blackened by hydrogen sulphide emissions.

But it was a Montserratian, Matthew Shiel, who had a peculiarly apocalyptic vision for his island, which he called 'a great and holy place'. His idea of nature was of a 'great and terrible' phenomenon. Shiel was, significantly, writing in 1901, just after a time of natural disaster – with hurricanes, flooding and earthquakes all occurring during the 1890s. The emotionally extravagant Shiel wrote: 'God cannot let it [Montserrat] be, but is ever at it, it would appear, to destroy it . . . my eyes have filled with tears of love and pity for it, and all its turbulent epilepsies, and its despondent manias and Orestian frenzies, and coming doom.'[17] Shiel's gothically inspired 'coming doom' was a long time coming.

A second intense period of earthquakes occurred between 1933 and 1937, with the worst of the tremors taking place between December 1934 (when the epicentre of the shocks came to within one mile of the surface) and the culmination of November 1935. This time the colonial authorities in London took notice. St Peter's church in the north of the island was destroyed as was the sugar mill at Molyneux, while St George's church, near a ravine at Harris, suffered bad damage in the tremors of both years. Not only churches but also Government House, the courthouse and the bank – all in Plymouth – were badly affected. On Jubilee Day 1935 the Salem school was destroyed. A former pupil remembered that the whole of the north was shaking and that 'the beaches and roads wobbled like liquid rivers'.[18]

It was during this period that Frank Perret made twelve visits to Montserrat. Perret, who had spent many years researching the world's volcanoes, had been based in Martinique since 1929. He set up an observatory at Mont Pelée and his intense interest in that volcano made him a hero in St Pierre (indeed, his statue still stands in the reborn town's main street, while the Frank Perret Museum tells the story of the eruption).

In Montserrat, Perret's most important work centred on the soufrières. He set up an 'experimental station' at Gages Soufrière, noting that Gages Upper Soufrière had been reactivated by the most severe earthquake of 11 November 1935. His equipment, some of which he invented himself, consisted of a recording thermometer, gas recorder, gas syringe, U-tube manometer for determining gas pressure, microphones and a seismometer. He measured the increased carbon dioxide and hydrogen sulphide emissions at the soufrière, and at one point was overcome by fumes. In his search to understand the nature of seismic activity, and to 'secure some premonition of an imminent strong shock', Perret also studied the behaviour of parrots, poultry, horses and even the sensitive plant *Mimosa pudica*, pots of which he left at his field station. These experiments, however, revealed no precursory symptoms. Perret even bit into his metal bed frame in an attempt to detect tremors. What he did notice, however, was that the household silver at Gages turned olive-black, and that high pressure at the soufrière was 'seen, felt, and smelt unmistakably'.[19]

Perret, who much earlier in his career had worked at Vesuvius, was a dedicated researcher whose writings and photography provide an important record of early volcanological study in Montserrat. He hoped that his account of what happened there provided an 'objective view . . . of an extended series of extraordinary events'. He also provided information to the civil authorities. In public, he told Montserratians that he believed that there was little danger of a surface eruption. However, in his book *Volcano-Seismic Crisis at Montserrat, 1933–37* he said that secretly he had been 'troubled by the nearness to the surface of this latest centrum of dislocation' and he had conveyed this to the governor in a confidential report. He concluded that discussions about the evacuation of Plymouth had been approved 'in the case of any eventuality'. He described the events as a 'long-drawn-out crisis – a human crisis – in which all that was best in a disciplined people stood out finely as a noble example of fortitude'.[20]

Fortitude, though, was hardly enough for the people of Montserrat. They feared more than just collapsed churches and broken crockery. They wanted more than flattery. And in the autumn of 1935 'leading figures' petitioned the governor asking that action should be taken to determine the danger of a volcanic eruption. The governor contacted the Colonial Office in London, which referred the matter to the Royal Society for advice.

And so it was that in 1936, while Perret was back in Martinique, a Royal Society expedition arrived on the island armed with seven shock recorders and a seismograph, which was installed at the Grove agricultural station in Plymouth. The expedition team consisted of geologist A. G. Macgregor and physicist C. F. Powell. Both men spent eleven weeks in the field in Montserrat and published in the *Philosophical Transactions of the Royal Society* a full account of the 'volcanic history and petrology of Montserrat'. They concluded that they had too little information as to be able to forecast a volcanic event. The expedition, according to Sir Gerald Lenox-Conyngham, writing in *Nature* magazine, admitted that 'as we know nothing at all of the causes which determine the time and place of an eruption, it would be extremely rash to assert that there will never be another'.[21]

Perret's findings on this matter had also been inconclusive. He suggested that either this second bout of activity represented the maximum activity or, given that the second was stronger than the first, 'a third might still be stronger'. Whether the conclusions of the stolid Royal Society or of the imaginative Perret brought reassurance to Montserratians is another matter.

Whatever the case, the quakes subsided. As Howard Fergus wrote in his poem *Ignoring Ten*, 'the climb down in '35/and other climaxes/soufrière swallowing its tongue'.[22] In any case, Montserratians had other matters to attend to. In 1936 a new constitution was introduced: it was hardly a great leap forward. There were to be four elected members to the legislative council. Property and income requirements, however, restricted voters to a minority and it was not until 1951 that universal adult suffrage was introduced. Migration continued, as did the pernicious system of share-cropping, which eventually ended in 1959. Sea island cotton had become the island's leading twentieth-century crop, with more than 4000 acres under cultivation by the mid-1930s. The estate culture, however, kept workers in penury. In 1945 an official report described labourers in the cotton field at White's, on the eastern flanks of the Soufrière Hills, as 'underfed, dressed in strings, haven't had soap for weeks'. The trade union movement would not emerge until 1946, a decade later than in neighbouring islands.

The next bout of enhanced seismic activity occurred in 1966–7. By this time Montserrat – although still very much a British colony and dependent on British aid – had its own executive council, including its first chief minister, W. H. Bramble (1961–70). As a trade unionist and 'father of the nation', he had wrested power from the merchant-planter class to lead the island's executive council. A ministerial form of internal self-government was adopted with the British-appointed administrator (the name was changed to governor in 1971) chairing the executive council and maintaining control over such matters as the national security, the civil service and foreign relations. In 1967 Bramble, having represented Montserrat in the short-lived West Indian Federation (1958–62), rejected the opportunity to advance Montserrat to associated statehood status – a step that took its English-speaking neighbours towards independence. The size of the island and the state of the economy, said Bramble, prevented Montserrat from taking 'this bold step'. For Montserrat, this important decision effectively stopped the independence process in its tracks.

Colonial status was reaffirmed and Bramble's energies were engaged in a new cause. With agriculture and, in particular, cotton in decline, Bramble sold off 600 acres of agricultural land as real estate. The purchasers were wealthy North Americans and, to a lesser extent, Europeans. It was an extraordinary venture, which brought an economic boom to the island. It was needed. Writing about the collapse of the sea island cotton industry at the end of the 1950s, George Abbott wrote: 'Wages are appallingly low and the standard of living near subsistence level.'[23] Instead of work with a cutlass in the hot sun, there were now jobs in the construction industry and part-time work in the service sector, as maids, gardeners, pool cleaners and so on. The expatriates were to enjoy their villas, the golf course (also former prime agricultural land), cocktail parties and invitations to Government House; they supported charities but largely ignored the politics of their little 'paradise'.

Dependency on the villas or 'beachettes', as they were first known, and the creation of white suburbia in part of a poor Caribbean island became, from time to time, an issue. But, in general, it appeared that this tourism hybrid worked. J. A. George Irish, a Montserratian radical, wrote in *Alliouagana in Agony* (1974): 'Most white North Americans will never get a clue as to what exactly is going on in the souls of the black people but if they are willing, they can retire peacefully, enjoy what they can, and leave us to work out our own destiny by ourselves without animosity and without conflict.'[24] Villa construction improved the housing stock of the island and its general infrastructure. Montserrat was gaining the trappings of a modern society.

But the ancient force in the Soufrière Hills was showing its hand once more. In 1966–7, as in the other periods of intense seismic activity, the magma stirred within the earth's crust. Yet, at that point, the volcano did not erupt. How close it came to an eruption is not known. In 1966 a small surveillance system had been put in place, which allowed for more precise monitoring. This had revealed several seismic changes around the Soufrière Hills. The renewed stirrings were characterised by earthquakes, the doubling of heat flux at Galway's Soufrière and an occasional radial uplift. Magma, the 'fuel' of volcanic eruptions, said the scientists, had moved to within perhaps 4 or 5 kilometres of the surface. In the wake of the crisis, a manned seismograph station was also set up at Grove's agricultural station near Plymouth.

This work was done by the Seismic Research Unit (SRU), originally known as the Volcanological Research Department, founded in Trinidad in 1952. Its mandate was (and is) to provide an earthquake and volcanic surveillance throughout the English-speaking eastern Caribbean – an 'early warning system' is how Richard Robertson, one of its scientists, described it. Through monitoring the behaviour of the volcanoes on its doorstep, the Unit provides advice to governments, writes regular reports and liaises with other regional institutions concerned with disaster preparedness. Since its inception the Unit has established seismic monitoring equipment in ten eastern Caribbean islands and has monitored some eleven volcano-seismic crises. The SRU played a major role in St Vincent during its eruptions of 1972 and 1979, but its work in Montserrat in the mid-1990s was to be its most challenging.

Through the work of the SRU, the behaviour of the volcanoes of the Lesser Antilles had, by the mid-1980s, to some extent been identified and explored. At a meeting on hazard mapping in the Caribbean in 1987, John Shepherd, a British volcanologist working at the SRU, said that it was 'generally possible to predict the time and place of onset of West Indian volcanic eruptions, although predicting their intensity is more of a problem'. He went on to say that all such known eruptions in the region had been 'preceded by precursory symptoms'. Of these, the most common were swarms of small earthquakes at shallow depth close to the volcanoes and increases in the emission rates of steam and other gases from hot springs. With an efficient monitoring system in operation, 'there is no reason why any future West Indian volcanic eruption should occur unexpectedly'.[25]

What worried Shepherd, however, was the level of earthquake and volcanic monitoring in the Commonwealth Caribbean. The SRU was, he said, the sole organisation working in the region; it employed only three scientists (while there were twelve studying hurricanes); there were 'virtually no funds' for the training of young scientists; and many of the island governments, which funded the SRU, were in arrears. The situation on islands where there had been recent volcanic activity, he added, was somewhat better. Following the eruption of 1979 on St Vincent, for example, the United National Development Programme had funded a project to help monitor the soufrière.

Around the same time as the 1987 meeting, two pieces of research were investigating the long-term prospects for volcanic activity in Montserrat whose hills had been in 'reasonable repose' since 1967. Crucially, both had a 'planning dimension'. Not only did they address the potential hazards of volcanic activity, they also suggested that development plans for Montserrat should take account of that potential hazard. Both based their conclusions on residual evidence from past volcanic behaviour.

In 1985, Peter Baker, who had done the work on carbon dating, wrote a paper on the volcanic hazards of St Kitts and Montserrat, assessing the possibility of future eruptions. For Montserrat, he concluded that although a recurrence of volcanic activity was around the order of every 10,000 years, 'persistent

fumarolic activity and intermittent shallow seismicity in the
Soufrière Hills region suggest it would be inadvisable to dismiss
the possibility of a future eruption as remote'.[26]

Baker also identified the areas at greatest risk. According to
Baker, the configuration of the Soufrière Hills made the Tar
River the 'most susceptible' to any pyroclastic flow activity.
Aware of a plan to build a road through Tar River estate to
Roche's estate, Baker advised that the potential volcanic hazard
should be taken into account in any plans for significant devel-
opment in that vulnerable part of the island. Baker went on to
speculate that the zone ranked next on the hazard scale was
almost the whole of Plymouth. He considered that the leeward
coastal area, from north of Plymouth to the north of Garibaldi
Hill, would be 'unlikely to be affected to any serious degree'.
However, there was, he thought, a very slight possibility that
pyroclastic flows could pass through the narrow gap between
St George's Hill and the Centre Hills into the Belham River.
(Indeed, the Belham River was to become a key point – a
crossing point both literally and metaphorically – during the
volcano crisis, when it became at times the boundary of the
exclusion zone.)

Baker's paper was overtaken by the work of Wadge and
Isaacs. Their research forecast the reawakening of the Soufrière
Hills volcano. Unlike many scientific papers, which get tidied
away in academic minds and libraries, the report by Wadge and
Isaacs was to play a key role in the crisis. Its opening statement
reads: 'Soufrière Hills volcano is active and will erupt again. It
is a potential threat to many of the people that live in southern
Montserrat.'[27] The report had been funded by the United
Nations Disaster Relief Organisation at the initiative of the
SRU as part of a programme called the Pan Caribbean Disaster
Preparedness and Prevention Project, based in Antigua. It was
also addressed to the government of Montserrat. It was particular
prescient.

'The report forecast many of the effects of the eruption with
considerable accuracy,' said Professor Steven Sparks of Bristol

University when he addressed the House of Commons' International Development Committee in London in 1997 in their inquiry into the Montserrat crisis.[28] It had achieved this measure of accuracy by using a model called a sequential hazard zone map. With a series of computer models, Wadge and Isaacs produced a map of the areas which would be 'covered by an eruption becoming increasingly more energetic'.[29] They did this by simulating the geological record of past eruptions in Montserrat or where these were lacking evidence from eruptions of similar character, for example, Mont Pelée. The map, said Wadge and Isaacs, 'is of value in deciding evacuation priorities'[30] by showing the likeliest chronology and affected areas during a future eruption. They claimed rightly that it would centre around Castle Peak in English Crater.

Wadge and Isaacs believed that the likelihood of a new eruption at the Soufrière Hills volcano was low. The probability of 'recurrence of hazard from eruption products' was, they said, around 1 per cent per century although this figure increased to 10 per cent 'for a small area within English's Crater to the east coast'. They were, however, mindful of the responsibilities of the emergency planners. They hoped that their map would be of 'practical use to government authorities during the few days to weeks immediately before and immediately after the start of the eruption'.[31] They also provided three different types of scenario to assist the non-existent planners. 'A small eruption within English's Crater' would affect the people of Long Ground and would trigger mudflows, specifically in Fort Ghaut above Plymouth. 'A moderate to large eruption' of pyroclastic flows as a dome begins to build was the second option. In such a situation, 'most of southern Montserrat should be evacuated', with only Richmond Hill and Cork Hill spared. The third possibility was 'a collapsing dome/lateral blast eruption. This is a very remote but dangerous possibility. The conditions leading up to it may be detectable in advance and once diagnosed immediate evacuation of the relevant 180 degree sector of the volcano would be required.'[32]

Early in 1987 copies of the report were handed to the project organisers, Christopher Turner (governor of Montserrat in 1987–90), the government of Montserrat and the chief of police. And there – on various desks – the report, it is assumed, rested. (And when, in 1997 the International Development Committee inquired whether either the Department for International Development or the Foreign and Commonwealth Office knew of its existence, both departments replied in the negative.)

Despite the report (a scientific paper by Wadge and Isaacs on the same theme was published in 1988), there appears to have been little official (as opposed to scientific) consternation about any volcanic threat. Arthur Watson, governor of Montserrat in 1985–7, said that he had met Wadge and Isaacs when they were in Montserrat in 1986 for their research. But apart from that, there had been, said Watson, 'no attention paid to volcanoes'. David Taylor, governor in 1990–93, also denied any knowledge of the report. 'Volcanoes were never talked about,' he said.

So what did happen to the report? Both governors Taylor and Savage surmised that it might have been blown out to sea during Hurricane Hugo in 1989 when papers were lost in the maelstrom. More prosaically, speculated Professor Wadge, it was a question of a lack of corporate memory. 'It is a genuine problem in small places and small organisations, all it takes is for a couple of people to leave, and the whole memory system goes.'

Whatever the fate of the lost report, a more serious charge remains – that the authorities made few attempts in the years before the onset of the volcano crisis to weave the possibility of volcanic damage into either official planning or public consciousness. The government of Montserrat was reluctant to invest in planning for a future emergency. In 1987, for example, a plan was drawn up by the Montserrat Disaster Preparedness Office. Under the heading 'Chapter 10: Volcanic Emergency' was the comment 'To be issued separately'. It never was. In 1989, prompted by increased seismic activity, the SRU added two more seismic stations to the one at St George's Hill. All three were destroyed by Hurricane Hugo and not restored until early 1991.

When Frank Savage arrived in Montserrat as governor in July 1993, he learned that the Caribbean Disaster and Emergency Response Agency rated Montserrat at the bottom of the disaster preparedness league. As governor, Savage was responsible for internal security so he got to work, along with the government of Montserrat, to upgrade the island's disaster preparedness committee, which he, as governor, chaired.

The British government funded a hurricane-proof office, while Savage also asked a regional consultant to draw up a disaster preparedness manual for Montserrat. It was delivered in the first half of 1995. 'We opened V for volcanoes and there was nothing there,' said Savage. No V for venting or V for viscosity, just V, apparently, for void.

This was set against a background of increased seismic activity, which had begun in 1992. Some volcanologists might have said 'told you so', for the timing coincided with the 'thirty-year gap' theory. Perret, in the 1930s, for example, had drawn attention to the 30-year gap (or a multiple thereof) between activity throughout the eastern Caribbean. He pointed to the fifty-nine years between the Guadeloupe activity in 1843 (with serious earthquakes in Montserrat and Antigua) and those of Mont Pelée and St Vincent in 1902 and the thirty-one years thereafter until the onset of increased seismic activity in Montserrat in 1933. Perret concluded that 'There exists for this volcanic province a periodic magmatic expansion about three times in a century, which has migrated back and forth along an extended line and has given rise to localised, concentrated effects under and through the various previously formed island centres.'[33]

Contemporary scientists would distance themselves from such conclusions, claiming that the other Caribbean volcanoes do not, at present, show a similar periodicity. They would, however, agree that although a century is a very short time in the lifespan of a volcano, there has been volcanic activity in the

Soufrière Hills roughly every thirty years: 1896–7; 1933–7; 1966–7; 1990s. Yet scientists are, as Professor Wadge points out, reluctant to predict: 'The trouble with geophysical periodicity is that a lot of people have made themselves look foolish – by getting it wrong.' He was, however, regretful that he had not himself paid more attention to that hypothesis.

What Perret had jauntily called 'Plutonic attentions' started to afflict Montserrat again, as Wadge said, 'almost bang on time'. In 1992, a new seismic-volcano crisis began when the seismicity increased above 'normal/background levels' with periodic swarms of tens and sometimes hundreds of earthquakes. The elevated seismicity, with a particularly acute phase at the end of 1994, prompted the SRU to increase the number of seismic stations on the island and to reoccupy three sites to measure ground deformation. Scientists from Guadeloupe also worked with the SRU at Gages Soufrière taking gas and water temperatures and monitoring heat flow.

Montserratians were aware of the increased seismic activity. Glenn Lewis, an electronics engineer from Richmond Hill, was particularly interested because he had become fascinated in the possible link between the patterns of seismicity and the cycles of the moon (Perret had suggested that earthquake shocks occurred at periods of the new moon). Lewis was also aware that the monitoring at St George's Hill was affected by the power cuts that plagued the island from time to time. He complained to the electricity company that something should be done about it: 'I knew that it was important for the SRU to be able to read the signals,' he said. 'The intensity of the volcano seemed to be getting stronger although at that time there was no visible sign.'

The accountant Simon Maty lived closer to the volcano in a two-storey house at Broderick's, on the south-western flanks of the Soufrière Hills. It was, he said, the last house below Chances Peak. Familiar with the earthquakes, he would sometimes hear a kind of rumbling. It sounded like a jet plane and Maty thought it might have been Concorde taking off or landing at the nearby island of Guadeloupe. He didn't think it was anything to do with a volcano. However, Sharmen Thompson, a psychiatric nurse, who also sometimes stayed at Broderick's with her parents, was less certain. The earthquakes and the strong sulphur smell concerned her. She thought the volcano would erupt.

On the other side of the Soufrière Hills, at the village of Long Ground, lived Fred 'Mountain Man' Lee, a well-known farmer and building contractor, who had returned to his home village in 1988 after decades in north London. He had built a large stone home and wood-panelled restaurant, the last house under the mountain. He reckoned that the volcano was coming to life. Six months before July 1995 his land on the usually fertile slopes of the Soufrière Hills had stopped bearing. 'Fifty bags of white potatoes, usually worth EC\$20,000 and I didn't get one. The potato had a black streak in it. We planted potatoes from October but we never reap a crop.' He went on to say that the whole sweep of the agricultural belt on the edge of the Soufrière Hills had been affected: everywhere, the potatoes failed; something was taking water from the plants.

Meanwhile, the SRU continued its monitoring, public education work, training and reporting to local officials. Professor Sparks told the International Development Committee that the scientists had at that time made it 'clear in discussions with local officials that there was a potential problem'.[34] Glenn Lewis believed, however, that more could have been done. 'The scientists were treated as insignificant. They were reporting to government all the time. The government was saying "Let's get on with development policies" while the scientists were saying "we have trouble".'

The SRU was still afflicted by a lack of resources and staff to cope with its extensive regional responsibilities; by 1995 it had fifteen members, five of them professional scientists. SRU scientist Robertson said that, given resources at the time: 'I don't think anything more could have been done prior to the eruption in terms of monitoring. Additional ground deformation monitoring may in hindsight have been much more useful – we had little and it was not being adequately monitored.' However, even with extra staff, funds and closer monitoring, Robertson did not believe that this 'would have fundamentally changed what happened in terms of our actual forecasting of events prior to July 1995'. Professor Sparks agreed. 'It is easy to exaggerate the idea that the scientists should have anticipated the eruption,' he said. 'In fact, similar earthquake swarms are common with volcanoes and do not lead to eruptions.'[35]

Certainly Governor Savage said that there were no messages passed down from the SRU at the time 'to the effect that an eruption of the volcano was imminent. Neither ministers, government officials, nor the department of agriculture had picked up anything that they regarded as out of the ordinary.' Some people said in hindsight that they had a premonition or a dream of what would happen. But, for the most part, it was only the crazy and the street-corner preachers who had intimated a fiery future. There was, for example, Brother Hammy White, known as God's Messenger, a farmer from Harris. He had preached for years that the volcano would erupt because of the people's sin. For those not given to prophecy, however, volcanoes were the stuff of faraway dramas or television documentaries. Howard Fergus explained that people had forgotten that earthquakes and volcanoes could be linked. 'We were seeing earthquakes as earthquakes – we were not making the link.' And neither the guidebooks nor the Montserrat Tourist Board mentioned the ponderings of the scientific community, continuing to promote the Soufrière Hills as a fine tourist attraction. The soufrières – the surface spillages of the discomfort of inner earth – remained a fascinating 'marketing' feature of the 'Emerald Isle'.

So what sort of island was Montserrat in the days 'before the volcano'? As a colony of the United Kingdom, as a dependent territory, it was locked into a complex set of political and economic relationships. Power in a dependent territory is a triangular structure: there is the elected local government, the British-appointed governor and the British government in Whitehall. In the case of Montserrat, the governor, who is appointed by the Queen on the advice of the British foreign secretary, retains authority over foreign affairs, internal security, off-shore finance, the judiciary and the civil service. The island's elected government, headed by the chief minister, is responsible for all other matters, governing through an executive council, presided over by the governor, and a legislative council. In 'normal' times, Montserrat had a devolved model of internal self-government.

Montserrat's public image, the way it liked to sell itself – to tourists at any rate – was as 'the way the Caribbean used to be'. This discomfiting slogan, suggesting a lost Caribbean paradise (ignoring slavery, share-cropping and the lack of democratic rights), was used to promote Montserrat as a gentle, crime-free Caribbean island, with an Irish legacy, a pretty capital of neat pastel-coloured buildings, and 10,000 or so 'friendly' people, unthreatening to outsiders.

If, at one level, such a description was accurate, it disguised some fundamental problems. Some of these were described in a development plan for Montserrat, prepared by its government in 1989. It put Montserrat's problems on the line: 'chronic emigration, horrendous balance of trade situation, a failure to share in the region's tourism boom, a budgetary cliff-hanger' and so on.[36] Looking towards the year 2000, the government had a conservative solution – to increase tourism and service-related investment as a way out of its difficulties. More hotel rooms and villas and a cruise ship berth and marina were identified as the 'only feasible course' for the island.

Even so, many Montserratians had come to enjoy a comfortable enough standard of living, priding themselves on their high-quality homes and cars and good education system. In 1987, for example, Montserrat's per capita GDP of US$3532 was the highest among the seven-member Organisation of Eastern Caribbean States; its infant mortality rate was the lowest, its persons per doctor and its staff/pupil ratio the highest. By 1994 its GDP had risen to US$5000. The welcoming economic and social environment also attracted Air Recording Studios, where some of the world's best-known rock stars went to record, and an off-shore medical school, the American University of the Caribbean whose students contributed to the booming GDP.

Montserratians lived predominantly in the south and along the saddle of the central corridor, with a growing middle class concentrated around Plymouth. The smallness of the society was both part of its attraction and a function of its malaise. The intimacy of relationships, close family connections and village life made, at one level, for cosy cohesion and a caring atmosphere. At another level, such conditions provoked petty quarrels, the personalisation of politics, a lack of accountability and the undermining of authority. In effect, it was an underdeveloped civil society.

While Montserrat had been out of budgetary aid since 1981, its economy fell far below that of other Caribbean dependencies, such as the Cayman Islands and Bermuda, both of which had developed successful off-shore banking activities. Montserrat's brief foray into that sector in the 1980s – at one time a total of 347 banks had been registered on the island – had ended with UK investigations into the brass-plate bank culture and its links to drug money and money-laundering. A few years later, John Osborne, a former chief minister (1978–91), was prosecuted – and acquitted – on corruption and bribery charges. Britain had responded to the banking scandal by clawing back its power over the off-shore sector, arguing that it fell under the mantle of foreign affairs.

This was a backward constitutional step for Montserrat. But then independence had never been a central issue for the island and had been vigorously opposed by the business class.

As chief minister, John Osborne, a self-made millionaire, had loudly claimed a pro-independence stance, but had never campaigned on the issue. Independence was not a vote-winner, although there were a few people who believed that some sort of political change could and should evolve. Political parties remained somewhat ephemeral: they existed during elections but faded away in the years in between. In common with many Caribbean islands, Montserrat suffered a brain-drain of disillusioned, bright potential leaders. Those leaders who remained saw themselves as somewhat patriarchal figures, looked up to for their ability to deliver patronage to a grateful population.

And then came another natural disaster – Hurricane Hugo, on 17 September 1989. Twenty per cent of homes were totally destroyed, and 50 per cent severely damaged. Nearly a quarter of the population was made homeless. In response, a £16.8 million capital aid programme was approved by the British in 1991: a new parliament building, government headquarters, a library and an improved hospital – all in Plymouth – and two new schools were to be built.

In the shadow of Hugo, political power changed. The elections of 1991 brought Reuben Meade, a young development economist, to power as chief minister on the platform 'Give Youth a Chance'. Meade was well educated, had lots of energy, contacts in international institutions and was a modern kind of political leader. His solution for the economy, however, was largely on the same lines as his predecessor's: inward investment and up-market tourism as a vehicle for providing jobs and earnings.

According to Governor Savage, a sense of purpose infused the island at this time. 'There was hope that the future was bright. It was all very positive.' This was reflected in renewed economic wellbeing. As one Montserratian teacher put it: 'I would meet someone and say, "Oh, I haven't seen you recently, where have you been?" The answer would be, "Oh, I was in New York shopping."' There were attempts to re-establish Montserrat as an off-shore centre: a rice mill was processing Caribbean rice for the European market; the construction industry had a boom; real-estate flourished; expatriates returned. There was some agriculture, while kitchen gardens and provision grounds allowed for self-sufficiency, especially for the elderly. A different interpretation, however, was reported by the development agency Christian Aid, which posited that this economic activity had taken a toll on reserves of local capital. Montserrat, as ever, remained to a large extent dependent on inputs from abroad. As Christian Aid's report put it: 'It has imported food to eat, aid to run the administration, private cash to sustain its lifestyle.'[37]

A post-Hugo reconstruction climate continued right up to the dawn of the volcano crisis. The builders were still painting the new library in Plymouth, the new government headquarters had yet to hold a legislative council meeting and the improved hospital had yet to receive a patient, when the mood in the Soufrière Hills changed. This time it was not just earthquakes; this time the magma moved from the magma chamber and reached the surface. For whatever reason – and scientists still do not know why – the Soufrière Hills were to begin a cycle of activity that was to change the landscape and the lives of the people of Montserrat for ever. It was 18 July 1995.

3

Collapsing Domes and Dangerous Uncertainties

Gertrude Shotte, headmistress of Kinsale Primary School, south of Plymouth, was driving back from the funeral of the island's education officer with a friend on the afternoon of 18 July 1995. 'When we were driving down Kinsale Road, we smelled strong sulphur. We didn't associate it with the volcano. Then I said to my friend, "You hear that sound?" It sounded like a plane, a struggling jet plane. The volcano was the last thing we associated with that sound. It was the last thing on our mind. Then ash started to fall . . .'

The first reports to the police, in early to mid-afternoon, came from coastal Kinsale. Those, like Shotte, who heard the constant rumbling and saw and felt the dusting of ash were experiencing the fall-out from a phreatic eruption. Two steam vents at Castle Peak and Lang's Soufrière had opened up inside English Crater. Underground water had come into contact with rising hot magma, expanded and turned to steam. Emerging under pressure from the vent, the steam had shot out along with ash particles. The Kinsale community had been the first to see this.

Governor Frank Savage was at his offices at Government House, a rather fine gabled colonial mansion surrounded by sloping lawns outside Plymouth. Savage didn't hear the sounds at the time, but looking to the south he could see 'dirty clouds'. With the first reports coming in, he sent a reconnaissance force to the mountain, and, as darkness fell, Savage went with Frank Hooper, the island's British Police Commissioner, to the top of Amersham estate, a suburb of Plymouth, below Gages Soufrière. 'From there,' said Savage, 'you could hear this jet engine sound and feel the sensation of standing in dry rain. When we turned the car headlights on, it looked like bits of soot.' (The 'sounds of canon' that had alerted the people of nearby St Vincent to their volcano in 1902 had become a jet plane at the end of the century.)

As head of the island's security, Governor Savage immediately opened an Emergency Operations Centre at the police head-quarters in Plymouth. The then Chief Minister Reuben Meade, who had been at a funeral in Long Ground, arrived to confer. That evening Savage telephoned Trinidad to contact the Seismic Research Unit. Lloyd Lynch, a Jamaican seismic technician from the Unit, was already on his way to Montserrat on a routine visit, but the SRU also sent its chief scientist, William Ambeh from Cameroon, and a visiting colleague, Joseph Devine, from Brown University, Providence, Rhode Island. They would arrive the next day.

Savage remembered his feelings in those early hours of the crisis. 'That first night I certainly didn't start thinking the end game. I thought it was necessary to get a good scientific briefing, not to overreact but at the same time to ensure that we were not risking anybody's life. That was my philosophy throughout the following years. The only important thing that mattered was the protection of each man, woman and child on the island.'

That afternoon Rose Willock, manager of the radio station, had been at home in Amersham. 'The neighbour's kids were chilling out and came to tell me, "You hear what is going on in the mountain. The volcano blowing." "You've got to be kidding," I said. But then I heard the throbbing.' Willock went to work. The radio station was to become a key source of information about the volcano for the islanders. But at first the broadcasters had no more knowledge than anyone else. Meade was concerned that the scientists should make their assessments and that the people should not panic.

But it was hard not to be alarmed. The situation was unsettling. Savage went on the radio that evening. On the strength of an initial assessment from Trinidad, he told Montserratians that there was no immediate danger but that if anyone felt frightened they could pack a bag and spend the night north of Plymouth in a school that would be opened as a shelter. Simon Maty, the accountant from Broderick's, remembered that after the radio announcement, there was a sense of panic. In town, there seemed to be people and cars everywhere. Radios blared and telephone lines were jammed. All over the island Montserratians were calling each other while Montserratians overseas were trying to find out what was happening back home. By nightfall, not only Montserratians but the rest of the world had heard the news.

The next day the Global Volcanism Network of the Smithsonian Institution in Washington, DC, put out its first 'Montserrat Update' on the internet. It had contacted the SRU scientist Richard Robertson in Trinidad, who was in close touch with Montserrat. Its report concluded: 'This eruption appears to have been a small phreatic event with minor ashfall being spread around the island by local winds.'

That same day Lloyd Lynch led a team of foresters and members of the Royal Montserrat Defence Force deep into the Soufrière Hills. They reported minor explosions thrusting ash and steam 40 metres up in to the air every twenty minutes. The following day William Ambeh approached the hills from the north, venturing into the Paradise Estate area. He also set up more monitoring equipment near Long Ground.

At this point, enter – albeit temporarily – the West Indies guardship, HMS *Southampton*. Governor Savage told the island on radio that he had spoken to the Foreign and Commonwealth Office and had asked for the guardship to 'divert to our area' as a precaution. 'I would like the assurance that we would have professional assistance on hand should it be needed,' he said. Only the faintest echoes of imperial grandeur surround the guardship, the British frigate that patrols the waters of the Caribbean from Belize to the British Virgin Islands. Its role is to defend British dependencies, support civil authorities of independent states in anti-drug trade work, provide emergency help in times of natural disaster, and put on cocktail parties to island élites on the Queen's birthday. In this instance, the HMS *Southampton* provided a helicopter to make an aerial reconnaissance and take the first aerial photographs of the events in the Soufrière Hills.

Meanwhile, the SRU team had set up what would become the Montserrat Volcano Observatory in Plymouth, next door to the Emergency Operations Centre. The government of Montserrat had also approached the Volcano Disaster Assistance Programme of the United States Geological Survey (USGS) for help. As Reuben Meade explained: 'We knew about them. We watched American television, not British television. We didn't know about the British Geological Survey at that time.' So it was that five American scientists arrived in Montserrat. It was their equipment that was used during the crisis. Volcanologists stress how crude their science is and how much there is still to be learned about the behaviour of each and every volcano, but by the mid-1990s observation techniques were becoming more sophisticated. Even so, although scientists are able to interpret the processes of the volcano, they can not reliably predict how the processes might evolve. For a worried and impatient population, this is extremely frustrating. The limitations of their knowledge also make decision-making and hazard assessment particularly tricky.

One week into the crisis, Cathy Buffonge, a local journalist, wrote, 'For the first time it was officially announced that areas in the south, including the south-east, would be more at risk in case of an eruption, and that areas north of Belham River would be safer ... The area said to be more at risk includes Plymouth, as well as the airport.' She wrote that island life continued as usual, 'with shops and offices open, and other activities such as pastry-making classes for adults and summer schools for children going on as planned'. Yet, as Buffonge pointed out: 'There is an undercurrent of unease as the emergency services quietly and efficiently go about the business of preparing for a possible disaster.'[1]

An extremely complex and crucial set of relationships between scientists, politicians and population was evolving. In an analysis of two earlier Caribbean volcano crises, in Guadeloupe (1976) and St Vincent (1979), Richard Fiske of the Smithsonian Institution wrote: 'When a potentially explosive volcano enters a period of crisis, interested scientists and a concerned, if not terrified, local community are brought into what euphemistically might be called a challenging relationship.'[2] This was certainly to be true in Montserrat.

Part of this challenge also turned on the relationship between the scientists themselves. In every volcano crisis, scientists from all over the world converge on the 'hot spot', bringing with them a disparate array of skills, expectations, interests and attitudes. In Montserrat, those who gathered around the bubbling soufrière pot were just such a mixture. First on the scene were the SRU scientists from Trinidad. Mainly seismologists, they were experts at monitoring Caribbean volcanoes and earthquakes. Close behind them were the USGS scientists, who arrived in a fire-brigade capacity. They were not familiar with the volcanology of the region, but they had vastly more money and controlled more equipment. The British scientists, some of whom were old hands from the SRU and who eventually dominated the work on Montserrat, were the third group to arrive.

Very early on, a difference of opinion began to emerge as to how the volcano would behave. Some of the American scientists had been at the sudden eruption at the Pinatubo volcano in the Philippines in 1991. There, more than 300 people had been killed but many thousands more would have died if the area had not been evacuated. The Americans thought that the Soufrière Hills volcano was showing a similar behaviour pattern to

Pinatubo, and that the situation in Montserrat might get worse – fast. According to Reuben Meade they were even uncomfortable about being based in Plymouth: they wanted to move to Salem, well to the north of the Soufrière Hills. Meade said he had asked them to think about what sort of signals a move to Salem would give to the people. 'I told them – you are not moving ahead of the public.' The SRU team agreed with Meade. They thought that moving would send the wrong signals; it would also remove the scientists from the Plymouth-based decision-makers. The SRU team represented the 'keep calm, don't worry' tendency. They were basing their opinions on their regional knowledge, in particular, of the events in St Vincent in 1971 and in Guadeloupe in 1976, when early signals had not materialised into major activity. The arrival of more scientists would only add to the various points of view.

Governor Savage was beginning to realise that the implications of the scientific uncertainty were causing serious dilemmas. The scientists would tell him: 'Jump too quickly and there is a danger; do not jump quickly enough, there could be the same consequences.'[3] Both Savage and Meade were taking a crash course in the nature of scientific method and the behaviour of volcanoes. Both were concerned to learn to trust the scientists. As Meade said: 'I had to develop confidence in the scientists. I wanted to learn and they were very open. I went to the mountain to see what was happening so I could communicate with the public.'

None of this was simple. Savage felt that his attempt to understand the situation was not helped by the battery of experts, so he decided to ask the British government for a special adviser, a kind of scientific 'broker'. The man first appointed to this task was William Aspinall, the British scientist who had worked at the SRU and knew the region well. When Aspinall arrived at the end of July 1955, he found that the scientists were 'not singing from the same hymn sheet'. The government and governor, he said, were asking the scientists for their latest opinion: the scientists would meet for half an hour and would fail to come up with any consensus; they would meet for an hour and again would not come up with an agreed position. And so it would go on, said Aspinall. No progress and increasing dissent.

While disagreement is an essential part of the internal process of scientific discourse, wide-ranging views were articulated in those first months, with meetings degenerating into shouting matches. One of the main disagreements centred on whether the phreatic eruptions would herald the growth of a volcanic dome, or whether they would stop and the volcano thus go back to 'sleep'. The American veterans of Pinatubo became convinced of the similarities, in terms of seismic and steam emission patterns, between the Soufrière Hills and Pinatubo. That, they said, made a magmatic eruption more likely and thus had serious implications for long-term planning. The SRU retained its 'let's wait and see' attitude.

To try and unify scientific opinion, Aspinall introduced a methodology, first used by the European Space Agency, but never applied before in volcanology. This procedure brought the scientists together by asking them key questions and weighing up the answers – according to the ability, propensities, experiences and judgement of each scientist. The answers were then put together and a conclusion reached via what was called a 'synthetic expert'. Aspinall, who became the facilitator of this process, said that it had been helpful in Montserrat; the decision-making process became more efficient and there was a structured framework for debate, if not for consensus.

This process, however, could not disguise the evolving friction. As well as scientific dissension, the tension was also to do with personalities, culture and funding. The difficulties were highlighted in the first month of the crisis when a large steam explosion enveloped Plymouth in volcanic ash and darkness on 21 August. The scientists felt that they could not guarantee that events would not get more hazardous and so an official evacuation of the south was ordered. That was the first of the three occasions during the crisis that the decision was taken to evacuate the whole island south of Belham. As Savage later wrote: 'The scientists were not able to tell us if magma and hot ash clouds would follow the phreatic eruption which caused day to turn to night in Plymouth and therefore there was no alternative but to ask people to move to the North.'[4] For Reuben Meade it was a very difficult decision: 'Plymouth was the seat of government, the business centre. Psychologically, it was like moving Washington, DC.' Richard Robertson of the SRU, who had witnessed the eruption on his home island of St Vincent in 1979, said that to know when the 'right' time would be to advise evacuation was always difficult. From his own personal experience, he also knew how traumatic it was to have to leave home.

Two weeks in to the August evacuation, a difference of opinion opened up between the SRU team and the Americans, with the latter thinking it was too dangerous to return to the south. In the event, the evacuation order was reversed when Hurricane Luis struck Montserrat on 5 September. Sheltering from the hurricane became imperative. The evacuated islanders who were in tents in the north were now sent back to the south where, at least, there were hurricane-proof shelters. The people returned home, grateful to be back, but sceptical about the necessity of the evacuation.

Difficulties persisted, in particular in the relationship between the governor and his staff and the then chief scientist, William Ambeh of the SRU. Communications started to break down and an extraordinary stand-off situation developed. One version of events was that Ambeh declined to co-operate with the governor's office, except on his own terms, refusing to provide scientific reports as requested by the governor. In an atmosphere of increasing mistrust, the SRU leadership believed that the governor was also seeking behind-the-scenes advice from other scientists outside Montserrat.

In this fraught and mistrustful atmosphere, Governor Savage did indeed decide to augment the information he had to hand with scientific services from elsewhere. And it was at this point that scientists from the British Geological Survey (BGS) were brought in to monitor the volcano's activities. They were eventually to play the major part in managing the volcano.

The SRU scientists, poorly funded by the University of the West Indies and somehow reluctant to ask for more from the overstretched government of Montserrat, were living on daily allowances a great deal less than those of the UK scientists, who were supported by universities, independent research money and, later, by the BGS. The lack of proper funding for the SRU scientists, which was not resolved until January 1998, two and a half years in to the crisis, hardly improved relationships.

Whatever the primary causes, the effect of all this dissension was the gradual sidelining of the SRU, the 'home team'. Robertson said that its 'role as primary manager of the scientific effort had been slowly eroded' and had become largely secondary. In contrast, the British scientists, with their better financing, their links with the colonial power and their understanding of the workings of the British government, inevitably began to enjoy a greater influence and a higher profile. Even so, what had come to be seen as the marginalisation of the SRU for a time caused considerable bitterness.

While the negative aspects of the first months did not characterise the scientific handling of the rest of the crisis, this was of little help to the people of Montserrat as they anxiously inquired as to what was happening to their little island. They watched the steam and ash pumping out of the still green Soufrière Hills; they admired the pictures of local photographers who had ventured close to the volcano; they tried to carry on with daily life; but most of all they worried and talked about the volcano itself.

Delicate strategies are required in managing a volcano crisis, and building the people into the equation is one of them. Christopher Kilburn wrote in *The Guardian* one month after the onset of the crisis: 'It is crucial during emergencies that the advising experts and local authorities obtain the trust of vulnerable communities, to explain the nature of volcanic activity and the limits of eruption forecasting.' This was especially important if the people have had no direct experience of a volcano. 'When the danger is not perceived,' he wrote, 'enforced evacuation may be resisted; when it is exaggerated, a panicked exodus may ensue. An invariable result of both extremes is civil unrest and an increased lack of faith among everyone concerned.'[5]

Montserratians were new to life under an erupting volcano. They began to learn a new science and a new vocabulary: words such as volcano-tectonic earthquake, vent, phreatic and seismicity. Later there would be pyroclastic flow, block-and-ash flow, surge, pumice, lapilli. These were words which would feature in scientists' reports, be reported on the radio, interpreted in poetry and song, and discussed by street vendors, rum-shop habitués, cabinet ministers, farmers, schoolchildren.

The islanders also began to learn about the management of other volcano disasters in the eastern Caribbean arc. The most dramatic one was, of course, at St Pierre in 1902; there, scientific ignorance and political decisions over an impending election had taken precedence over the safety of the people. Far more recently, the consequences of poor relationships between scientists, between scientists and the media – and consequently the public – had been in the spotlight in Guadeloupe in 1976. There, as Aspinall himself had witnessed, when an eruption threatened, there had been 'gross scientific uncertainty in the full glare of publicity'. Enhanced volcanic activity at La Soufrière volcano close to the town of Basse-Terre had prompted the governor to order an evacuation of 72,000 people. Two teams of French scientists rowed in public about the behaviour of the volcano. These disagreements appeared in the press, creating even more confusion and alarm. Eventually, the volcano quietened, and the people returned home. The exercise had cost the French us$300 million; in terms of their reputation, it had cost the scientists far more.

The lesson from Guadeloupe had not, however, been learned nine years later. The Nevado del Ruiz volcano in Colombia caused the deaths of 23,000 people when mudflows submerged the town of Armero. This enormous disaster was blamed, not on the behaviour of the volcano itself, but on 'cumulative human error', including official paralysis, lack of emergency plans, bureaucratic delay and poor communications systems. And while it was the politicians and officials who were largely to blame, the disaster had again drawn attention to the need for improved communication skills among scientists. 'If you don't try to convince, you are not a good volcanologist,' wrote the late Maurice Krafft in assessing the lessons of the disaster.[6]

Yet communicating with the media (let alone the public) has not traditionally been part of a scientific education and culture. As Peter Baxter, the expert in charge of health issues on Montserrat, said: 'Scientists are hopeless at dealing with the media. They are trained to study rocks not social impact.' This may be changing, for volcanologists are now keen to point out that they have become more aware of wider responsibilities. Scientific papers, for example, examine communication problems and suggest ways of minimising them. In Montserrat, the scientists, at one point, had asked the British government for a public relations adviser. The request was turned down. It was, perhaps, a serious omission. Public anxiety had been intensified by the squabbles among the scientists. Picking up on the difficulties of the early months, Christian Aid wrote of 'a widespread scepticism about the scientists and at the same time an intense, almost obsessive interest (and investment) in what they say'.[7]

In many volcano emergencies, the scientists remain isolated from the local people. Their responsibilities remain unclouded by the needs and feelings of the people at risk. 'The traditional scientific view has been to draw a clear line between science and socio-economic effects. Anything else is anathema,' said Aspinall. 'We're trained that it's not our business, but on a small island like Montserrat you get involved.' The scientists at the MVO certainly became aware of the suffering of Montserratians: they engaged with their distress, worked with them as colleagues and met them regularly in daily life.

Inevitably, the Caribbean scientists bonded better with Montserratians than the scientists from outside the region. As the local journalist Keith Greaves observed: 'Caribbean scientists know Caribbean people.' Richard Robertson believed that the SRU scientists were able to gain the people's 'trust and confidence in a way that other scientists were never able to', that they were able to offer a more sympathetic response from a more familiar point of view. The rank and file of Montserratians had also trusted the judgement of the SRU's William Ambeh – and he had got on well with Chief Minister Meade. 'He was held in high esteem by most Montserratians,' said Franklyn Michael, then head of the Emergency Operations Centre. 'He was able to establish a rapport with the people. He took risks – going by foot into the Soufrière Hills. He went on the radio, became part of the community and, most important, he seemed to have an understanding of how people lived.' In contrast, the experience of the August evacuation, for example, had not endeared the islanders to the US scientists (who had left, as planned, at the end of August) while the credibility of the governor's office had also been compromised by that episode.

The colonial status of Montserrat was again part of the equation. The British scientists were sometimes caught up in the islanders' underlying mistrust of the British. There was a perception, said Greaves, that foreign scientists might have an ulterior motive in exaggerating the gravity of the situation. 'There was a feeling that UK scientists were working for people in the UK. We asked what is their role and their agenda?' Somehow or other the feeling was that different people were being told different things. In the difficult and often suspicious circumstances of the time, these perceptions were not surprising. As Christian Aid put it: 'We see no reason to believe that scientific reports have been politically influenced but the perception that they have is itself important.'[8]

During the first months, while Meade and Savage regularly broadcast on ZJB radio, the scientists were 'only occasionally seen and heard on the media'.[9] According to Meade, the scientists were initially reluctant to go on the radio or to raise their public profile. Then daily MVO reports began to be broadcast, but at first most people thought they were incomprehensible. Montserratians needed clear and accurate information and they needed to believe what they were being told. When information began to leak out about things they had not been told, there was even greater unease. For example, an internet report by the departed American scientists alluded, among other things, to their disquiet about the management of the volcano. Montserratians read this report, and the perception that information was being suppressed or withheld grew. Rose Willock at ZJB was the focus of countless calls from people wanting to know what was happening. 'We needed things explained,' she said. 'We were getting more and more frustrated, but we didn't know what we wanted to know.'

Things changed, however, in October 1995. For a start, the scientists came out of their corner. They began to explain openly about volcanism, and, in particular, about what they understood was happening in the Soufrière Hills. The scientific reports became easier to understand. The scientists began to visit schools and villages in an effort to explain what was happening. Montserratians employed at the MVO were also increasingly used to spread the word. In the end, the Observatory became proud of its communications record. Richard Robertson of the SRU said he knew of 'no other place where so many different ways have been tried to get the message of volcanic hazards across to people'. Inevitably, some people thought that there was, in time, too much information; or too much information of the wrong sort; or information that either underplayed or overplayed the danger. As time went on the Observatory reports, sometimes broadcast twice a day, were even ignored as the public became indifferent to hearing familiar jargon day after day. Such were the difficulties of a learn-as-you-go-along public information system.

Local culture also influenced the way the volcano was managed. Montserratians had lived with hurricane, earthquake and flood for generations. Among less educated islanders there was a strong fatalistic streak. In such a culture, persuading people of the dangers had been hard. As the Irish-born Catholic priest Larry Finnegan explained: 'It was difficult convincing some people of the dangers because everything is governed by God's will.' There was also a sense that no one could bear to face the worst and so failed to confront realities and plan for the future.

All these complex relationships and responses were part of a pattern familiar to observers of volcano crises. Peter Baxter, who had worked in many volcano crisis situations, said: 'You have elected representatives and a population who don't want to hear the bad news. Populations resist outside scientific advice. Why do these people want us to leave our homes and so on? Local people gang up against the scientists and accuse them of scaremongering.' He said it was the same in every crisis. The tensions were not unique to Montserrat.

The Soufrière Hills volcano itself, however, was behaving in a particularly odd way. While every volcano is unique, the activity in the Soufrière Hills was to prove a conundrum. Not only was it a surprisingly long-drawn out emergency, its fundamental peculiarity lay in the way it evolved. 'We usually think of volcanoes as being very violent and active at the beginning and gradually slowing down and going to sleep,' said Professor Sparks. 'This volcano has done exactly the opposite. It started out very slowly and has gradually built up.' The result, according to Sparks, was that everyone was 'running to keep up with the volcano and how it has escalated and developed'.[10] It was an extraordinarily complicated business. Geoff Wadge pointed out that there was no way to forecast this pattern of growth: 'We had no precursory signals that this is the way it would develop. This had a huge effect. With a gradual development you were constantly on the back foot because it kept getting more serious.'

There was another constraint in coping with the volcano. That was the size of Montserrat. If the island had been any smaller, total evacuation would have been the only reasonable option. If it had been any bigger, it would have had an adequate hinterland. In Montserrat, there was somewhere, but only somewhere small, to run to. This factor had important implications for the politicians, but also added to the scientific pressure to look hard at the evidence and give as precise advice as possible about the hazards. As one official hazard assessment report put it: 'The scale of the eruption combined with the small size of the island and the desire to maintain a population presents unprecedented challenges for volcanological monitoring and risk assessment.'[11]

Every Montserratian was having new – and frightening – experiences. After the initial ashing of 18 July 1995, new vents opened within the Soufrière Hills and the ash continued to fall, largely to the west on the prevailing trade winds. And then, on 21 August, there was 'Ash Monday', a 'day to remember', or, as a young electrician put it, 'the first darkness'. A major phreatic explosion plunged everything into darkness. As the rolling black cloud of ash descended, car headlights became useless pinpricks of light. There was fear and panic. It was, perhaps, the end of the world. It lasted fifteen minutes.

Rose Willock remembered that day. At 8.00 a.m., she was in the ZJB studio. 'I looked into the hills and I saw the place getting dark. The technician was trembling. I thought I will tell the people there is nothing to worry about.' Her staff had left, but Willock knew that she couldn't go. She put on some gospel music. 'I don't know what I was saying, but I was very calm. I told the people to hold on to each other and not to go outside. I told them that it's OK. The fear was driving everything,' she said. 'I was alone in the studio with God.' The next day Plymouth and the whole of the south and east were evacuated north of the Belham River.

Although the people were allowed to return home in the first week of September, the crisis had, in fact, only just begun. Towards the end of that month the situation began to change again in the Soufrière Hills – with the first sign that 'something' had reached the surface. Kevin West, a local photographer, had trekked into the hills and, looking into English Crater, he had noticed a small protuberance near its rim. He showed his photographs to Geoff Robson, a veteran British scientist who had by then taken over from Aspinall as adviser to the governor. Robson realised that the change in colour and the heaping up of stones were signs of an emerging dome. At this stage, however, there was no new magma. What West had seen and recorded was, in fact, the old dome floor being uplifted. Then some weeks later new magmatic material began to emerge, pushing out toothpaste-like lava into the crater. This was the material that would grow to form the dome.

For some time the horseshoe-shaped English Crater could contain the growing dome. But five months after the dome's emergence, the crater could no longer hold the unstable lava. The dome breached its east edge for the first time. The age of the pyroclastic flow, those fast-falling fragments of rock, gases and ash, had begun. With the flows would also come the devastating surges, the 'hot hurricanes' of dilute clouds made up of gas-rich particles. Lighter than flows, they could spread outwards and upwards, burning rather than burying.

The first pyroclastic flows travelled 2.4 kilometres from the dome down the Tar River valley in April 1996. The ash clouds rose in tight grey curls, giant heads of broccoli rising upwards, outwards and downwards as the flows propelled themselves in a continuous leapfrogging, tumbleweed roll towards the sea. On 12 May the flows down the Tar River reached the sea, causing the water to sizzle and a new grey-dead spit of land to form at its delta.

This pattern of activity continued as the dome grew and grew, switching its focus of growth from one direction to another over the months. At one time it seemed to threaten the east, then it moved to the north-west and back to the east. At the end of July 1996 the extrusion rate of the magma was estimated at 10 cubic metres per second. This process continued until 17 September 1996, when there was an unexpected development: the first 'explosive event' of the Soufrière Hills volcano. The scientists at the MVO were alerted to the eruption just before midnight: they heard the jet-engine rumble of the eruption itself, of thunder and lightning and the howling of dogs. By the time the scientists reached the east, the Tar River valley was glowing. Houses in Long Ground were on fire: the first to burn was the fine stone house and restaurant, built by Fred 'Mountain Man' Lee, the farmer who had reported the failure of his potato harvest early in 1995. Another casualty was the old Tar River estate house. Wiped out by a surge cloud, only the shell of this elegant old home, owned by the Osborne family, remained when daylight came.

Locals still in the area reported 'falling stones', 'fire from the mountain' and buildings 'pushed', as if by a strong wind. Adolphus Morson, who had been staying with friends in Cork Hill, had gone back to the eastern village of Tuitt's to 'relax and do a little cooking'. He got up to see fire coming down the mountain. 'I was rushing around looking for the keys of the vehicle and couldn't find them. Then I ran for my life. I saw a man ducking from the thunder and lightning, and told him, "get in man, get in man." That was the worst experience of my life.'

This explosive eruption had been triggered by a massive collapse of up to 30 per cent of the dome. In turn, this had decompressed the gas-rich magma swirling around inside the dome and in its conduit. The effect was like uncorking a champagne bottle. The explosion hurled rocks – like the ones to hit Long Ground – up to 1 metre in diameter some 2 kilometres from the volcano. Missiles of various sizes fell far and wide – pumice clasts up to 5 cm reached more than 3 kilometres north of the airport and to the outskirts of the villas of Old Towne on the west coast; gravel pelted onto roofs even further away. Nearby, in Fox's Bay, a resident reported that, come morning, no light could be seen through the bedroom windows. 'They were caked with mud. What we had taken for heavy rain was really a downpour of volcanic mud. About two inches of drying mud had piled up against each outside door so we had to cut through one of the screens of the veranda to get out. The mud was an inch thick on every flat surface . . . the grass was almost invisible. Trees and shrubs were bent low or broken by the weight. The swimming pool looked like strong tea.'[12]

That day, 17 September, some 600,000 tons of ash fell over Plymouth and south-west Montserrat. Roofs collapsed under the weight of the ash. Trees, shrubs and plants were once again under a grey blanket. The coconut palms would eventually turn yellow and die; so would plants such as hibiscus and allamanda that graced suburban villas. The tough-leafed oleander would survive best. Daylight came but earth and sky remained grey. The ash lay on the plants and the land, and subdued the birds and animals. It reached everywhere: inside and outside the house; on the body and in the body.

The physical discomfort of living with the ash was real enough, but at the beginning the potential dangers of the ash to human health were unknown. The Christian Aid report of May 1996, for example, said: 'The clouds of ash that are vented by the volcano harm plants but do not directly endanger life, though people who are caught in thick ash obviously experience some difficulties in breathing.'[13] Yet Susan Edgecombe noted that, by 1997, health officials were telling the public to wear ash masks when it was 'ashing' or on visits to ashy areas. This was different, she said, to 1996 when 'no mention of breathing ash as actually being dangerous was ever mentioned'.[14]

The first report by Dr Peter Baxter, drawing attention to the toxic effects of the ash and the possibility of long-term health problems such as silicosis, was presented to the British government in October 1996. Baxter and his team went on to investigate the possibility that the ash might contain harmful amounts of a toxic silica called cristobalite, a mineral which is capable of causing silicosis. What Baxter's team discovered was that the respirable volcanic ash contained 10 to 25 per cent cristobalite, which was about twice as toxic as that found in, for instance, coal mines or quarries. What research had yet to reveal, however, was the risk to human health in terms of short-term and long-term exposure to the cristobalite of the Soufrière Hills. In

December 1997 Baxter's team reported that: 'Exposure in the impacted communities has not yet been long enough to lead to the development of silicosis and it was considered very unlikely that anyone would be adversely affected if exposure to ash were then to cease.'[15] A survey of asthma in schoolchildren showed that living in areas of moderate to severe ashfall exacerbated the sufferers' symptoms. Monitoring the ash levels in different parts of the island continued throughout the crisis, with readings in May 1999 suggesting that in parts of the south the background level of resuspended ash in the environment remained high.

For more than a year, from the end of 1995, the major characteristic of the volcano had been dome growth and, from April 1996, dome collapse. As bits of the unstable dome continued to fall off, new material filled the scar piling into the void left by an earlier collapse. By New Year 1997, for example, a new dome had grown within the hole left by the September explosion. Dome growth was faster than ever. Its focus continued to shift position, as if moving from one foot to another, to pose a threat in a new direction. In March 1997 another part of the crater wall once again collapsed, and this time pyroclastic flows poured over the vulnerable Galway's Wall, on the southwest edge of the crater. These flows destroyed the well-loved tourist attractions of the Galway's Soufrière and the Great Alps waterfall, before coursing down the White River. All was gone.

The scientists then detected that the dome could pose a threat to the northern flanks of the volcano. By mid-May 1997 the dome's highest point was 981 metres above sea level, peaking the island's previous summit, Chances Peak (915 metres). Pyroclastic flows intensified, filling the ghauts as flow piled upon flow. It was such a process that caused the deaths of 25 June. That day there had also been 'secondary pyroclastic flows', which had condensed from ash cloud surges to travel in directions different from the main flows, in this case, down Dyer's River and then down the Belham River valley as far as Cork Hill.

In July 1997 the flows turned westwards. At the beginning of August flows poured down Fort Ghaut towards the sea at Plymouth creating a landscape of razed earth and the smooth surface of a sepia-brown ski slope. The flows and surges feasted on the empty ghost-grey capital, its people long evacuated. They scorched and began to bury it. The only remaining sound was the swishing of the waves against the sea walls; the only colour was from a sometimes turquoise sea.

Plymouth was being laid waste and the dome kept growing. And then another new and 'ominous' phase began. For four days, in early August 1997, the volcano exploded at twelve-hourly intervals. This appeared to be a different sort of explosion to that of September 1996. This time, in a process known as 'fountain collapse', mixtures of ash, pumice and gas were 'explosively discharged and collapsed under gravity to form pyroclastic flows'.[16] On 7 August the eruption column reached 12,000 metres, while pumice and pebbles fell like grey hailstones on the north, and islanders were warned to remain indoors, cover windshields and stay away from glass windows. The scientists speculated that the explosions might become larger. The risks were great. The MVO report for 14 August described Salem, the small town north of the Belham Valley, as 'highly vulnerable' and pointed out that the crisis had 'now entered a stage for which there is little precedent in other well-documented eruptions'. In a special report for the Montserratian and British governments, the scientists described the situation as 'currently at its highest level of sustained activity yet', adding that 'the trend is towards more violent and hazardous behaviour'.

Up until this point, Salem and the neighbouring villa communities of Olveston and Old Towne had been thought to be safe. (Indeed, there had even been plans to build a permanent volcano observatory at Fleming, close to Salem.) But the explosive eruptions had shown that volcanic fall-out could reach that far. The scientists assessed the risk as follows: 'An eruption ten times greater than any seen so far has an estimated probability of between 1 in 10 and 1 in 100 over the next six months.'

The response to this increased risk was for Salem and its surrounding areas to be declared unsafe for night-time habitation from 15 August 1997.

A further report on 3 September reinforced the earlier forecast that activity would 'continue at similar or somewhat elevated levels' over the next six months. This report had drawn for its opinions on e-mail discussions held between the MVO scientists and international colleagues. These had formed the basis of an 'expert elicitation' along the Aspinall model. The result reinforced the potential dangers to Old Towne and Salem. The scientists reckoned that: 'Explosions only slightly larger than those in early August would be sufficient to transport dense pumice clasts with an equivalent diameter of 10 cm into Salem.'[17] While hazard was less in the north, the scientists said that 'the threat to the north is not zero'.

Then between mid-September and mid-October another phase began: seventy-six 'vulcanian' explosions 'spaced at a mean interval of 9.5 hours' over a month-long period provided a *son et lumière* performance. It was extraordinarily beautiful. 'A magnificent pink and purple sunset reflected the colours as the explosion rose up expanding and churning in the sky – a night to behold,' as Susan Edgecombe wrote of one of these events.[18] Fiery-red rocks cascaded from the summit with theatrical exuberance. By day, the dome appeared neither rounded nor symmetrical. It was bulky and slate grey, a heap of jagged rubble with a large deep crater. Sometimes fingers – spines – of rock stuck out from its profile like a castle battlement. Often it remained hidden in cloud. But it was there and its energy was prolific.

By that time, there was real concern. Was any part of the island safe? In December 1997 two major risk and hazard reports from the scientists were published. They were reviewed by the UK's chief scientific adviser, Sir Robert May, whose conclusions were both comforting and troubling. May concluded that individual risk on an annual basis was less than one in 100,000 for those living in the north. The scientific advice, which May quoted, stated that this likelihood 'should be viewed in the context of other natural hazards to which the island is continuously exposed'.[19] The remaining Montserratians, now clustered in the north, could live with that.

However, Sir Robert emphasised the 'inherent uncertainty' in the analysis and 'recommended in the strongest possible terms' that Montserratians should leave Area 3, otherwise known as the buffer zone. This was an area north of Salem, where Montserrat's remaining middle class lived and where the governor had his relocated office. In the event, the evacuation of the buffer zone never happened. Residents largely ignored the recommendation. What did occur, however, was the largest volcanic event of the whole crisis.

In December 1997 the dome was still growing vigorously. Its volume totalled 120 million cubic metres. It was 1 kilometre across and had reached a height of 1020 metres. By then, the dome had been growing at the rate of a small truck per second. Then, on 26 December, at 3.00 a.m., the volcano performed an unprecedented trick: down the south-western flank of the crater came landslide, pyroclastic flow, ash cloud surge, tidal wave and what scientist Simon Young called a 'violent and energetic lateral blast'. It was the extensive sweep of damage – from Kinsale to O'Garra's – that shocked the islanders. Every feature of a familiar landscape, both natural and manmade, disappeared across an area of nearly 7 square kilometres. At sea, a delta 1.6 kilometres in width formed at the mouth of the White River, with debris from the collapsed Galway's Wall piled 30 metres high around it, while a tidal wave, at least 1 metre in height, came in at Old Road Bay, north of Plymouth.

In photographs, the arc of destruction shows a white, featureless mass edged by the sea; only the faintest shadowy remains of steep-sided ghauts that had once striped the Soufrière Hills are visible. From the air, less than a month after the Boxing Day 'event', it remained a sea of blankness. 'Terrible, terrible. It's very bad,' was all that former Chief Minister Bertrand Osborne could say as he peered out from the helicopter moving slowly over what had once been his constituency. Villages that literally disappeared that night were St Patrick's and Morris; Trials and Kinsale were horribly damaged. Alone in the emptiness was a row of steps – climbing to nowhere. Bent steel structures straining away from the volcano and towards the sea had once been St Patrick's police station. 'Galway's Estate was somewhere down there,' indicated the helicopter pilot. Black sticks stood as markers for trees. Only the stone Reid's Hill sugar mill was left. It was hard to identify anything more. When Dunstan Roberts returned home to Montserrat in October 1998, he went to Trials to look at the ruins of his home and search for his piano. All he found were the piano wires.

The massive Boxing Day collapse – some 45.9 million cubic metres of dome material – did not deter the dome from filling up again. In fact, it was filling up as fast as ever. Then one day after the first week of March, everything changed. The dome suddenly stopped growing. Magma no longer reached the surface. At that point, the dome's height was 1031 metres, its highest ever. It had extruded nearly 300 million cubic metres of rock since it had begun to grow in November 1995, some twenty-eight months earlier. It was enough to fill 3000 Royal Albert Halls.

Why it stopped then and there is not known. As Aspinall explained: 'We are dealing with non-linear dynamic systems. There are different processes working for and against each other. The volcano itself doesn't know what is going to happen next.' The most likely thing, he speculated in April 1998, was that it would 'gracefully decline'. No one could say for certain. By July 1998 the scientists reported that the volcano seemed to have entered a period of repose: the probability of no further magmatic eruption in the next six months was put at 95 per cent. A year later there had been no reappearance of the magma. Even so, the danger remained. Pieces of the hot dome rock would continue to collapse, creating pyroclastic flows, sometimes to fall towards the north, the east and sometimes again over Plymouth, while the magma beneath the dome continued to degas and release heat.

For Montserratians, one of the keenest points of loss was Plymouth, involving both personal and national grief. Montserratians are sentimental and stalwart, outgoing and private. Some could not bear to know what had happened to their homes and businesses; others wanted to look, to rescue what there was to salvage.

From the end of 1997, in periods of relative calm, islanders began to be allowed weekly trips into Plymouth under police escort. The meeting point was McChesney's, the relocated office of the governor, in Olveston. McChesney's had been the luxurious if dull home of a soft-drinks millionaire who had retired to Montserrat. Now there were stray donkeys on the lawn. People anxious to inspect their homes and businesses or to extract a precious piece of furniture or equipment would gather there. Once their names had been checked, the police sergeant would deliver instructions about the rules governing entry, ending with the words: 'I have a radio, siren and PA system. If we get the call, I'll alert you. If I say get out, it may be your only chance to get out. Drop what you have and go.'

The road from McChesney's to Plymouth passes through changing landscapes. The looping road is edged with empty villas, their driveways dipping towards generous car porches, huge verandas and swimming pools. From Olveston, the route goes through Salem, then on to Old Towne, past the Vue Pointe Hotel with its view of the volcano and Old Road Bay, Montserrat's first settlement. The vegetation has become battered, but in this area not defeated, and often as glistening and green as in any Caribbean island. The villas here have names such as Connemara and Bay View and overlook the golf course at the mouth of the Belham River, its greens and fairways now littered with pumice stone and bathed in mud.

And then the greenness fades away into greyness. From the top of St George's Hill, Fort Ghaut had become a flat pyroclastic flow deposit sloping towards Plymouth, now a pale, washed-out alpine town in an out-of-focus photograph. To walk on that flow meant walking on what had been the suburb of Gages, of which little remains – apart, perhaps, from the remnants of a shop called Celeste's Fashions. At least, that's what a young man who used to go to Celeste's to get buttons for upholstery thought. Peering at some lumps of concrete, he said: 'I remember the building had stucco outside; it was cream, but there's some flaky pink paint here. Look. Yes, that was at the back.' What he was looking at had been a two-storey house. Its ground floor was buried, its top floor was ripped off and all that was left was the steel reinforcements bent down towards the sea, and a corner of concrete with lipstick-pink paint. Below Celeste's was a rock. It was as big as a two-storey house. It sat in the middle of the pyroclastic flow. It had been hurled down the mountainside.

Close to Gages is Lover's Lane, a road that runs in a straight line from the suburb of Richmond Hill, north of Plymouth, to Fort Ghaut and the corridor road to the east coast. Lover's Lane had survived; it was just gaunt and grey, more bombed out than obliterated. Here had been the rice mill and M. S. Osborne's timber yard, one of the biggest businesses on the island. zjb radio station was also on Lover's Lane, purpose built and almost new, with three studios and editing suites. Some of the other buildings were lopsided with ash; some had lost limbs. The road was studded with rubble and burned trees. Again there was no colour. The ash scooped up by the wind, swirled and settled again.

In the centre of Plymouth, past the cricket pitch (where early in the crisis the ash had been deposited in neat piles) and past the cemetery was a war memorial and a British red telephone box. Gradually, those traditional images became further and further entombed in ash.

In some places in Plymouth the ash was so deep that a first-floor veranda had become a ground-floor entry point – push the shutters and you could walk straight into a first-floor sitting room. Inside a house at the bottom of George Street, the family furniture was untouched: a chaise-longue, the canework filtering the ash, a carved table, a television. Outside, galvanised sheets torn from some roof were draped like brown towels. Montserratians sometimes lost their way in Plymouth because nothing familiar was left in the boulder-strewn landscape. 'Turning left at the Royal Bank of Canada we really lost our bearings. Where were all the familiar buildings?' wrote Susan Edgecombe, who had a real estate business in Plymouth. 'A few foundations only. We thought we recognised the Printery walls. The next thing we realised was that we were actually standing on top of the prison and could see down into the cells.'[20]

There were curious details among the ruins of Plymouth, snapshots of what had once been. At Angelo's Food Centre, with its signs for Whiskas and Pedigree, the shelves were empty except for the odd jar of peanut butter or tin of coconut milk. At the Legislative Council, the plastic chairs had melted but the frames remained. Outside the still-standing Anglican Church, the delicate ironwork on the gate had been bent by the heat towards the sea. The Catholic Church was a shell, although the cross remained on its steeple. In a room in the police barracks, an officer's uniform still hung in a tiny wardrobe behind the door, his cap rested on the end of the single bed. In a corner of an office, a computer poked out from a mass of ash while a coffee percolator rested undamaged on a ledge. Sometimes, little remained except tangled steel frames and stone walls.

Plymouth was written about as if it had become a post-nuclear war zone or – the most popular invocation – a tropical Pompeii. The same had happened in St Pierre, Martinique. The American Angelo Heilprin, who visited St Pierre soon after its destruction, had a similar experience to visitors to Plymouth nearly a century later. He wrote: 'The most massive machinery was bent, torn and shattered; house-fronts, three and four feet thick, crumbled and were blown out as if constructed only of cards. The great cathedral bell lay buried beneath the framework of iron which had supported it, tossed from the church to whose chimes it had so long added its sweet music.'[21] St Pierre, however, somehow rose again; within months people were squatting in the ruins as flowering vines began to thread their way through the rubble. That is not the way with modern disasters; our way is to turn the ruins into a heritage site. Tourism is the way the Caribbean makes its living. Even so, it would be years before such ideas could become reality in Plymouth.

The Soufrière Hills were not yet safe, even if the magma was no longer disturbing the surface. In October 1998 chief scientist Keith Rowley told the *Montserrat Reporter*: 'The volcano must still be considered as very active, even though there is no growth, there is the disintegration of the dome, which makes it still very dangerous.'[22] That was still the case in mid-1999, with dome collapses, small explosions and huge ash clouds being expected to continue. Scientists believe that the continued instability of the dome is caused by the rise of pressurised volcanic gases from magma deep in the earth. The high gas emissions and fluctuations in activity could carry on for many years. 'The overall level of residual activity is not clearly in decline,' reported the scientists cautiously in June 1999. And on 20 July a dome collapse resulted in surges, devastating areas in the far south of the island previously untouched by the volcano.

Gradually, however, the boundaries of the 'safe' zone in the north were being extended south. The health experts suggested that Isles Bay, just south of the Belham River mouth, could be reoccupied in April 1999, although Cork Hill and areas further south remained 'unsuitable for reoccupancy' at that date. While the north continued to be the centre of the new Montserrat, the desolate retreat from the volcano had finally ended.

Over the years of the crisis, the work at the MVO had attracted up to fifteen scientists at a time – from the Caribbean and the United Kingdom, with support from French and North American scientists and, via e-mail, from many more. Enormous amounts of knowledge had been acquired. The Soufrière Hills had become, as the MVO team wrote in *Science* magazine, 'one of the most closely monitored volcanoes in the world'.[23] Professor Sparks described the MVO's work in his memorandum to the International Development Committee as 'outstanding', a 'major achievement' with 'beneficial impacts in future volcanic eruptions in other parts of the world',[24] while Simon Young said that the amount of data gathered had been 'unprecedented' and the learning 'wide-ranging'.

In the field, the scientists went on foot or were dropped by helicopter into the exclusion zone, such complex operations complementing the work done at the Observatory. Gases were monitored, ash was measured and deposits – from vast ballistic blocks down to the finest ash – were analysed. In volcanology, the scientists learned about the behaviour of magma and the magma chamber, about pyroclastic flows and gas levels. Important advances were made in seismology, in understanding how dome growth works and about ground deformation. The MVO team described how laser range-finding binoculars were used to measure changes in the shape and volume of the dome: 'Repeated weekly helicopter surveys, combined with precision ground surveys and photo analysis, have enabled reconstruction of lava flux over time; the resulting data is unprecedented and crucial to the understanding of magmatic processes.'[25]

'Montserrat has been one of the most important eruptions of the century in terms of learning about volcanoes,' said Dr Baxter. Yet, despite all the research, all the monitoring, much uncertainty remained. As Sue Loughlin, deputy chief scientist at the MVO, said: 'What has been highlighted is the great complexity of volcanic systems and the general lack of precursor signals which can be used as precise predictive tools for future activity.' The scientists' forecasts sometimes proved right, sometimes wrong. 'There was always a lot of uncertainty as to how far the scientists should be believed,' said Baxter. And always there was some luck. 'Scientists in Montserrat came out unscathed, but if they had made a bad call, it would have been a different matter,' he concluded.

While not denying the difficulties of the first months, the MVO scientists patted themselves on the back. Responding to a critical news report in *Nature* about the scientific handling of the Soufrière Hills volcano, Barry Voight of Pennsylvania State

University wrote in 1998 in stout defence of the MVO scientists. They had performed, he said, 'meritorious service under exhaustive and frequently dangerous circumstances for the past three years . . . I cannot think of any volcano emergency in which more effort and ingenuity have been applied to ameliorate an enduring crisis in which complexity and exasperation reign supreme.'[26]

The MVO, which had moved from Plymouth to the Vue Pointe Hotel, to Old Towne and then, in September 1997, to a large house on Mongo Hill, in the far north, was relatively open, unstuffy, welcoming and, unusually, without a rigid bureaucracy. There, amid the photographs and the equipment, the boots and the fire suits, the messages and the warnings, was a sign. It read: 'How well did we do? – Geoff Wadge.' Well enough, was the verdict of Wadge's fellow scientists in respect of the Wadge and Isaacs report. 'Extremely useful,' said Professor Sparks.[27] The report had predicted the Tar River as the most vulnerable area and it had established Salem as the northern limit of a worst-case scenario. The forecasting of Wadge and Isaacs – the 1 per cent chance of a volcanic eruption – had come to pass.

As the emergency ebbed away, the status of the MVO changed. In 1999 it became a statutory body, funded by UK aid and with the British scientist Simon Young appointed as its first full-time director. The tossings and turnings of the volcano had given unprecedented opportunities to local young men and women to train as scientists. Those who had become involved in the work at the MVO and had gone abroad to study would return. There would still be a need to keep watch over the 'inherent uncertainties' of the Soufrière Hills volcano, by day and by night.

4

'Refugee in me own Country'

Randall Greenaway, a Montserratian teacher, wrote a song inspired by the volcano called 'Refugee in me own Country', which tells how it feels to live in internal exile. So do the lyrics of 'Woman in a Shelter', another of his poignant songs.[1] Both are tales of loss and displacement and of life in the shelters of the 'safe' zone, where many Montserratians spent not just months but years. The shelters were inadequate and often squalid, and they came to represent everything that was unacceptable about the management of the crisis. Alongside the collapse of the education and health services, the lack of proper housing and land were the key issues of the emergency.

The housing problem had been drawn into sharp focus by the nineteen deaths on 25 June 1997. A number of those who died had either refused to move to the shelters or had temporarily returned to their homes from a shelter. That was understandable, as even Governor Savage acknowledged: 'I would not describe the majority of those who died as irresponsible. By and large, they had just about had enough of the deprivation in the north of the island.'

Chief Minister David Brandt gave evidence to the International Development Committee in the high-ceilinged, wood-panelled Committee Room 13 in the Palace of Westminster in

October 1997. 'Several persons have said that they would prefer to die rather than to live in those conditions in the shelters,' he said, 'and they would prefer to stay in their houses rather than suffer the indignity of living in shelters like that.'[2] His oratory, part preacher, part lawyer, is a style fixed in Caribbean culture. He told the eleven committee Members of Parliament that the shelters were not as good as the conditions 'in which they keep cattle' in the United Kingdom, and that they were 'synonymous with the barracoons that they used when they brought us over'.[3] He went on to describe life in the shelters. 'It is not easy,' he said, 'if you want to sleep and somebody is playing a radio; if you want to change your clothes and somebody is standing up looking at you; you cannot get to bed; you want to go in the toilet and five people are there before you; you want to go to toilet, you have a belly ache.'[4]

The shelters – tents, churches, schools and purpose-built buildings – had been a solution to the problem of mass on-island evacuation right from the beginning. The first major evacuation had been in the wake of 'Ash Monday' on 21 August 1995 when, with little warning, Plymouth and areas in the south were evacuated. After two weeks the population returned home, but at the end of November there was another mass evacuation. This time it was better organised and phased over two days, lasting until mid-January. In April 1996 the third evacuation took place. Once again, the whole of the south and east – some 2600 people – trudged north. This time, there was no return.

Sumptuous villas, old town houses and humble village homes had to be abandoned to the ash. When the evacuation sirens sounded, it was time to tune in to the radio, listen to instructions and prepare to move north. Those who had transport took to the roads, others collected at pick-up points in their communities to await buses and trucks. There might be just time to go home – to turn off electricity, water and gas supplies, to secure the house and to collect an emergency kit (two weeks' supply of clothing, food, medical supplies, drinking water for two days, and personal items, including passport and birth certificate, credit cards and flashlight).

After 25 June 1997, the exclusion zone was extended again: that meant the evacuation of the 1500-strong community of Cork Hill. Finally, in September 1997, Old Towne and then Salem, the little community which, after the 'fall' of Plymouth, had been targetted as Montserrat's safe 'new' capital, were evacuated. By then 64 per cent of the island's surface had become unsafe.

The social fragmentation, the evacuations and relocations, the conditions in the shelters, the shrinkage of the island, the decline in the quality of services, such as education and health, all hastened the island's disintegration. The result was the departure of two thirds of the population – from nearly 10,500 before the volcano, to 8069 in July 1996, down again to just over 5000 in July 1997, and by the end of that year to over 3000. The population then gradually increased, building to an official figure of 4400 (which many disputed as too high) at the end of 1998. While details of the demographic changes were not recorded, it was clear that many professional and middle-class families left, in particular, women with school-age children. Opportunities in the more productive sectors had dwindled. The civil service, including teachers, police, nurses and engineers, lost many of its top people, as did the private sector.

The small minority of Montserratians who did not leave the island became internal exiles in the north. Some went to live with family or friends or rented any property they could find. Some went to the shelters. Some even lived in sheds, boats, abandoned cars or half-built houses without doors or windows. Families moved not just once, but two, three or four times as their original place of safety became hazardous or as their options diminished or as their money ran out. The rich as well as the poor lost their homes, although it tended to be the poor and the elderly who stayed long-term in the shelters.

At one time, after the evacuation of Salem, 1580 people were living in shelters, more than one in three of the population.

Although these numbers fell (mainly because people left the island), there were more than 1100 people in shelters for 'a long, long time', according to Richard Aspin, information officer of the Emergency Operations Centre. By April 1998, when the total population stood at around 3500, there were still more than 500 shelterees, roughly one in seven of the islanders. One year later, the shelter population stood at 372, at which point Governor Tony Abbott admitted: 'Shelters may be with us for some time.' By this time, the crisis was nearly four years old.

Back in July and August 1995 the British army put up tents at Gerald's Park, near St John's. The area, which became known as Tent City, is flat, but windswept and unprotected. Marcell Ryan, a young woman from Webbs, just south of Plymouth, lived there for a time with her mother. Once inside the tent, Ryan looked up and saw it was spiked with holes. When the wind and rain came, the tents fell down, and the people got wet. As Ryan explained: 'The Lord blew them down and knew what was best.' Not only God, but also Montserratians knew that 'tents don't work at Gerald's'. As Reuben Meade, then chief minister, explained: 'We said they wouldn't work, the British military said they would. No one listened to the local views.' Eventually the tents were thrown out and burned.

Life at Gerald's Park was, according to Ryan, 'just horrible'. 'Imagine. It's like a refugee camp . . . all standing in line. They issue you with a cot and blanket.' The people cooked over open stoves. The sanitation consisted of pit latrines less than 2 metres deep. They were intended to be in use for two days. They were, in fact, used for more than two years. When it rained, the pits overflowed. 'It is not uncommon for users of these ODA [Overseas Development Agency] toilets to have their bottoms splashed with liquid excreta,' said an appeal to the United Nations High Commission for Refugees (UNHCR) on the conditions in Montserrat. In a home video by Don Romeo, who became a persistent chronicler of shelter conditions, a woman said: 'We refuse to go to the tent. But we're not given a choice. They've no toilet facilities, no bathroom. If we have

Explosion from the Soufrière Hills volcano in October 1997. This was taken during one of the most intense periods of activity, with 'vulcanian' explosions occurring at regular intervals

Plymouth, the capital, in December 1995, with Chances Peak and the volcano in the background. Plymouth was to become vulnerable from the ash carried on the prevailing winds, and later from pyroclastic flows, surges and mud flows. The town was evacuated permanently in April 1996

Plymouth in February 1999. By then it had been almost completely laid waste

The first pyroclastic flows descended on Plymouth in August 1997. This large building on George Street lying deep in ash was reduced to skeletal walls and mangled steel

A buried car at Spanish Point, an expatriate residential area on the east coast destroyed on 25 June 1997

One of the three pyroclastic flows which poured down the northern slopes of the volcano on 25 June 1997 burying villages and killing islanders in their homes and fields

The body of one of the 19 Montserratians who died on 25 June 1997

Streatham village in the wake of the 25 June disaster

Looking towards the dome from the Tar River valley on the eastern flank of the volcano. The valley was the site of the first pyroclastic flows in March 1996

Living in tents at Gerald's in the north of the island, August 1995, during the first evacuation of the south. The tents blew down, leaked and were eventually burned

An elderly man outside St Peter's Anglican church – many churches and schools became shelters during the crisis. At one point, more than 1500 evacuated Montserratians were living in shelters in the north

Moving house. A lack of proper housing was one of the main reasons why two-thirds of Montserratians had to leave the island

Waiting for the ferry. After the closure of the airport on 25 June 1997, a ferry service from Little Bay to Antigua was the only means of entry and exit for most Montserratians and visitors

Surviving the ash. Montserratians had to cope with ashfalls: unpleasant, demoralising and, in the long term, potentially dangerous

Simon Young, director of the Montserrat Volcano Observatory, measures the temperature of pyroclastic flow deposits at Trant's

(*Above*) David Brandt became chief minister of Montserrat at the height of the crisis in August 1997

(*Above*) Frank Savage, governor of Montserrat, July 1993 to September 1997

Montserratians remained defiantly proud of their island

New, post-volcano housing at Davy Hill in northern Montserrat, financed by the British. A 'housing estate' layout was unfamiliar to Montserratians

to go to the tent, we might as well go back to our houses.'

The first prefabricated, emergency structures to house the evacuees were opened in April 1996, nine months after the start of the crisis. These shelters were built on a ridge of land at Brades. Made of metal, they looked like freight containers and would sizzle in the hot sun. At first they were dormitories, with cots on each side. Later, wooden partitions divided the shelters into tiny rooms with a narrow central corridor. Each room had half a window. In the afternoons, it was unbearably hot. 'We can't stay in them in the day,' said a woman resident who worked in the hospital kitchen. 'We call them our little jail cells.' A British housing specialist and consultant for the Department for International Development wrote, 'The accommodation is wholly inappropriate for long-term residential use.'[5] More than three years after the first evacuations, those gleaming shelters remained occupied.

Many relocated Montserratians squatted in schools or churches, the only institutions with space larger than a private home. Schools – including a brand-new one – were requisitioned, while Catholics, Pentecostalists, Methodists, Anglicans and Adventists opened their doors to the evacuees. In all, thirty-eight schools or churches became sanctuaries. Communities were, where possible, moved together – those from St Patrick's, for example, went to the Salem Catholic Church and Salem Anglican Church, while those from Harris went to Brades Primary School. 'God was pleased with having people sleeping in the church,' said Pastor Joan Meade of Bethel Methodist Church, but at times she had found the change of use difficult to accept. 'I once saw sanitary towels on the pulpit,' said the compassionate Pastor Meade. 'Then there was the time when people misbehaved – a lady and her sons were having a rum and a smoke. But it was her birthday. At first I shuddered at all that, but then I thought the church was perhaps offering a better service than before.'

The problem was that although these shelters – especially the churches – were adequate for brief stays, they, too, were unacceptable for long-term use. The officials' guide to evacuation procedures, written and produced by the Emergency

Operations Centre in November 1995, said: 'Many of the shelters were not designed for such purposes and therefore showed a number of deficiencies during use.'

The most obvious deficiency was the overcrowding. There were rows of cots and often no screens between family units; there was nowhere to store possessions. Sanitary conditions were also poor. At one former school, Brades, 145 people shared four toilets; at the Seventh Day Adventist Church in Salem there were two toilets for the same number of people, according to the appeal to the UNHCR. The private had become public. This was not easy for Montserratians. As Christian Aid put it: 'In a rather private culture, familiar with physical catastrophe, where people do not advertise their personal difficulties, much of the population feels under strain.'[6]

Tom Peters and his wife were among many elderly people who endured life in the shelters of the north. In their younger days they had spent years labouring in the cotton fields of neighbouring Nevis. Back home in Montserrat, in the hilly village of Trials, south of Plymouth, they cultivated some 5 acres of land, kept sheep and cattle. They lived, like many rural Caribbean people, an independent, self-sufficient life. This life ended when the volcano came. 'The big thing did come. The mountain is tumbling,' remembered Mrs Peters.

Their particular shelter was a tiny, isolated stone building on a windy, sloping ridge with a magnificent view of the sea, perched above the northern village of St Peter's. Beulah Pilgrim Holiness Church became home for twenty-one people, from the church's congregation in Plymouth. Outside, beside a spindly line of pigeon peas, was a cover for a generator. Like many items of emergency aid provided by the UK, it had a Union Jack flag stuck on its side and the words 'Gift of the British people'. 'We cluster together,' commented Mrs Peters, using the verb to express not comfort but clutter.

You can see St Peter's Anglican Church from Beulah. It is mid-way down the hill, not far from the sea. St Peter's is more establishment than Beulah, more like an English village church with squat stone features and a square tower. It, too, became a shelter. Inside, it was dark. The stone font at the entrance had been covered up; the pews were pushed aside or turned into divisions or shelving. The shelter was crammed with personal possessions: a cabinet, plastic washing tubs, suitcases, shampoo, a wheelbarrow here, an old stove there. There was nowhere to sit, to eat, to talk, to study, to read, to relax except on the cot beds. It was a pokey, makeshift kind of life. Some people had brought no more than what they were wearing. They had left at short notice and in a panic. 'We walk with nothing except our papers,' was a familiar phrase.

Helen Corbett, a slight, rather stylish woman, had arrived with her husband at St Peter's. 'We are only here because we couldn't do any better. We had nowhere to go. We are having a rough time.' Her fridge was with her in the church, but: 'They mash up me fridge when they bring it out.' She had photographs with her of her old home; they showed a modern sitting room and 'centre table', potted flowers, sofas and maroon tiled floor; a tidy kitchen where, as she pointed out, she 'keep me pot on the fire' and 'the towel that hang up' and the toaster. For now, however, she had only her 'mashed-up' fridge.

Outside, in the graveyard, where the long grass roughly brushed the headstones in the wind, washing dried. Also in the graveyard were two plywood kitchen areas. There was a Calor gas stove, a sink and some shelving. Dolores, a young, gap-toothed mother of two children, used the kitchen as and when she could. As she fried chicken, carefully turning it and adding a seasoning of onion, garlic, green pepper and ketchup, she said: 'Shelter life not easy.'

Shelter occupants relied on the government for much of their food supplies. Evacuees to the north had been told to take two days' worth of food with them. The supplies were erratic, especially at the beginning. Before vouchers were introduced in September 1995, there had been food rations. Many of these supplies were regarded as less than nutritious. Don Romeo interviewed a woman who described for him the hand-to-mouth existence of shelter life. One woman said: 'Someone gave us some meat. I begged a breadfruit and bits and pieces, just to make a pot of soup. Does the government expect us to live on tinned food? We're used to dasheen, not macaroni and rice.'

In December 1996 Romeo had drawn up a catalogue of needs of the shelter people. In letters to the governor, he described poor ventilation, unhygienic and inadequate cooking facilities, minimal toilet facilities, lack of storage space, washing in buckets, health risks, lack of privacy and so on. In a 'shelter needs assessment', dated December 1996, Romeo derided the authorities for such conditions. 'It is unconscionable and callous to expect that Montserratians, British dependent citizens, should be expected to continue to exist in these human "warehouses".'

It was not until after 25 June 1997, after the deaths of the nineteen people and the further escalation of volcanic activity, that international media coverage began to draw attention to the conditions in the shelters. In August 1997, for example, William Reid, an occupant of the St Peter's church shelter told the British newspaper the *Daily Mirror*: 'I cannot stress enough how bad the conditions are – the heat, the smell, the flies. It is so hot at night you can barely sleep . . . Please, please, please, tell everybody who reads your paper in Britain we need proper help and we need it soon.'[7]

The British government eventually began to pay closer attention to the crisis and sent its Chief Medical Officer, Sir Kenneth Calman, to visit Montserrat in September 1997. His report stated that there was 'serious overcrowding' in the shelters which were particularly inadequate for the elderly and the young. He also drew attention to poor sanitation, the potential for disease and the likelihood of fires (in March 1998 a fire destroyed two shelters at Manjack; thirty-five people, who had lost almost everything from the volcano, lost the rest of what they had from the fire). Visitors were appalled at what the people were enduring. 'The squalor of it all. No one should be living in such conditions,' said Baroness Symons, Parliamentary Under-Secretary of State at the Foreign and Commonwealth Office.

Giving evidence to the Select Committee, she commented that the people were 'facing their difficulties with extraordinary courage and dignity'.[8]

Father Larry Finnegan was Montserrat's Catholic priest during the long years of the crisis. A tall, Irish-born missionary of the Divine Word Society, he lived in Salem Catholic Church with eighty-four other people for many months. The church, which had three showers, toilets and a kitchen in the basement, was better equipped than many of the other shelters. Even so, conditions were hard. 'We slept an exhausted type of sleep. You were always tired. I slept in my trousers and shirt and my car became my wardrobe,' said Finnegan, who remembered queuing up in the morning to use the toilet as one of the key moments of his experience as a 'shelteree'. 'We became used to living together,' he added. Even so, it was not just the physical conditions that made life in shelters full of hardship and tensions. There were arguments to resolve: complaints about babies wetting the cots, about radios being played too loud, or the toilets not being cleaned properly, about who cooked when (some people got up in the middle of the night to prepare their meals). With a good shelter manager, problems could be solved and systems put in place to ameliorate the hardship, but the toll on some was great.

It was particularly hard, said Finnegan, on the older people. Their dignity was lost because they could no longer hide physical problems such as incontinence. Conditions were also stressful for parents, who were anxious for their children, in particular teenage daughters. There were reports of sexual abuse of young girls, and the alleged rape of a thirteen-year-old. While Caribbean culture publicly articulates a strict moral code, in reality, sexual and physical abuse of children, teenage pregnancies and so on are not uncommon. It was then not unlikely that shelter culture would intensify this problem and make parents anxious to protect their teenage daughters. Finnegan noticed that a number of young women chose to sleep close to him. 'Father, we feel safe with you,' was what they told him.

The mentally ill also increased the tensions in the shelters, but also inspired kindness. In one of the metal shelters at Brades, Alfred White, a small, round-faced man, who had spent many years in north London, cared for the former bellringer of the Anglican church. White had looked after the bellringer and had also saved a substantial sum of money for him. He was trying to find him a secure place to live.

Dependency became a feature of shelter life, something unknown 'before the volcano' except in the context of remittances from overseas. Rose Willock of the local radio station and a displaced person herself, was aware of what was happening. 'In the shelters, everyone is dealing with severe trauma. It is good to have support for a short time, but people have to get out of there before a sense of dependency develops.' Many of those in the shelters had been farmers. Lydia Ryan, the shelters' liaison officer for the Emergency Operations Centre, said: 'They used to do agriculture. Now they have to sit and have no garden. They have lost everything. Now they just sit all day.'

Some people coped better than others. Sara Dyett's home was as sparkling as her brightly printed dress. She lived with eight others in one of the wooden shelters at Brades. 'Come let me show you,' she said. The narrow corridor was painted pink, the toilets gleamed and sea-blue tiles decorated the shower. In the small living room, there was a television, surrounded by a cabinet of plastic flowers and a cheery china dog collection, a bead curtain and religious poetry on the wall. The kitchen – like everything else in the shelter – was immaculate. 'We try to link together,' said Dyett. A few metres away there was an identical shelter. Inside, the atmosphere was listless and depressing: in the kitchen, a broken cooker and dirty dishes; in the living room, only a collapsed sofa, a cot and a television covered in a black plastic bag. 'The strain sometimes wore away endurance and resilience,' said Father Finnegan.

If life in the shelters was particularly testing, those living in private accommodation also found conditions stressful. They, too, had lost their homes and businesses and had left behind their possessions. They found themselves dependent on the goodwill of friends and relatives. Many had to pay rent for the first time in their lives. This affected both the rich and the poor – most people had owned their own houses, whether large or small. Throughout the crisis, many also continued to pay the mortgage on homes in the south that they might never live in again.

The internal refugees piled into homes built for one family, now bursting at the seams with up to twenty occupants. For those who took people in, it was an opportunity to express neighbourliness, but it provoked tensions too. 'How long a neighbour going to tolerate us putting things in their fridge and using their bathroom?' asked a woman from Trant's, very early on in the crisis. 'Thanks to them for giving water, food, use of fridge. But who is going to pay?'[9] The food vouchers, which were introduced in September 1995 and replaced by cheques early in 1997, were worth EC$120 per month per adult (EC$60 for children). Everyone who had been evacuated, not just those in the shelters, was eligible.

For those relocated, the financial and physical strains were compounded by a sense of emotional loss. Tracey Skelton, a British geographer who had lived in Harris a decade before the volcano crisis, went back to talk to some of those displaced villagers. 'I miss the breadfruit tree, miss the paw paw tree, I miss the big stones in the yard, I miss the lime tree,' said a nurse from Harris. 'I miss our neighbours, used to go by the house, sit down and chat, I miss the field, overlooking the field there, I miss walking down the road and saying hello to everybody that I meet . . .' A common thread among Skelton's interviewees was the importance of a familiar and treasured physical landscape. 'The softness of the land, the richness of the earth, the fertility of the trees and plants . . . the land provides them with what they enjoy and they are free to partake of it,' she said. 'The North cannot provide in such a way and they don't have the freedom to take what little it can offer.'[10]

A sense of dislocation and domestic uncertainty affected

everyone. Rose Willock lost her much-loved home at Amersham, on the outskirts of Plymouth, in August 1997. What possessions she still had were in boxes and garbage bags. Accepting the loss of her house, she had not dared hope that some of its contents might have been spared from the ash and fire. Most especially, she worried about a trunk containing fabrics, crystal, glass, her father's briefcase, and a photograph of the grandfather who went to Panama – like so many thousands of Caribbean people to build the canal – and never came back. The trunk was about her past – and her future. When she was finally able to have someone find the house and rescue what was salvageable, there was her trunk. She feared to open it, but the key worked. She looked inside. Everything was safe.

Almost every Montserratian had a story of things lost – or sometimes saved – connected to their homes and possessions. The loss of home, the lack of housing and the enforced life in shelters were among the most emotional of the issues that afflicted the island.

Other key services, such as education and health, were also seriously disrupted. In education, schools were either closed or turned into shelters. The technical school in Plymouth and the sixth form college closed. The number of pupils plummeted from 2672 before the volcano down to 620 in September 1998 as more and more Montserratian families moved abroad. Teachers were also affected: as the school rolls declined, staff members were made redundant or left of their own accord. The number of teachers declined from 200 in 1995 to fifty-four in 1998.

For those who stayed, the first challenge for the school system was to deal with the fear of both children and staff. Randall Greenaway teaches physics and maths at the Montserrat Secondary School. At first, he said some teachers could not control their own fears. 'We had plans in place, but once, during a phreatic eruption, things went topsy-turvy.' Eventually, the staff gained a better understanding of the situation and learned how to cope. Gertrude Shotte was headmistress of Kinsale Primary School. 'I had to look after the staff, parents and children,' she said. 'I didn't think about me. I pushed everything else to the back of my mind.' Kinsale was the first to be affected by ash and often school was cancelled when ash fell into the classrooms. There were crying children to comfort and worried parents to attend to. In April 1996 Kinsale School was evacuated – to tents on the Salem School campus, which at that time was still in the safe zone. When the sun shone, the heat bore down on the tents, when it was windy, the tents blew down, when it rained, teachers and pupils had to sit on the desks to avoid the water. 'We were in a no-win situation,' said Shotte. 'I would rather take lessons under a tree.'

One of Shotte's mechanisms for helping her pupils deal with the situation was to encourage them to write prose and poetry about the volcano. The result was published in 1996, under the title *Out of the Mouths of Babes*. The poems express the children's fears and wonder but also their knowledge about the volcano. 'Even a five-year-old could tell you the difference between a pyroclastic flow and a phreatic eruption,' said Shotte. It was important for the children to learn about the awesome force that had changed their lives. Another book of poetry, called *The Voices of our Children*, was written by pupils of St Augustine's Primary School, the Catholic school relocated from Plymouth.

The Montserrat Secondary School, the island's only secondary school, moved to its Salem campus, where it operated under a shift system. There was little space and few resources. And when Salem was evacuated, the school had to move again, to Lookout – in the far north – where it took over a new primary school. Even so, the school did not open until October 1997, with no sixth form and fewer than 200 pupils (the figure had risen to 250 by January 1999) compared with 600 before the crisis. Both staff and pupils somehow managed, but the disruptions were damaging, especially for older children.

In the primary sector, there were even heavier losses. The school roll at St Augustine's fell from 135 to thirty. The youth group was down from thirty-seven to three members. At one point it looked as though no primary schools would open for the September 1997 term. In desperation, Father Larry Finnegan asked the government for three teachers and appealed for sponsors for children who could not afford the fees. When St Augustine's reopened at a house in Palm Loop, in the safe north, with thirty-seven pupils, there was a feeling that the haemorrhaging of skills and people could perhaps be stemmed. By Christmas 1997 it had one hundred pupils. 'People who were anchors in the community had left because there was no education for their children,' said Carol Osborne, who was involved in the new school. 'If there's no education, forget the future.'

There was criticism that the lack of schools and of support for teachers had hastened the migration of Montserratians. The government was accused of failing 'to plan properly for education' and thus undermining 'the potential for schools to provide an oasis of the stability lacking in other areas of children's lives'.[11] According to Gertrude Shotte, the teachers had received little official help from an administration that gave the impression that nothing had changed. 'They wanted us to be normal in an abnormal situation. But that was impractical. We were under a lot of strain.'

In the health service, there were similar problems: workers under stress, the migration of skilled workers and dislocation and curtailment of services. The brand-new extension to the sixty-eight-bed Glendon Hospital in Plymouth had been built by British money in the wake of Hurricane Hugo. The hospital was evacuated three times. For John Skerritt, Permanent Secretary at the Ministry of Health, moving the hospital from Plymouth to the north had been the most stressful time of all. 'There was lots of ash. We had little information, you're trying to move sick people and equipment, and you didn't know what was going to happen.' The people in charge were dealing not only with all aspects of life under a volcano, but with their more private problems and worries.

The new home for the hospital was a primary school at St John's. It was hardly adequate. Sister Valerie Lewis, the principal nursing officer, said that the hospital had managed to cope but that the situation had been challenging. There was a lack of space and equipment; much of the heavy equipment, such as the x-ray and dental machinery, had been left behind in Plymouth. 'The environment was poor,' said Sister Lewis. 'The floors were concrete and the patients had to walk outside to a toilet.' There was also a staffing problem. According to Sister Lewis, 50 per cent of the nursing staff, and most of the qualified ones, left. There was a minimum of medical support, especially during 1997 when there was no resident surgeon. 'We managed to cope,' said Sister Lewis, 'mainly because we had less patients and the critically ill were sent overseas.'

In his report on medical conditions in Montserrat, Sir Kenneth Calman described the improvised hospital premises as 'grossly substandard' and without an adequate sanitation system. He drew attention to the distance between the wards and operating theatre (1.6 kilometres) and noted that members of staff were undertaking complex treatments for which they were 'not always accredited'.[12] The British MP Jenny Tonge, who had visited Montserrat with the Select Committee, ventured to comment that Florence Nightingale would have been ashamed of the conditions.

The old and the mentally ill were particularly at risk. Calman stated that in September 1997 there were approximately 250 frail, elderly people requiring some level of institutional care, while there were 120 mentally ill people, of whom twenty had chronic illnesses 'not appropriately managed'. In many cases, the support systems of village life, which had sustained the vulnerable, no longer existed. If you were old it was hard to accept the hitherto unknown concept of institutional care. The Red Cross opened a shelter at Brades and another at Cavalla Hill. The Red Cross was also to build the coyly named Golden Years Home for the Elderly. In fact, there was some evidence that there was too much institutional care. 'We found elderly people who were hale and hearty but had ended up living in institutions because social and family support had broken down,' said one British social policy adviser.

The volcano laid waste Montserrat's population. It also destroyed its economy. In the first year of the crisis, economic activity contracted dramatically, with a minus 20.16 per cent growth rate compared to a 2.53 per cent growth rate in 1993. The tourist sector collapsed and the volume of cargo through Plymouth's port declined by 25 per cent. Tax revenue was down by 18.8 per cent while current expenditure rose by 26.6 per cent, largely as the result of emergency relief projects. Costs rose as supplies declined. By 1997, the government's current balance, which had stood at EC$1.7 million in 1995, was −EC$35.4 million.

The focus of economic life had been Plymouth. With the capital abandoned, many businesses closed. Others − in a severely modified form − moved north, squatting where they could. Some relocated into the villas of Old Towne, Olveston and Woodlands, where the sound of lawnmowers was replaced by office telephones ringing beneath the glass chandeliers. Smaller businesses moved repeatedly. Carlisle Shoe Centre, for example, relocated from Plymouth, to the owner's home, then to Cork Hill, to a container in St Peter's and finally to Sweeney's. The Bank of Montserrat colonised a former bar on the bend at Fogarty's Hill, using the bar as its counter; the post office occupied a villa with a yellow stair carpet at Woodlands. Every government department seemed to be crammed in someone's former living room, with filing cabinets in the kitchen and computers on coffee tables.

The desperate economic situation was compounded by the withdrawal of insurance cover. For those with policies (many Montserratians had been unable to afford the increased premiums imposed after Hurricane Hugo), the volcanic activity prompted the insurance companies to 'impose major changes designed to reduce their liabilities' in May 1997.[13] Christian Aid submitted that 'insurance companies were acting unreasonably in response to claims and had reduced the level of payment' to 55 per cent and then 25 per cent.[14] Worse was to come. In August 1997 the insurance companies simply announced that all policies were invalidated.

Basil Lee was one of many Montserratians to suffer from the withdrawal of the insurance companies. Lee had owned a tile and paints business in Plymouth and lived in a large, brand-new, two-storey home in Trials. The volcano damaged his business premises and burned down his house. Both buildings and their contents were fully insured, but like many other Montserratians his insurance policy had been cancelled on 24 August 1997. Lee received a tiny percentage of his claim. He was pursuing vigorously the insurance company but his hopes for financial recovery were slight. 'I couldn't start a business now. I have no overdraft facilities. I have no money at all – everything was in the business,' he said. 'I've always worked, even since I left school, but look at me now, I just sit here all day.'

After the loss of housing, homes, land, social services and education, the cancellation of the insurance policies in August was one of the most distressing events in what was to be one of the grimmest weeks of the whole crisis. It also coincided with the affair of 'the golden elephants', a phrase which few Montserratians are likely to forget.

5

From Golden Elephants to White Elephants

The gift of a blue silk tie with a golden elephant motif to Chief Minister David Brandt from a Foreign and Commonwealth Office official. A calypso band called 'The Golden Elephants'. A headline in the *Montserrat Reporter*: 'Golden ones are out but here's our own White Elephant' in a story about the new temporary government headquarters. How did such non-Caribbean images – more appropriate to Britain's imperial outings in the East than to its supposed partnership with a beleaguered Caribbean island – come to play a part in the crisis? Apart from the volcano itself, 'golden elephants' became the one phrases that the outside world now associated with Montserrat.

The answer lay with Clare Short, Britain's Secretary of State for International Development. In August 1997 Short had been in government for less than four months. The Labour Party had won the May general election and in one of its more radical moves it upgraded the old Overseas Development Agency, the aid arm of the Foreign and Commonwealth Office, to a full-scale ministry, the Department for International Development, with a seat in the Cabinet. Short had already announced that her new ministry would focus its efforts on the elimination of world poverty. Yet the aid programme for the remaining British dependencies, including Montserrat, also had to come out of the Department's budget. This was based on the entrenched principle that 'the reasonable needs of the Dependent Territories will be first call on the British aid budget'.[1] With aid to the remaining colonies having nearly doubled since 1992, and Montserrat accounting for two thirds of that aid since 1995, there were implications for this 'first call' duty. Alongside the UK's contingent liability responsibilities for the Dependent Territories, it would have forced some constraints on Short's priorities to focus on the 'poorest of the poor'.

So whenever Short tried to reassure Montserrat about the best intentions of the UK government, she also felt bound to mention her Department's obligations to the rest of the world. When Montserrat had brought her, as she put it, 'a shopping list' to London at the beginning of August 1997, it included 'more houses, a new hospital, a new airport, helicopter service, roads and a transport system in the north, a restitution fund for uninsured assets and support for financial services'. The Department blanched at this. 'I reminded them,' Short wrote in *The Times*, 'that the budget exists to assist the poorest people in the world', that £40 million had already been pledged to Montserrat and that her ministry was accountable to British taxpayers.[2]

It was Short, too, who made the damaging reference to 'golden elephants'. That came in a front-page story in *The Observer*. Under the headline 'Short's "Golden Elephant" Gaffe over Volcano Isle', the article quoted her as saying: 'My Department's budget is designed to help the poorest people on the Earth, and I have to be very responsible about how it is spent. It would be weak politics if I said, "They are making a noise and a row. Oh dear, give them more money." People in Britain do not get compensation if they suffer.' She accused the government of Montserrat of 'talking mad money'. 'They say 10,000, double, treble and then think of another number. It will be golden elephants next. They have got to stop this game. It is bad governance. It's hysterical scaremongering, which is whipping people up.'[3] The so-called 'gaffe' had been prompted by the then new Montserratian chief minister, David Brandt, who had complained about the size of the British-funded relocation grant for Montserratians wishing to leave for another Caribbean island.

Short's comments, which she later said she 'completely and absolutely' regretted, made her deeply unpopular. The minister, better known in Britain for her generosity of spirit and radicalism, became something of a hate figure in Montserrat. 'Anyone here will say she is a bitch,' said one American resident with uncharacteristic lack of restraint. The islanders were hurt and angered by her accusations of greed. Brandt's response reflected both sorrow and anger. 'She has no right to talk about us in this way and is only doing it because she knows we are broken and in no position to fight,' he said. 'No Government should be so rude about its subjects – and we are British subjects even if we are thousands of miles away. I have people starving, with their houses, their crops and their cattle all burnt.'[4] Distrust, which had never been far away in this crisis, became acute, fanning feelings that Britain had never really cared about Montserrat and that it had treated the islanders shabbily. Other leading British politicians, such as Foreign Secretary Robin Cook, later tried to patch up the public relations disaster by visiting the island. Short never did.

That August, the relationship between the UK and Montserrat faced its lowest moment ever. The 'golden elephants' quote had come at the worst possible time for Montserrat. The gods of the volcano were roaring and unpredictable. Everything seemed to be fragmenting. The future of the island was in doubt.

During that month the first pyroclastic flows poured into Plymouth, burning and burying homes, public buildings and businesses. Heartbroken people watched Plymouth on fire. Debris, the size of pebbles, fell as far north as Salem. A series of explosions then shook the island for four days and neighbouring Guadeloupe reported that a full-scale evacuation of the island was imminent. The reports were speedily denied by the Emergency Operations Centre, which added that Guadeloupe would help if an evacuation became necessary and that plans were in 'continuous revision'. Nevertheless, such rumours caused both alarm and anxiety.

Next, Salem became vulnerable. Once again, what had been declared safe was now unsafe. Salem had become a substitute little capital and had four shelters, including Salem Catholic Church where Father Finnegan and his flock had found sanctuary. Now this whole community of 2000 people had to move, wearily, again. The decision to evacuate Salem was a considerable blow. 'It killed us dead, dead, dead. People had reinvested in Salem,' said one senior official, 'but they had no more money. They had to leave Montserrat. The government of Montserrat allowed their own fears to dictate the situation under pressure from the UK and the governor.' Also in August there was extreme economic insecurity: Barclays Bank closed; W & W Electronics factory folded; the Montserrat Building Society was suspended; many small businesses collapsed; and insurance policies were cancelled. (Many blamed George Foulkes, Short's deputy, for precipitating the insurance companies' decision when he mentioned the possibility of a 'cataclysmic' eruption.) The opportunities for what was left of a 'normal' life on Montserrat were dim.

The British had always argued – although they were desultory in turning words into action – that Montserratians must be offered 'informed choices' about their future. Short wrote in *The Times*: 'It is wrong to trap people on the island. They must be able to make their own choices.'[5] In contrast, the government of Montserrat had resisted British plans to offer help to Montserratians with, for example, free air fares to Britain. It was anxious to keep the society together and perceived the British proposals as offering unequal choices.

However, that August, the deteriorating situation, in particular the closure of Salem and the lack of housing in the north, finally persuaded the Montserratian government to accede to the British. On 16 August Chief Minister Bertrand Osborne told the islanders that due to the deteriorating situation a 'voluntary evacuation scheme' paid for by the British would be put in place. Montserratians could choose either to go to the UK, where they would be entitled to all benefits, or they could go to the country of their choice in the Caribbean region and receive a sum of money to support their settlement there. At that point Osborne could give no details either of the timing or the sums involved; only that the islanders who wanted to leave would be taken to Antigua, where they would remain in some sort of holding operation. Montserratians were confused and angry. It must have seemed very much as if a closedown of the island was imminent, although Osborne said no enforced evacuation was in the offing.

It was at this point that the people – for the first time during the whole crisis – publicly expressed their frustration. The demonstrations (described by the international press, to the distress of the islanders, as riots) were held over several days. They were peaceful ('more a rum and patties event', said one onlooker), although the sight of police in riot gear was unprecedented. They showed that even Montserratians needed to put a public face to their private passions. It should have signalled how bad things were, for Montserratians are not prone to exhibit their feelings. Their restraint throughout the crisis had, in fact, been extraordinary.

The immediate cause of the protests was that no one knew the details of the voluntary evacuation scheme. At a deeper level, the protests were a response to a general sense of helplessness. The Concerned Group of Citizens, an *ad hoc* association including many young people, led the protest. Julian Romeo, one of the organisers, said: 'We were concerned about the total evacuation and what would become of our country and our lives. What would happen to our culture? Where were we going?' The demonstrators marched past the royal palms to Governor Savage's office at McChesney's alongside some Rastafarians who later, separately, burned tyres and blocked the road in Salem. The anger swirled around like the volcanic ash. 'There was a period when life was very tense. What people don't understand is that everybody had been living with this for two years. Everyone was stretched to breaking point,' said Savage, remembering this period. It was the worst time, reflected a senior Montserratian official. 'We had no leaders, we were tossed on the sea. We were in despair.'

At this point David Brandt, then an independent back-bencher, flexed his muscles. 'I was vocal in expressing the ill-treatment of Montserratians by the UK,' he said. 'The people were asking, "What's in the package?" The people needed to know.' Brandt went on the radio and leaked the figures under discussion. Montserratians who wanted to stay in the region would receive an average two years' salary package (although how this would be assessed was unclear) of EC$40,000 for a head of household, EC$30,000 for other adults and EC$20,000 for children. Brandt put himself forward as a more forthright defender of the people than the accommodating Osborne, who was beginning to be seen as a political liability. Osborne, a conservative businessman often described as a 'complete gentle-man', was seen to be too pro-British and too colonial in his approach.

The negotiations on the relocation package had taken place in the Department for International Development's Aid Management Office (AMO) on Montserrat. As with many other events in this crisis, there are two versions of what happened during the discussions. According to Brandt, it was the AMO, then headed by the well-respected Frank Black, which came up with the sums for the compensation package. According to Governor Savage, it was the Montserratian politicians who proposed them. Whatever the case, the figures were agreed in Montserrat. The financial proposal 'was put to London,' said Savage. 'I don't know if there was any hint of a green light from the AMO that it was likely to be accepted.' London, how-ever, thought otherwise.

Without any consultation with the government of Mont-serrat, the Foreign Office phoned Governor Savage on the morning of 21 August. He was told to inform the chief minister that the package would be announced at 10.00 a.m. London time. It would consist of £2400 for every adult and £600 for every child under eighteen to be paid in three separate instalments over six months. Those with savings or assets of more than £10,000 were excluded from the grant. Savage told the Foreign Office that this would bring down the chief minister. It did.

Now that they knew the real size of the package, the people, angry and hurt, then turned on their own government. Protestors marched to Osborne's office. Despite his plea that he, too, found the package 'totally unacceptable', they demanded his resignation. Osborne resigned within hours when three of his ministers withdrew their support. Brandt then made his move. Brandt, known as 'the heavy roller', is broad-shouldered and nervously alert, in contrast to Osborne's small physique and diffident presence. Originally a village boy from Windy Hill, Brandt had used his brains to succeed as a lawyer, was generally admired for his shrewdness and speaking skills, although some disliked his brashness and did not trust him. But at that moment, he was the people's champion and 'the best man for the job'. He was sworn in on 22 August.

The three chief ministers to lead Montserratians through the volcano crisis had little in common except their title. All, however, were the victims of the volcano as their power crumbled in the face of British intervention in the management of the crisis. There was no disguising Brandt's frustration. Unlike Reuben Meade, the energetic modernising technocrat, and Bertrand Osborne, the reserved, conservative businessman, who had negotiated behind the scenes, Brandt had a more public style. Certainly, Brandt needed to make a mark and, as Savage said, 'If you want to grab the regional headlines as the chief minister of a dependent territory, the sure fire way of doing that is to attack the British.' And attack the British he did. He has, as they say in Montserrat, 'lot of mout'.

'All we are asking for is a chance to rebuild our own lives,'

Brandt told *The Independent*. 'The British government is not giving us that chance.'⁶ Brandt's view was that Montserratians should be given 'real choices'. The choice, he said, between a ticket to London with housing and benefits, and the squalor of shelter living on Montserrat was spurious. Brandt believed that what the UK wanted was as small a population as possible on Montserrat. The smaller the population, the fewer the resources required or justified. It was not a new attitude. Indeed, Reuben Meade had also been 'absolutely certain' that this was what the UK had been angling for as far back as 1996. 'That year, before the hurricane season, there were monthly visits from the MOD adviser in Barbados. They were saying even then that they would like to get the population down to 4000–5000 because of the hurricane season.'

Rumours about the deliberate depopulation of Montserrat by the British coursed through the whole crisis, never quite going away even when the diplomatic smiles were widest. The UK always emphatically denied the rumours. 'The "theory" that we wanted to depopulate the island is rubbish. But we didn't want to force people to stay,' said George Foulkes, echoing a slate of British politicians before him. 'Everyone on the island [had the idea] that the British had this underhand plan to take everyone off. And I was going around assuring everyone that the British had no such intention,' said Savage. Short was also clear about this. 'It [depopulation] has never been the case, never even considered as a policy option, that I am aware of in any forum where I have been.'⁷ Even so, in Montserrat, it had become a permanent undercurrent of the crisis, especially in the second half of August 1997. The off-shore presence of the West Indies guardship of the Royal Navy had done little to reassure. As the Montserratian journalist Keith Greaves said: 'We felt that one day we would wake up and a British ship would come and take us off. Although the British kept saying, no, they wouldn't take us off, people didn't believe that.' And for some the closure of Salem was another 'clue'. 'The evacuation of Salem was a strategy to close the island,' was the view of John Watt of Plymouth, who had had to move his ice-cream business to Salem; Watt had decided he would never leave – he would be on the last boat after the last boat.

Montserratian fears were also centred on not knowing what would happen if, indeed, volcanic activity forced a mass evacuation. Emergency evacuation plans had been made very early on in the crisis. Ministry of Defence personnel had organised contingency accommodation in Antigua, at Camp Lightfoot, a military warehouse. 'It was cupboard space for 1000 people,' said one official of the Department for International Development. None of this was officially made public. Indeed, even in 1996, when revisions were made to the original plan – and hotel accommodation was substituted for Camp Lightfoot – Montserratians were not officially informed, although rumours, an important factor in the whole crisis, abounded. As Greaves said: 'No one knew about an evacuation plan. We were asking for specifics, such as where do we go? All we were hearing is that there is a plan.' Even when the International Development Committee began its investigations into the Montserrat crisis in October 1997, it was told: 'If there were an emergency evacuation Montserratians would not know what to do.'[8] Operation Exodus, as the plan was called, was constantly being rewritten in response to the changing situation. It was finally made public in May 1998.

The Ministry of Defence was, for its own reasons, fundamentally against an empty Montserrat. Left uninhabited, Montserrat would have needed a garrison. The Ministry does not like garrisons because they are expensive. A spokesman said that in this particular case the Ministry was further 'resistant to the idea of a garrison because it had no responsibility for drug runners'. The thinking was that Montserrat would have been swiftly reoccupied by Colombian drug cartels.

Rob Cunningham was working for Christian Aid on Montserrat in August 1997. He believed that a closedown of the island had been on the agenda. 'There was a lack of resolve to do anything about the north and a lack of reassurances. People wanted to stay but they didn't get the support quickly enough.' There was much talk locally of it being 'easy' for Montserratians to leave and 'difficult' for them to stay, wrote Cathy Buffonge, in her reports for *Caribbean Week*.[9] Bennette Roach of the *Montserrat Reporter* believed that 'If there had been no package, and the people had not left, then the British would have to have done more to solve the accommodation problem.' Belief in a 'conspiracy' theory perhaps said more about the Montserratian leadership's lack of familiarity with the ways of the British establishment than about the reality of the situation. But Britain's management of the crisis had, at that point, largely put paid to any rational response.

The British MP Bernie Grant, a member of the International Development Committee, arrived on Montserrat on 29 August – less than a week after Short's 'golden elephants' comment. He found the atmosphere 'very bleak', with Montserratians feeling that they had been abandoned. Brandt had asked to see him because he thought the UK government was not listening, so Grant had gone to Montserrat: he went as an individual MP but with the British government's blessing. 'I went to calm things down,' said Grant. He found a 'thorough shambles'. There was no one in overall control, everyone was working separately, no one knew what anyone else was doing. 'I had never seen anything like it in my life.' Immediately on his return to London, Grant spoke to Bowen Wells, chair of the International Development Committee. Grant suggested that the committee should investigate Montserrat, and at the beginning of September it was announced that an urgent inquiry would be held into the current situation on Montserrat.

Grant was immediately followed to the island by George Foulkes, Short's deputy. Foulkes is a cheerful, bluff sort of politician with a considerable knowledge of the Caribbean. It was, however, his first visit to Montserrat. 'I went in the knowledge that they were fearful about the future. There was pessimism and uncertainty,' he said. Prime Minister Tony Blair had asked Foulkes to get the message across that the UK would never abandon the people. More significantly, Blair told him to come back with plans for the future. Foulkes's reference to a 'cataclysmic' disaster had made him not much more popular on the island than Clare Short, but he was met on his arrival, he said, with 'a bear hug from David Brandt'. In fact, his visit was something of a watershed. The key moment was a meeting with the National Consultative Forum, a loose grouping of the private sector chaired by Bennette Roach. At that meeting the seed for what became known as the Sustainable Development Plan was first planted. This idea became a blueprint for the future development of Montserrat. The very existence of the Plan, committed to 'provide the level of services and infrastructure appropriate to the needs of the community', meant that Montserrat would not be abandoned. It had a future.

Foulkes's visit allowed for some patching up between the two governments. Brandt spoke of 'not wanting to fight with the British government' and of being 'partners giving each other mutual respect'. The visit triggered, too, the resumption of various projects, which had been 'put on hold' by the Department for International Development during the uncertainties and fears of the previous week. Some projects never took off again: a new hospital did not materialise, neither did a new prison at Mongo Hill. Priorities had been rejigged, but at least the bulldozers began to move again in the 'safe north'. While the volcano continued its destructive work in the south, the north was now the landscape with a future.

The north was all that Montserratians had left. Before the volcano, for many Montserratians the north was separate and different. Most islanders had lived in the south, around Plymouth, the central corridor or in the east. As one teacher said: 'If you were from the south, there was no reason to go north. I went there on school visits but I would say to myself, "What am I doing in the north?"' Or people would go for a family picnic or to celebrate St John's Day. Some also went there to enjoy the island's only white-sand beach at Rendezvous Bay, to drink at the local bars or to sample goat water, a hearty soup of goat meat and vegetables that constitutes Montserrat's national dish, at Mrs Morgan's restaurant in St John's.

And there were, indeed, goats grazing the tired soil with its sparse vegetation of acacia and cactus. Those on the scrubby land at Little Bay had retreated to the hillsides when the new jetty, the only port, had been formally opened in June 1997. Since the closure of the airport, the port became the poignant point of departure for the thousands who had left. It was also the sole point of arrival for everything and everyone (except for the élite who travelled by a newly inaugurated helicopter service). The ferry to and from Antigua operated (usually) twice a day, the cooking gas supplies came (irregularly) from St Kitts, fruit and vegetables arrived (sometimes) from Dominica, container loads of tinned and frozen food for Ram's supermarket from Miami, timber from Guyana. All basic means of survival were unloaded through this little coconut-strewn bay in the north-west.

By the end of 1997 the north had come to mean the area deemed safe for occupation. The north is 15.52 square kilometres, less than one quarter of the island's surface. It tapers from the bulk of the uninhabited Centre Hills to the squared-off cliff faces of the far north that edge the furthermost contours of the Silver Hills. While its south-western extremities are pretty and gently wooded and its centre deeply forested, much of the north is exposed, in parts almost bleak, with the prevailing trade winds blasting in from a shimmering sea. There were once large sugar estates in the north, but by the mid-nineteenth century the clay soil and low rainfall had triggered their collapse. Migration was particularly high from the north; but those who went away, to the oilfields of Curaçao and Aruba, for example, often returned richer than they left and bought land for cultivation.

For a time, in the first half of the twentieth century, sea-island cotton had provided a livelihood for northern smallholders, although in the long term this had caused further erosion of the dry, thin soils. Apart from farming, the people of the north, who saw themselves as 'independent', turned their hand to building trades, fishing, sailing and smuggling. They were somewhat better off than the other islanders. Like the east, they were also largely Protestant (the Methodists had opened a school at Cavalla Hill in 1838), in contrast to the more Catholic south.

Yet the relative wellbeing of the north was deceptive. By the 1990s the land was underproductive and there was little infrastructure – poor roads, no port, no sizeable town. It was unattractive to investors, being remote from the businesses in Plymouth and the golf course. Richard Aspin of the Emergency Operations Centre listed its problems: 'There was no employment in the north, no development, no single building had been built, the school was poorly equipped, the roads had deteriorated. It was also an area without a strong political voice. We are now paying the price.'

This then was the small world that by the end of 1997 had to protect and nurture a total island population of 3381, more than twice the north's normal population. It was a fragmented and demographically distorted population: a high proportion of men to women (56 to 44 per cent respectively); many elderly (18 per cent were more than sixty years old), and many children living with a single parent (58 per cent). There was a disproportionate number of the mentally ill, who would sometimes be found wandering aimlessly with their bodies and clothes covered in ash. Seventy per cent of the 'new' population had been relocated from the south, of whom 18 per cent remained in shelters at the end of 1997.[10]

Among the 'stayers' was a smattering of key business people: for example, the Osborne family (tourism, timber, import/ export); the Romeo family with their hardware shop; Manu Chandaramani of Ram's supermarket; Arrow, the calypsonian. There were also a few skilled professional people, civil servants and members of the political élite, as well as a core of expatriates, church leaders, farmers, trades people and construction workers. 'We love this little island of ours,' people would say. There was fierce devotion both because of and in defiance of the suffering.

For everyone, the north would have to be a new-found land.

These were the people who had to shape a future for Montserrat, who had to create wealth, provide services and work out the dynamics of a new society. They were exhausted. Even so, they were to summon their energies in hope, seeking to evolve some sort of partnership with the British, including the new governor, Tony Abbott, who had replaced Frank Savage in September 1997. For it was the British who had the money. Grappling with the future shape of Montserrat had barely begun. Normal life had been suspended. It was still 'one day at a time', as Arrow's song lyrics reminded everyone, although it was the long term that really mattered.

The sounds of construction began again. Some buildings were temporary, including the unpopular government headquarters at Brades, which looked like a trailer park; others, such as Arrow's Man Shop (painted red, yellow and green) and Norman's supermarket above Brades, were permanent. The sounds were of hammers and chainsaws, the sights were of pick-up trucks and dumpers, excavating machines and containers, timber and breezeblock. 'Cement, cement, cement,' sighed one woman with some satisfaction, sitting in the back of a bus as it swung past bags of cement being unloaded at M. S. Osborne's new business site at Brades.

It was such developments that made Montserratians begin to feel a little easier about the future. However, the key to making the hope tangible was the Sustainable Development Plan. Clare Short had described it as identifying the key policies to provide all kinds of basic needs for 'decent life, decent housing, decent health care, decent education and decent care of the elderly'.[11] The government of Montserrat described it as a goal for the island's development. After innumerable drafts had been shunted backwards and forwards between Whitehall and Montserrat ('London says it's too specific,' said Chief Minister Brandt in April 1998. 'They are delaying implementation . . . they want to measure the waves.'), the Sustainable Development Plan was eventually agreed. Alongside a physical development plan, it concentrated on the strategic targets of that development. Full of good intentions, this was the sort of document of needs and objectives about which only the devil could disagree. There was, however, little indication as to how such proposals would turn into reality.

Then in June 1998 Clare Short told the House of Commons that £75 million had been allocated to Montserrat for a three-year period, until 2001. This worked out at a 25 per cent increase in expenditure from the Department for International Development to Montserrat over the £59.3 million of the previous three years. It was estimated at £25,000 per capita. While the Sustainable Development Plan remained 'the overarching framework', it was the three-year Country Policy Plan, up to April 2001, that became the key document. It outlined budgets, programmes and how to achieve them. There were tight objectives to be met for each sector, health, education, housing and so on, and a detailed action plan with a timetable for each year.

To look at the Country Policy Plan is to become aware of the enormous loss suffered by Montserrat and the long climb back to reclaim what Clare Short called 'an acceptable standard of welfare'. The Plan aims to achieve not just economic revival, but also to rebuild the island's social, cultural and political life. It is important not just in its major concerns ('Continue renovation and upgrade of hospital facilities at St John's compound' and 'Develop and review options for providing appropriate surgical facilities') but in its inclusion of all those needs (absent from Montserrat since the volcano) that contribute to a decent quality of life. To develop, to improve, to strengthen, to review were all central components of the Plan, for example in sport ('Commence construction of netball and basketball courts in Lookout'), legal action ('Clear backlog of criminal cases caused by suspension of assizes'), parliament ('Review filing system at the Clerk of Council's office') and agriculture ('Support for formation of Farmers Association'). There was much to be done.

Not surprisingly, it was new housing that was central to the development of the north. The building programme was desperately needed but it had been very tardy in starting. As Governor Savage had said in October 1997: 'It was not enough and it was too late.'[12] Fifteen months later, Chief Minister Brandt, in a speech following the signing of the Country Policy Plan, said that the tranche of the £75 million allocated to housing would 'not fully satisfy the needs of all those who have lost access to their homes'. He suggested that an additional £25 million 'be ring-fenced for housing and resettlement'. Whether or not such a statement was labelled another 'golden elephants' demand is unrecorded, but it was clear that the housing programme, which promised less than 300 new houses by the summer of 1999, did not go far enough to meet the needs. It was estimated that 800 more homes were required, not only to encourage Montserratians resident abroad to return home, but to cope with the needs of those who had remained on the island.

Besides the number of homes, the ways and means of their delivery provoked further tension. In July 1997 the UK had agreed the first substantial tranche of money earmarked for housing: £6.5 million to build 250 houses. Work went ahead quickly, and fifty prefabricated, two-bedroom homes at Davy Hill, close to Carr's Bay, were ready for occupation by November. The first tenants (rent: EC$150 per month, with the option to buy after three years) were those who had been in the shelters longest. Among them were Mr and Mrs Peters, who had spent so long in the Beulah shelter on the hillside above St Peter's.

The Davy Hill houses are laid out in rows on a steep slope. From above, the housing estate looks like a grid of pale pastel boxes. One adviser called it 'a mind-numbing layout'. It was certainly not traditional Caribbean housing – 'too neat', said someone else. At first, there was no shade, no greenery. This was partly because animals sauntered into the small unfenced garden plots and destroyed everything. Tom Peters wondered what would grow there; within months there were pigeon peas and sweet potatoes around some homes. There was a sense that people were adjusting. 'The volcano scatter and the volcano

bring together,' said Peters as he pointed out his new neighbours, from White's, Long Ground and his own village Trials.

Living on a housing estate had been unknown in pre-volcano
Montserrat. Most Montserratian homes had been designed so
that extensions could be added on here and there, as dictated
by size of family and financial resources. The prefab design
was rigid and inflexible. Furthermore, the room layout was
unfamiliar. As the British geographer Tracey Skelton pointed
out, in traditional Montserratian homes the bathroom is close
to the bedrooms, so that residents can move quickly and easily
between the two, dressing in the bedroom so as to leave the
bathroom free for the next person. 'In Davy Hill, the bathroom
is on the opposite side of the living area from the bedrooms
and so people effectively have to walk right across the house
and pass the open front and back doors,' said Skelton. 'People
said they found it embarrassing to do this and felt they had lost
some of their privacy.'[13] Indeed, Davy Hill was public housing,
in both senses of the word.

After Davy Hill, the next stage of the British-funded building
programme was for 200 houses at Lookout Yard, a wild and
windy spot exposed to sea blast. The cost was met from development aid and the houses were constructed differently and to
different specifications to the Davy Hill prefabs. While half of
them were partly prefabricated and the other one hundred were
of block material, the designs were to a high standard. The
exterior detail had attractive fretwork, while inside there were
fitted kitchens and cupboard space. Some of the new tenants
of these homes were civil servants – for the first time the government of Montserrat had had to think in terms of a housing
allocation policy. A £2.72 million scheme for the purchase of
materials for 320 self-build homes was also set up, which was
what most Montserratians would have wanted all along.

Apart from housing, what was most needed was access to
land and, allied to that, access to mortgages. Both were problematic. The Davy Hill housing had been built on a small portion
of government-owned land. The rest of the land in the north

was privately owned. With the volcano crisis, the cost of land escalated. A significant amount of the land in the north is 'family land', to which members of one family have common rights. This system, characteristic of many parts of the Caribbean, often means that the land is not registered. So tradition, bureaucracy, speculation and the law all made it hard for Montserratians to find land to buy. The government of Montserrat, funded by the Department for International Development, eventually compulsorily purchased the housing land at Lookout which was valued at EC$3.3 million. The Country Policy Plan emphasised that among its objectives was the identification and acquisition of land for accommodation, not only for government ministries but for the 'displaced population' whether on or off the island.

The land issue had also affected the future of agriculture. Many of the displaced people were farmers, but only small patches of land seemed available. Eventually, farming land at Upper Blake's was leased by the government and access roads developed. The Montserrat Council of Churches, funded by Christian Aid, helped fifteen farmers to begin to grow much-needed vegetables. While there was some ambivalence about the potential for agriculture in the dry and overgrazed north, the Country Policy Plan was committed to the participation of farmers in the decision-making and the development of a more efficient and more responsive Ministry of Agriculture.

Even when land was available to buy or rent, many people no longer had access to funds. For many their savings had gone, in part from the disastrous closure of the Montserrat Building Society, leaving savers with access to, at first, only 35 cents in every dollar of their savings. Fifteen per cent of the population of the north who had homes in the exclusion zone were also still paying a mortgage at the end of 1997. Home ownership had been the norm in Montserrat. Some islanders had paid off their mortgages with their insurance money for homes they would never again reoccupy. With no capital, no land and no collateral, many Montserratians could no longer meet the terms of any bank. To address this problem, a soft mortgage scheme had been promised by the British government. But by September 1999 it had still not found a financial partner to co-finance its proposals.

The delay in setting up the mortgage scheme slowed down the redevelopment of the north. So did the decision of the British government not to provide financial support for the Montserrat Building Society and its refusal to underwrite cover after most insurance was withdrawn in August 1997. The International Development Committee drew critical attention to the government's policy not to intervene. It said: 'The Government does not address the fact that in the case of Montserrat we do not merely have the unfortunate losses of a few thousands of individuals but an imperilled society. The normal rules cannot apply.'[14]

Even the equable Cedric Osborne of M. S. Osborne felt as late as October 1998 that 'the UK was deliberately dragging its feet'. Osborne was also looking for other incentives to rebuild, for example changes to the tax system, which would allow him to write off capital investment against profit. The Osbornes had never thought of leaving. They had lost all their property in Plymouth and had then moved the business to their hotel, the Vue Pointe, where the tennis court became a timber yard and the conference centre was turned into a church and shop. Then, when Vue Pointe was finally evacuated in August 1997, the business moved to a piece of land at Brades where containers and timber crammed the yard. 'We have given hope to people by staying,' said Cedric Osborne. 'We wouldn't pull out now.'

M. S. Osborne was the largest business to stay, but other relocated businesses sprang up around the north, especially at Brades where the much disliked temporary government buildings had been built – people called them a 'white elephant' because they had cost far more to build than the original estimate. Just up the road from the Osborne business were Johnnies Mecca Fashion, Montserrat Stationery Office and Economy Bakery, whose old shop signs adorned the new wooden premises. Across the road was Tina's, a new restaurant, prettily painted in green and white, serving pizzas. In blustery St John's, Bessie's provided lunches from a tiny wooden building (in the old days, Bessie had cooked the desserts and catered for the cocktail parties at the Vue Pointe Hotel), while at the Emerald Café, the sign read: 'Due to the volcanic situation, we do not give credit.'

A small business funding programme of £450,000 was established in April 1998 and managed by the National Development Foundation. The new scheme offered credit loans of up to £22,000, largely for those in the farming and service sector. In October 1998 new portacabin offices for the Foundation opened at Davy Hill, while another portacabin offered space to micro businesses. Among them was a craft shop selling volcano ash souvenirs.

When the dome stopped growing, in March 1998, Montserratians were given hope that the worst was over and that evacuated areas might at some time be reoccupied. But it was not until the end of September, one year after its original evacuation, that Governor Abbott announced that Salem and adjacent communities were deemed safe for reoccupation. Peter 'Dr Doom' Baxter, the ash expert, said that the ash should be cleared before residents returned. In October the Catholics initiated a clean-up of Salem Catholic Church, a former shelter. Mops and buckets, brooms and brushes were put to use inside, while outside volunteers mowed the high grass and cleared away the debris. Suitcases, old candlesticks, shoes and mildewed schoolbooks were hurled out of the church into skips. Ash and more ash was cleared from the pews and the fire department was called in to hose down the walls, ceilings and floors. The church eventually reopened in March 1999.

Such initiatives continued, but renewed residency in Salem remained a trickle well into 1999. The people of Salem had gone – mainly to England. It was easier to return if you had moved to the north of Montserrat. Clerical officer Lynette Farrell, for example, had gone to live at Brades for a year and was now back home, busy tidying the yard. She had been frightened to stay in Salem, but that was now in the past. Her neighbours had fled further and there was a long journey back for them. 'Everyone run, everyone gone to England from this street,' she said. The once neat gardens surrounding one-storey concrete homes were filled with the detritus of flight: trainers and refrigerators, suitcases and, most of all, cars, some with covers still on, others crippled by ash. Overgrown hibiscus hedges sparkled with red flowers; and the fruit trees had survived, too.

A few businesses reopened in Salem. Andy's, the tomato-red restaurant made famous by its former rock star clientèle, such as Elton John and Mick Jagger from Air Recording Studios, was closed, but Arrow's Man Shop and the Montserrat Stationery Office were back in Salem by the end of 1998. Jimmy Wilson's Bar was also open, serving good fried chicken as it had always done. The drunks at the rum shop next door took up their usual seats, too. Every sound of a grass cutter or the rat-tat-tat of a broom in a yard, every extra car moving down the road, was a sign of reoccupation. In May 1999 it was announced that the police station at Salem would reopen and that the first cricket match at Salem Park was to be played.

For many Montserratians, however, especially those in the business community, a key aspect of survival lay with an airport. 'It will save our island,' said Cedric Osborne. Chief Minister David Brandt had extracted the promise of an airstrip out of Tony Blair when the two had met at 10 Downing Street in September 1997. But where exactly would it go and how much would it cost? The discussions turned on familiar issues: how much money was available, how far could the British be trusted, and what the volcano would do next.

At the start, there were three options: Thatch Valley, Gerald's and Blake's. The choice of the government of Montserrat was Thatch Valley, an uninhabited area in the far north of the Silver Hills. Its view was that an airport at Gerald's would 'sterilise a large area of otherwise prime development land' and destroy the only remaining flat sports area on the island, while one at Blake's would use up potential agricultural land. During public discussions in September 1998 it was made clear to the British consultants that Thatch Valley was also the people's choice. Those discussions also revealed, according to the *Montserrat Reporter*, that the consultants had overestimated the EC$383 million (more than three times the cost of the other locations) for the Thatch Valley option. Doug Houston of the Aid Management Office admitted that there had been problems, that the consultants were 'inadequately prepared' and that the audience had 'latched on to their shortcomings'. Even the most moderate members of the business community were suspicious. Cedric Osborne, for example, said: 'We assumed that they have deliberately overpriced it.' There was an air of unreality about the consultations. Were the British really interested in local opinion? Had a decision already been made? As one of the limericks printed weekly in the *Montserrat Reporter* put it: 'Her Majesty's visiting heralds/Are gauging our airport referrals/They are eager to know/Where we think it should go/Before they locate it at Gerald's.'

When Richard Teuten, head of the Montserrat unit of the Overseas Territories Unit in London and known as 'Clare Short's money cruncher', went on the radio in Montserrat, he did not improve his standing with the community. As Carol Osborne said: 'They pretend that we participate and make decisions, but in reality the Department for International Development make all the decisions. We have no real options about the airport. Thatch Valley would cost £90 million, but we only have £75 million for three years – for everything.' Indeed, Teuten explained that the Thatch Valley option was included in the discussions 'to make it clear' that it was not an affordable option. And when the Department commissioned yet another consultancy to re-evaluate the costs of developing the site, the reported conclusion was that, 'if anything, the sum of EC$383 million undervalued the cost'.

And then it was suggested that the old W. H. Bramble airport, which had been nearly destroyed on 25 June 1997, might be brought back into use. At first Montserratians were amazed. The danger from the volcano to the airport had surely been amply demonstrated. Austin Bramble, son of W. H. Bramble, a former chief minister, was now Minister of Agriculture, Trade and the Environment. He said: 'It is ludicrous for anybody to suggest that we should go and spend millions of pounds to go back to that.'[15] However, as the months drew on, it appeared that the decline in volcanic activity might make the reopening of Bramble airport feasible sometime in the future. In April 1999 Chief Minister Brandt announced that Bramble would, indeed, be rehabilitated; there were funds to do that, but not, he admitted, to build at Thatch Valley.

Another cornerstone for the development of the north had been the creation of a new town and commercial centre. Little Bay had long been identified as the strategic site for a new town and the reason why the government of Montserrat, which owned 230 acres at Little Bay, had turned down the area as a site for housing development. One private developer, Landbase International, had made some proposals for a new town there. In the event, neither the Montserrat government nor the British government offered Landbase support, and eventually it withdrew its offer. (At one point, in the feverish atmosphere, in Britain, if not in Montserrat, following Princess Diana's death, there had been an expatriate suggestion that the town be called Port Diana, despite the fact that the dead princess had never been to Montserrat.)

A central platform of the redevelopment was private sector involvement and inward investment, especially in the tourist sector. But until a local contractor began to build a twelve-bedroom hotel at Sweeney's, there were no hotels in the north. The energetic director of tourism, Ernestine Cassell, saw that a new strategy was needed to attract visitors back. Only a few of the snowbirds would return now that there was no golf course. The new tourists would become volcano watchers: there were attempts to bring day tours from Antigua – to dive, to hike, to watch a 'live volcano which can be viewed from a safe distance', and later, possibly, to pick over the bones of the now lost city of Plymouth. As one early day-tripper commented: 'It has been a pleasure to see the damage.'

All this renewed activity in the rebuilding of the north meant jobs. But the small population and the lack of skills had caused a labour shortage. At first the Montserrat government was reluctant to employ outsiders, but growing numbers of Guyanese, Jamaican and Dominican workers began to arrive. Like all migrant labour they were perceived to work harder – and for less pay – than local people and were prepared to put up with poor living conditions. The local response was predictably critical; a weakened society felt threatened by the newcomers. Stereotypical views about foreigners became part of misplaced local gossip: they bring AIDS, they abuse our women, they are dishonest (the Guyanese, in particular – with their gold jewellery and gold teeth – faced accusations of thieving).

The lack of available skills for professional posts had also caused an increase in overseas appointees. There were not enough skilled local people to fill specialist jobs. There was disagreement among Montserratians as to the impact of British appointees. 'My only concern is that they do their work hard. And they do,' was one senior civil servant's comment. Others, however, felt that the British were clawing their way back. 'We'll soon have a British permanent secretary and under-permanent secretary. They'll never let us go,' said a top Montserratian businessman.

Such suspicions about the British continued despite the growing optimism. Even the most stalwart pro-British Montserratian, such as American-born Carol Osborne of the Vue Pointe Hotel, who had once described herself as a 'Royalist', continued to feel 'let down'. The British style did not seem to generate trust. As one British adviser had observed: 'The development of the north will not be achieved without the people's contribution. You need a sense of ownership to make a sustainable community possible.'

Apart from the British, aid had come from individual member states of the Caribbean Community (Caricom), the Caribbean's 'common market', of which Montserrat is a member. Many countries offered small amounts of money, holidays for children, food, medical supplies and skilled staff, such as nurses, but such support was limited – the Caribbean saw Montserrat as the UK's problem. P. J. Patterson, Prime Minister of Jamaica, chastised the United Kingdom for not moving fast enough to rebuild the north. 'A lesson in how not to respond to a disaster of this nature'[16] was Patterson's view of Britain's approach. However, the only significant Caricom contribution to Montserrat was also slow in coming. Work on the US$500,000 'Caricom village' of thirty houses at Lookout, begun in 1998, stopped by the end of that year and eventually resumed in June 1999.

Help from Montserratians in the diaspora had been a feature of the crisis. In the UK, for example, the Montserrat Overseas People's Progressive Alliance (MOPPA) and the community organisation known as MAC89 sent food, supplies and money. They had been exhibitions, poetry readings and benefit concerts by and for Montserratians. The glitziest concert was at London's Albert Hall in September 1997, organised by Sir George Martin of Air Studios, the former recording studio on Montserrat. Arrow played, so did Sting and Paul McCartney and others who had spent time at Air Studios in the days when Jimmy Buffet had recorded the lines 'I don't know where I'm a gonna go (when de volcano blow).' The Albert Hall benefit and further donations made a total of nearly £700,000 raised for Montserrat by Sir George's fund. Out of this, £100,000 was contributed to the Montserrat Project in the UK, while institutions to benefit in Montserrat itself included the St Augustine School and the Golden Years Home for the Elderly (a Montserrat Red Cross project), as did fishing and agricultural programmes. (A poultry scheme proposed by Christian Aid was opposed by the fund's vegetarian lobby, led by McCartney.)

So Montserrat was able to move on from the days of its greatest loss, both of land and people. There was no longer the sense of always being on the move. Things were settling down. By the time radio ZJB had moved to its new home in Sweeney's in late 1998, it was its sixth relocation. As station manager Rose Willock put it: 'Soon we hope that the term "relocation" in the Montserrat context will be an experience of the past . . . an experience to draw on in the future to teach lessons of survival, of perseverance and hope.'[17] Progress had been made, but renewal was slow. The determination of the islanders and the commitment of the British government had – for now – guaranteed the possibility of a new Montserrat arising from the ashes of the old. Yet the Golden Elephants episode seemed to have been only too characteristic of the tensions that had plagued the relationship between Montserrat and the United Kingdom from the first days of the crisis. What exactly had gone wrong?

6

··

What Went Wrong

The deaths of 25 June 1997, the escalation of the crisis in late August that year and the exile of two thirds of the population were landmarks of the emergency, intensifying the fear and uncertainty. But underpinning all that was a growing sense that something had gone wrong with the handling of the crisis from the start. Why had people spent so long in shelters? How had the aid been spent? Why had so many Montserratians left? Why had the relationship between the UK and Montserrat become hostile? Why had people's personal fears been compounded by a sense of mistrust?

The ever-changing and unpredictable nature of the volcanic activity in the Soufrière Hills had certainly been one determining factor in the management of the crisis, but, fundamentally, the explanations lay with the political – rather than the volcanic – status of the island.

First of all, a long-term malaise in Whitehall had afflicted dealings with the small islands of the Caribbean. 'When something like this happens in the Caribbean, they [British politicians] have to look it up on the map,' was the trenchant assessment of Baroness Young, a former Conservative minister in the Foreign Office with a considerable knowledge of the region. 'With Montserrat, we were very slow off the mark,' she said. 'When the Falklands invasion happened, the Cabinet met immediately. With poor little Montserrat, the machine eventually cranked itself up to do something. It was a very, very, very long way down the agenda. So few politicians know about the Caribbean and so it gets neglected.'

The administration of the Caribbean Overseas Territories (formerly known as the Dependent Territories) – Anguilla, Bermuda, the British Virgin Islands, the Cayman Islands, the Turks and Caicos Islands, as well as Montserrat – had languished in the backwaters of the Foreign and Commonwealth Office. 'The Overseas Territories are not fashionable, and no one at the Foreign Office who is a high flyer would be involved in the Caribbean,' said David Taylor, governor of Montserrat in 1990–93. 'All that the FCO was interested in was avoiding trouble, escaping from trouble,' said Taylor, who wrote in his memorandum to the Select Committee inquiry on Montserrat that the dependencies were 'a potential source of embarrassment rather than a source of opportunity'. A similar view was taken by David Jessop, executive director of the West India Committee, who described the failure to pay attention to the Caribbean dependencies as a 'culture of dismissal' within a general policy which was about 'how to control, not how to encourage'.

In 'normal' times, Montserrat had been used to a devolved model of internal self-government. It was the most politically advanced of the Caribbean dependencies. 'I felt that Montserrat did not really accept the right of the governor to intervene and in my day I was the only British administrator on the island,' said Arthur Watson, governor of Montserrat in 1985–7. The system had allowed for a considerable degree of autonomy, although some governors had had occasion to hold it in check, for example Christopher Turner, in dealing with an off-shore bank scandal, and David Taylor, in handling the Scotland Yard investigation into alleged corruption. It was the volcano crisis, however, which most explicitly exposed the serious flaws in the triangular arrangement of power: the governor, the local government and Whitehall. As the Christian Aid/Montserrat

Action Committee report of 1996 concluded: 'Our visit led us to think that, in several respects, Montserrat has been living a political and economic fiction. The Soufrière has reminded all those in authority, if they had forgotten, that the island is a colony. Powers of decision in key areas of policy, and power over resources, remain with London.'[1]

And it was in London that the immediate difficulties in managing the crisis had their genesis. The two key departments involved in the Montserrat emergency were the Foreign and Commonwealth Office and the Department for International Development. The former is the main policy-making department, charged with the constitutional responsibility for the Overseas Territories while the latter controls the budget, for both emergency and development aid. When the Overseas Development Agency became the Department for International Development and a fully fledged ministry in May 1997, some felt that this move exacerbated already existing tensions between the two. As one senior Foreign Office official put it, none too delicately: 'You have a new secretary of state wanting to call the shots and officials with chips on their shoulders who can now say, "Up Yours to the FCO".' Whatever the relations between the two departments, the key point – fundamental to Montserrat – was that the division of powers began in Whitehall.

A further decision-making layer, the Dependent Territories Regional Secretariat (DTRS) in Barbados, sat beneath the Whitehall posses. It had been set up in 1993 by the Foreign Office to manage development aid in the Caribbean dependencies. However, in a complicated structure, its aid programmes had to be agreed with the Department's arm in Barbados. For the first two years of the volcano crisis, until it was removed from the decision-making loop, the Secretariat was responsible for the management of development aid to Montserrat. The management of emergency aid, however, remained in London, with a particular branch within the Department.

The result of this tortuous management hierarchy, both in Barbados and Whitehall, was that there was no one with both the authority and the money to serve the needs of the Montserratian people. As the International Development Committee rightly observed: 'Power, responsibility and resources have rarely been found in the same hands.'[2] One Department official described the decision-making as 'an alphabet soup where lines of communication were very complicated and lengthy', while a senior Foreign Office official commented: 'You have a problem when you have a problem that doesn't fit a structure.'

This bizarre situation stunned the International Development Committee as its members attempted to unravel the web of decision-making bodies. They even requested a diagram of the different authorities involved in the management of the crisis. Witness after witness agreed that the situation was impossible. Short herself said: 'A major part of the problem . . . is that there are so many players in the decision making that it is quite dreadful.'[3] At its simplest, the question was, as Bowen Wells, the sympathetic Conservative chair of the Committee, put it: 'We have to sort out . . . who is responsible for what in Montserrat.' That, at least, was clear.

Another layer in the power structure was the key figure of the governor. The role of 'Our Man' was the legacy of a nearly extinct British Empire, but it required more than a plumed-hat approach. In the days of the Colonial Office, there had been a large supply of recruits who would be trained to 'serve the Empire'. When the Office was abolished in 1966, the leadership skills ('for quelling the odd riot, dealing with the odd famine,' as David Taylor put it) disappeared. Furthermore, the job of governor of a small place was not one to attract high-flyers, despite the fact that small places often generated large problems requiring considerable diplomatic and administrative skills. 'The general problem – although the FCO won't admit it – is that to be a governor of a Caribbean island is not an attractive career move,' said Taylor. 'It might come at the end of a fairly ordinary career. You tend to get a solid citizen, who will not have the experience because there is not the experience to be had. Therefore he is not terribly well qualified to do it.' The problem was to some extent acknowledged by the Foreign Office. 'The FCO agree that the mechanism for the appointment of Governors in the Overseas Territories requires careful and sensitive consideration.'[4]

The governor's responsibilities are twofold: he (there has never been a woman governor) is the direct representative of the UK government and is also responsible for the welfare of the islanders. This can create a tussle of loyalties. 'Governors get schizophrenic,' said Frank Savage, 'because part of the time we are the government of Montserrat, part of the time we are representing HMG.'[5] Once again, in normal circumstances, the tensions in the role could remain to a greater or lesser extent dormant. In an emergency, the difficulties were exposed. George Foulkes recognised this when he acknowledged that governors sometimes become sympathetic to the situation on the spot. 'I once told Frank Savage: "Do not forget that you are the representative of Her Majesty's Government on the island." ' Meanwhile, Montserratian leaders were claiming Savage for themselves when, at his farewell dinner in September 1997, all three chief ministers – Meade, Osborne and Brandt – affirmed his support for them. Reuben Meade, for example, said: 'You fought as a Montserratian shoulder to shoulder. We never had a fear . . . as to whose side you were on. I knew you were always on our side.' London's verdict on Savage might have been less enthusiastic.

Yet it was crucial that Savage trusted London to support him and that London trusted his judgements. His evidence to the International Development Committee suggested that this had not always been the case. 'I do feel strongly as Governor that not sufficient weight was given to my views.'[6] The fact that Savage sent 400 telegrams – both routine and important – to London perhaps indicated either a lack of support from London or the governor's lack of confidence in that support. There were certainly FCO officials who believed that many of the difficulties would have been resolved if both politicians and officials in London had made a better job of backing their representative in Montserrat.

The problems with the British structures were not the end of the affair. The officials in Whitehall and the governor on the front line both had to deal with the island's internal divisions. Montserrat's political landscape had traditionally consisted of loosely organised parties to which loyalty was largely ephemeral and whose leaders were often offered only equivocal support by colleagues. During the emergency Savage said that he had tried to get the politicians together in a kind of wartime cabinet in an attempt to take party politics out of the equation. Instead, Montserrat held a general election in November 1996, in the middle of the crisis. The number of candidates was unprecedented. Commenting on this situation on the eve of the election, the surgeon Lowell Lewis wrote: 'At this time, Montserrat needs more than ever a government of national unity. It is sad that a less hostile atmosphere does not exist.'[7] The election went ahead after a commission, headed by Howard Fergus, had canvassed opinion about whether an election should be held in the circumstances. The results of the survey showed 54 per cent in favour. That election saw Reuben Meade's administration replaced by Bertrand Osborne's coalition.

There was regular criticism of leadership under all three chief ministers. The *Montserrat Reporter* commented in July 1997 that ministers were 'devoid of the mental, intellectual leadership, creative skills and capabilities that are necessary to take us out of the crisis'.[8] An opposition MP was quoted in the same issue as saying: 'It is very easy to hurl blame at the British government . . . But the government of the day cannot escape responsibility for the poor state of affairs now facing our people.' There was a sense that effective government had collapsed under the weight of the crisis. 'Our government had become figureheads. In fact, they made very few decisions. The government had literally allowed the governor to be in control,' was the view of Glenn Lewis, younger brother of Lowell. The forthright Richard Aspin, information officer of the Emergency Operations Centre, agreed: 'The government has done nothing to respond to the volcano. It's too big for them. It has no fuel to put into the engine to turn the wheels.' Brandt's frustrations were profound: the 'heavy roller', as he had been called, was now known as the 'powder puff'. The Antiguan politician Tim Hector described Brandt's position as 'like an ant kicking an elephant'. In effect, the government had become an interest group, often excluded from decision-making and unable to effect change, except by obstruction.

While political structures and leadership were weak, the civil service also faced a problem – the lack of skilled officials. This is not uncommon in small islands weakened by migration. But, in a crisis, and with many of its best people having left, Montserrat suffered acutely from having some officials promoted beyond their experience. As one senior Montserratian official put it: 'Public works and the water authority are working without skilled technicians. It's remarkable that we survive at all.' The civil service had to deal with new and extra responsibilities in a difficult and changing environment. The Ministry of Health, for example, had to cope with a sudden increase in the numbers of people in institutional care. As its permanent secretary John Skerritt said: 'We were dealing with the situation as it evolved. Every day we were learning something new. Mistakes were made but we were constantly adjusting and reacting – and without resources.' Inevitably there was managerial indecision and a lack of planning.

A failure to plan ahead characterised the entire crisis as it unfolded. Early uncertainty among the scientists compounded the political unwillingness – both in Montserrat and in the UK – to adopt long-term strategies. The initial British response, said Governor Savage, was 'to put a lot of emergency aid into Montserrat to hold the situation until the scientists can tell us a little more about what's going on'. At the same time, the UK also continued to regard a return to Plymouth as a possibility. As late as October 1996, Peter Vereker, the permanent undersecretary at the then Overseas Development Agency, endorsed a decision to remove ash from 'key facilities in Plymouth in expectation of an eventual return to most areas in the south'.[9]

So, while the UK seemed to enter the crisis with a policy of spending as little as possible for as long as possible, the government of Montserrat was, for different reasons, keen to maintain a 'business as usual' atmosphere. Its need was twofold: to keep the economy going and to persuade people not to leave. Could these objectives have caused the government to minimise the effect of the volcano? Governor Savage believed that the initial failure to put infrastructure in the north, including, most importantly, permanent housing, was partly prompted by the desire 'not to send the wrong messages . . . not to scare away all our residential tourists and investors from the island'.

The journalist Keith Greaves said that Chief Minister Meade had been reluctant to take drastic action because of the impact on people's livelihoods. Greaves's view was that 'everyone was hoping that the volcano would go away, hoping that things would stop'. The criticism of Meade was not fair, he said. Montserratians are a die-hard people who believe in their territory. It was, perhaps, stubbornness rather than folly to attempt to maintain what to many was an unrealistic position. When Janice Panton of MAC89 went to Montserrat in May 1996, she noted the reluctance of the islanders to articulate their needs. 'They are very proud,' she said. 'We asked: "how are things?" "We're coping," they said.' The people's refusal to articulate their losses was, she said, interpreted by Whitehall as an indication that Montserratians were managing. In reality, this was far from the truth. Panton's view was that there was a sense of denial among the politicians. 'Plymouth was in danger but people weren't taking it on board.' This perception was also endorsed, if less sympathetically, by a senior Foreign Office official in London, who said that – until 25 June 1997 – 'the politicians in Montserrat would not reconcile to the loss of Plymouth. They harboured the belief that they would go back so they didn't take the necessary decisions in the north of the island. I have no sympathy that they didn't acknowledge that. They failed to do their duty.'

The International Development Committee was also clear

about this. It asked why there was not a single person in proper new housing nearly two and a half years after the eruption began, despite the resources and expertise at the disposal of the UK government. It answered its own question with the comment: 'The decision of the Government of Montserrat in August 1996 not to apply for aid to construct housing is a significant cause of the delay in the provision of adequate accommodation.'[10] A UK aid package of £25 million that August had focused more on infrastructural development than on housing. At this point, according to Reuben Meade, it was British officials who had indicated that housing was not one of their priorities. The UK, said Meade, had offered tent-like structures with pit latrines. The government of Montserrat had rejected this offer, and had gone elsewhere to search for funding for housing. Meade only partly succeeded in obtaining money for housing from regional sources; there was EC$1 million from the Caribbean Development Bank, with which he constructed seventy-five two-bedroom wooden homes. He also energetically introduced self-help schemes for building, but such projects fell far short of the immediate need.

The lack of government-owned land in the north – for both housing and agriculture – also became a major problem. Land had to be acquired through compulsory purchase by the government of Montserrat. But to fund the purchase it had to approach the Department for International Development, which would not contribute unless told what the land would be used for. The Department would not fund land on a contingent basis nor would it finance a land bank. Only after the emergency of 25 June did it agree to fund the compulsory purchase for housing of the land at Lookout. There was also an urgent need for land for farmers – both for crops and grazing. The best farming land was in the exclusion zone. As it became clear at the inquest into the deaths of 25 June, there was no crop insurance scheme for the farmers; there was no compensation for their loss of livelihood; there was no alternative land. An attempt had been made to rent land at Blake's and Waterwork estates for grazing cattle; but the long process had proved unsuccessful. Behind all this was a lack of political will. Christian Aid was told: 'if the Government were to acquire land compulsorily it would generate acute ill-feeling among landholders who might be affected.'[11]

While Meade had decided not to press the UK for housing, partly because he thought he could get help from elsewhere, Governor Savage had thought otherwise. As early as September 1995 Savage had written to the Foreign Office to recommend the building of permanent accommodation for 1000 people in the north of Montserrat. His request was turned down. Development aid had to be agreed with the government of Montserrat and not the governor. This episode revealed another twist in the decision-making labyrinth: the governor, despite his leading role on the island, was not central to the delivery of development aid. ('DFID keeps the governor informed but there's no formal relationship,' explained Doug Houston, manager of the Department for International Development's Aid Management Office.)

The governor's role in the management of the shelters illustrates another example of the gap between power and resources. The governor, being responsible for the overall management of the emergency, had set up the Emergency Operations Centre to manage, among other things, the shelters. However, as Governor Abbott reflected: 'Although responsible for people in shelters, the Governor has no control over efforts to re-house them . . . nor does he have funds under his direct control to finance improvements.' This was the responsibility of the government of Montserrat, with funding, of course, from the Department for International Development.

The result of this extraordinary mish-mash of structures – in Whitehall, Barbados and Montserrat – was inefficiency and delay in the delivery of support and aid. It had not gone unnoticed. Montserratians were asking: 'Who is responsible for the aid? Where has it gone? We cannot see where it has been spent.' Short herself recognised this problem during the

International Development Committee's attempt to clarify the confusion: 'It worries me that a lot has been spent and yet people have not been well looked after. That is where my worry is.'[12] She had also come to the conclusion that the wrongs done to Montserrat were ultimately beyond her capacity to right. As she told the Committee: 'What we have here is a disaster of enormous magnitude that cannot be put right by my budget. That is a really important thing because part of the psychology is to keep saying, "If only my Department spent more money, everything could be put right". It is way beyond that capacity.'[13]

Up to mid-1997, the Department had spent or had approved for spending £45.8 million on the volcano crisis. Of this, nearly half (£22.5 million) was in emergency aid. Among the major costs were emergency housing (£6.5 million), the jetty at Little Bay (£2.6 million), ferry service (£1.6 million annually), scientific monitoring (£1.4 million for 1997–8) and food vouchers (£1.2 million). There was also expenditure on such items as sirens, ash masks, medical gas supplies, cesspool emptiers, triage tags, bulldozers, life jackets, privacy screens. This long list of the commonplace and the obscure reflected the extent of the disaster, the diverse and critical needs of the island and the lack of on-island resources.

It was generally agreed that emergency aid arrived speedily, but without full consultation between the British and local governments. The repercussion of such procedures and the division of responsibilities in the delivery of emergency aid was illustrated by 'the great sludge wagon scandal', as reported to the International Development Committee.

In the autumn of 1995 the Department for International Development was informed that the existing sewage system in the north of Montserrat was unable to cope with the extra sewage and that the cesspits were full. Its emergency aid arm was asked to provide a sludge wagon to deal with the problem. It found one, in Barbados; it arrived in a matter of days in response to the urgent need. The problem was that it was nineteen years old. A second, reconditioned, one was sent from the UK to replace the veteran one. When it became clear that the sewage problem was going to be long-term, a third one, this time a new vehicle, was bought in Puerto Rico at a cost of £50,000. This was not, however, the end of the story. According to Andy Bearpark, head of emergency aid at the Department, his branch provided the vehicles, but the government of Montserrat was responsible for emptying the cesspits. 'We were able to provide the sludge wagons that would be used, but those sludge wagons then have to be donated to the Government of Montserrat who then have control of their maintenance, which they may or may not carry out.'[14] The government of Montserrat, however, had a different version of events: the first vehicle 'never functioned as it was meant to', had no spare parts and no manual; the second one could not climb hills; the third, which had been bought in consultation with the Montserrat government, worked well and was properly maintained.

Short told the Select Committee of her frustration about the sludge wagons: 'I remain haunted by the fact that the sewers are not being properly cleaned,' she said. 'I have tried so many times, you have no idea, to get this sorted out and the fact that I cannot it seems to me is shocking, so there is something wrong with the procedures and the decision-making.'[15] While the British had suggested that the government of Montserrat was not fulfilling its responsibilities, the Montserratians argued that the lack of consultation in the delivery of aid rendered it ineffective and inappropriate. Each side, stymied by the system, blamed the other.

In contrast to the speed with which emergency aid (including the first fifty houses at Davy Hill) was delivered, the disbursement of development aid was a tortoise-like process. This is not unusual, as donor governments are mindful of their responsibilities to taxpayers and of the potential for corruption and waste. A project proposal, submitted by a claimant government, is subject to lengthy scrutiny. In this case, the urgent need for improved roads in the north had been subject to a rigorous appraisal by the Department, who had 'crawled over the project proposal line by line'. When the feasibility study was done it was sent to advisers in Barbados, who, according to an official from the Foreign and Commonwealth Office, 'sat on it and said the proposals had not allowed for bus stops'. In normal conditions, this might have been a reasonable consideration; in the middle of a volcano crisis, concern about bus stops must have seemed absurd. It was labelled a crisis gap.

Governor Savage believed that to talk of development aid in a crisis situation was inappropriate. And despite his marginalised role in the delivery of aid, he had made representations to London, not just about 'what aid should be delivered' but also about how decisions were made and about the speed of the delivery of development aid. 'It took far too long to bring programmes on stream. We battled with the UK government quite hard to get money for housing in the north. I was getting frustrated when consultant after consultant said yes, but we need another consultant to look at x, y, z. We needed development aid disbursed at the speed of emergency aid.'

The government of Montserrat was not only concerned about this slow pace, it was also suspicious. 'The UK government acted very expeditiously when it came to setting up the evacuation office but when it came to spending money for the development of Montserrat then there were great difficulties and delay,' said David Brandt. Such perceptions were fanned by Montserrat's impotence. As the crisis deepened, Montserrat had virtually no money of its own. It had to ask London. It was frustrating. Brandt was fond of saying: 'I can not spend a nail without consulting Clare Short.' Brandt perceived that the word according to the Department was imposed on him rather than discussed with him. For Brandt, it was not the system that was at fault but the political will. A sense of exclusion became a function of the crisis in the tussle between the government of Montserrat and that of Her Majesty.

A particularly vexed issue in this respect was the Department's appointment of Brown & Root, an international engineering construction company, for the Davy Hill and Lookout building programme. There was no consultation with the local government. The company's brief had been to build fast, and to use the maximum amount of local labour and contractors. From the beginning, Brown & Root faced hostility. 'Ever since the contracting firm arrived on island there were questions about their methods and activities,' claimed the *Montserrat Reporter*. 'The Chief Minister has been known to say, "If Brown & Root want to stay and work here they will have to work with the people of Montserrat."' There had been 'many public utterances', the article continued, that the company 'behaves like a government unto itself'.[16] Many of these criticisms centred around the claims that Brown & Root did not listen to local expertise and experience and disregarded local standards and regulations.

Brown & Root defended its position, saying it had to impose 'systems of work that we were familiar with and that we knew had a good chance of working'. Early in 1998 Leo Bedford, at that time the company's local manager, said: 'At the beginning there was no time for consultation. We had two weeks to come up with the concept. We hit the ground running, working twenty hours a day. I resent that people have forgotten what we achieved in two weeks.' The Davy Hill houses were finished in good time, but when Brown & Root came to manage the Lookout project in which a local architect, local contractors and suppliers were used, a new set of problems emerged. There were delays, said the firm, because local contractors were not able to complete on time, the specifications for the designs were time-consuming, there were labour problems and supplies arrived late. The problems rumbled on, and became another example of the tensions that characterised relations between the British and Montserratian governments.

The Department for International Development had an image problem on Montserrat. This was exacerbated by a perceived sense of secrecy. 'Getting information out of DFID was like pulling teeth,' said Aspin of the Emergency Operations Centre. Department officials, especially those on contract, appeared uneasy about their own positions and were unwilling to talk freely. One senior member on a short-term contract said that the Department failed to look after its own. 'People don't feel loyal to it,' he said. 'It sucks you dry and spits you out.'

Various consultants drew attention to the false premises set up by London. The idea of a partnership between the UK and Montserrat was a myth, said one British social policy adviser. There was no partnership: decision-making was carefully controlled and masterminded by London. 'I couldn't say anything unless it had been approved in London,' he said. 'We worked for a month before we were allowed to talk with Montserrat ministers. Every statistic was subject to so much scrutiny. We did draft upon draft. The whole of our relationship was to present an argument acceptable to DFID to put to Clare Short for her decision.' Another short-term consultant, a civil engineer who spent six months working in Montserrat, compared working for a non-governmental organisation with working for the Department. 'In an NGO,' he said, 'you work for the local government. DFID thinks it can stand apart. I don't like this top down stuff.' He argued that the local department that he worked for should have had financial control. 'We're here to build up confidence after a difficult period. I want to involve Montserratians more in decision-making . . . It's bad for the UK to be in control – the attitude that when the cavalry arrives that will solve everything.'

Glenn Lewis, who had watched the aid support system at work, believed that the British relied too much on their own consultants. They were always 'patching things up'. If there were a problem, they would just send in another expert, he said. Lewis felt that there should have been an understudy system for Montserratians to learn the skills. 'The British way just encouraged inefficiency,' he concluded. Pam Arthurton, of the travel agency Carib World Travel, also felt there had been a lack of local involvement in problem-solving. 'The British should have used Montserratians more,' she said. Arthurton also believed that the British needed 'to do some public relations. The British are doing things for Montserrat, but people don't realise it.' The Department for International Development had a public relations officer in Montserrat for a very brief time. 'Everyone is beholden to the British – that's the truth,' said Richard Aspin of the Emergency Operations Centre. 'But the PR has been atrocious coupled with some expatriates who rubbed people up the wrong way.'

The presence of specialist consultants became contentious in other ways. As Chief Minister David Brandt put it: 'I don't know how much these officials are being paid, but they drive expensive jeeps and live in six-bedroom, air-conditioned homes with swimming pools.' There was, indeed, a certain lack of sensitivity in the way that aid consultants (whether from the UK or the Caribbean) enjoyed life in empty luxury villas, rented by the Department, while Montserratians continued to be crammed into shelters.

Such divisions were sometimes made more acute by a lack of cultural awareness, despite 'background briefing prior to departure'. One adviser working with a specialist sector of the civil service told of 'dinner with his predecessor, and a cup of coffee and a chat with officials. It was a joke.' There was no read-ing list of local literature – neither E. A. Markham's poetry nor Howard Fergus's historical works – to prepare them for Mont-serrat, no attempts to introduce consultants to either the cultures of the Caribbean in general or Montserrat in particular. There was room for misunderstandings at best, and conflict at worst.

Father Finnegan remembered one occasion when the man-ager at Little Bay had called him to say that the workers were complaining that there had not been a blessing for the new port and could he come immediately to bless it. 'The consultants had no understanding of our traditional ways. For example, there is always a blessing for every new building or business that opens. There was no awareness of that.' Finnegan had also noticed in planning schemes that there was no place for the churches despite the fact that 'church communities are very important, an anchor in life'. Montserratians sometimes felt that their lives had become invisible. 'They don't see us. They don't hear what we say, they don't listen to local knowledge. They think they know best,' said one Montserratian. 'Our experience doesn't touch their soul.'

There were some, however, who became extremely engaged in the crisis and its people and uncomfortable with the situation. 'I feel an outrage about the way Montserratians have been treated. What are you going to call the book – "Outrage"? This is people's lives,' said one distressed British official. Others had worked in places where the level of suffering had been much worse. The laconic Doug Houston, head of the Aid Management Office, had, for example, spent years in Bosnia (there was a map of Sarajevo in his Montserrat office). 'This is a contrast. But I like the people here and I want to do my best for them,' he said. Yet others were 'frankly bored' or unsympathetic, or both, privately complaining about bureaucracy and the Caribbean work ethic (British sailors digging trenches while locals 'limed'), and there were those who found the Montserrat handshake 'like the flat palm of the hand' or the local attitude was a 'cargo cult culture of receiving gifts'.

When Rob Cunningham of Christian Aid arrived in mid-1997 to work with the Montserrat Christian Council in establishing an agricultural project, he was confronted by contradictions. 'I thought that the country was dependent. I asked myself, do they like it or is it that it's always been like that? Then with the demonstrations, I realised that they didn't like the dependency. I felt strongly about the tragedy and the sense of a lost island.' Brandt constantly spoke against the dangers of a 'dependency syndrome which you have in the UK. We want to help ourselves. Give us a chance to start all over again.' While the voucher system, later abandoned, was thought to encourage dependency, longer-term strategies for self-sufficiency, such as grants for small businesses, had taken many months to get off the ground.

The so-called 'dependency syndrome' worsened as both the economic and psychological situation deteriorated. As former governor David Taylor pointed out, the tension between wanting to be independent and dependent simultaneously was inherent in all the Overseas Territories; but perhaps it was particularly acute in Montserrat during the volcano crisis. Minister George Foulkes agreed that it was a general condition associated with Overseas Territories. 'The difficulty is that there's always the feeling that you can go back and ask for more. It is not peculiar to Montserrat. It used to be like that in the Falklands – now there has been a change from dependency to self-reliance, from dependency to authority and responsibility.'

There was also a lack of grassroots organisations on Montserrat, which one relief worker attributed to the extent of the dependency. 'The level of civil and social society was low,' said Jasmine Huggins of Christian Aid. 'There was no farming association, no fishing association, no advocacy. There have been very few public debates during the crisis, and nothing structured or continuous.' Christian Aid, one of the few agencies working in Montserrat, emphasises local partnerships and capacity building, and its agricultural project was run with the Montserrat Christian Council. Rob Cunningham set up systems for administration and finance, trying to give equal weight to long-term development. 'If you don't look at a longer-term strategy then you undermine the productive capacity of the people,' said Jasmine Huggins. The Department for International Development's methods in the emergency did not seem to promote local skills or empowerment. Under albeit difficult circumstances, it concentrated on infrastructural development and emergency relief. It could excuse itself by pointing to the lack of capacity on the island and the need for quick solutions to problems. But it did not find – perhaps did not seek – an alternative way.

Instead, the British response to the problems in Montserrat was to reorganise the structures and 'upgrade' the administrative handling of the crisis in Whitehall. In August 1997 delegated financial authority was withdrawn from the Aid Management Office in Montserrat. According to the Department for International Development, this decision had been made because it had been 'heavily criticised for decisions which had been taken by officials on the island'. The removal of delegated authority would 'ensure that all decisions took sufficient account of the political sensitivities of the programme.' In Montserrat this move was interpreted as London consolidating its power.

In the same month the Foreign Secretary Robin Cook announced the formation of a new, high-powered committee, the Montserrat Action Group, to co-ordinate the handling of the crisis. 'Our assistance strategy needs to be delivered speedily and effectively but requires co-operation across Whitehall,' said Cook in a Downing Street statement. The group, headed by the Foreign Office, was drawn from all departments (including social security and the Home Office) that were involved in the crisis. At the same time the Dependent Territories Regional Secretariat in Barbados had its responsibilities for Montserrat passed back to London, and new parallel units were set up in both the Foreign Office and the Department for International Development to deal with the Overseas Territories.

One of the central concerns of the International Development Committee had been what it called the 'main organisational weakness' of the crisis. The Committee had recommended that responsibilities and resources for the then Dependent Territories should be in the same department, thus avoiding 'unnecessary tensions and inefficiencies'. The British government had rejected this idea, but it did to a certain extent reorganise the way in which aid to Montserrat was delivered, making a more coherent structure out of the 'alphabet soup' that had existed earlier.

Many of the arguments and processes that had characterised the crisis were discussed in detail by the International Development Committee, which had its first sitting in October 1997. Its investigations ranged far and wide, with many of the main players in the crisis being questioned. From the sum of the evidence, the Committee reported in stinging terms, laying blame on institutions rather than individuals. The first point in its press release reads: 'The Committee was appalled at what they saw in Montserrat, at the conditions people were having to endure, and at the mismanagement and confusion which have been evident throughout the crisis.' The Committee criticised both the Department for International Development ('too many decision-makers in the delivery of aid'), and the government of Montserrat for its failure to ask for long-term aid. It commented on housing, the safety and health of the people, the science of the volcano, the 'inadequate' conditions for evacuees in the UK and the Caribbean, and the long-term development of Montserrat.

The Committee also held that the constitution of Montserrat had 'proved unequal to the demands of this emergency'.[17] Yet, interestingly, the short-term alternative was never applied. This was direct rule. The UK certainly had the power to exercise this (it had done so in the Turks and Caicos Islands in 1986 in the wake of an arson and corruption scandal). A few voices supported it, including the Labour MP Bernie Grant, a member of the Committee. Grant believed that the British government should have declared a state of emergency. 'The UK government was using the inexperience and naivety of the government of Montserrat to cover up their bad decisions,' he said. Grant's argument was that even if the UK had been accused of high-handed imperialism and racism, the people of Montserrat might have been better served. The matter was certainly discussed in London. However, Savage believed that both Labour and Conservative administrations held that the people of Montserrat should decide. 'No one on the island, no Montserratian,' said Savage, 'came along and said for God's sake get rid of our politicians.' The islanders, he said, wanted their own government. To have 'suspended the constitution is a major, major step. As long as the Montserratians wanted to manage this themselves, the British were going to support them to do so.'

What the International Development Committee achieved

was considerable. While it had no power to enforce its recommendations, it prompted changes in the way the island was administered and monitored the government's commitment to the Sustainable Development Plan. It also stimulated an overhaul of the administration of the Overseas Territories culminating in the White Paper of 1999 (see chapter 8 below). The range of its inquiries concentrated the minds of government departments. It forced ministers and officials to address the chaotic manner in which Montserrat had been governed and to articulate the difficulties that had loomed so large during the first two years of the crisis. After the Committee's initial report and its follow-ups, the authorities were no longer able to avoid addressing the problems that they had ignored for so long. That much had been achieved.

7

....

The New Diaspora

For Montserratians, there is nothing new about leaving. Migration has been central to the lives of most families for generations. It is part of the restless history, not just of Montserrat but of the whole Caribbean – the 'going up', the 'coming down', the 'back home', the 'up there'. The imperative to leave, the scattered families, the sense of exile, the memories of home and the anxiety of returning – all these elements are present in the histories and literatures of the Caribbean and, for better or worse, have helped to shape many features of those societies.

At times a higher percentage of Monserratians than people from any other Caribbean territory have migrated – pushed by a shortage of land and jobs. The process began in the post-emancipation period. By 1845 a colonial officer claimed that 2307 adults emigrated to Trinidad and British Guiana. He feared that continued emigration, which had been fuelled by the payment of bounties for transporting labourers from one colony to another, 'would in a short time have denuded this little colony of her adult population'.[1] The process never really stopped. Montserratians continued to leave for other English-speaking Caribbean colonies. Some also went to Panama (2000 Montserratians helped build the Canal, on which work began in 1881; many of them died there), others to Cuba and later to

Curaçao and Aruba to work in the oil industry. In the 1950s and 1960s the migratory route was to the UK, and then, to a lesser extent, to Canada and the US.

Migration provided an escape from rural drudgery and a promise of opportunities elsewhere. Official endorsement of migration was clearly stated in a letter from W. H. Bramble, trade unionist and Montserrat's first chief minister, to a local newspaper. In 1957 he wrote: 'I pray that one day I would see a ship big enough to take every working man and woman out of this island leaving only a few big men and their money . . . they are fleeing from share-cropping, from feudal landlords and from economic pressure . . . Help them go and let them go.'[2] And they went. Between 1955 and 1961, for example, 35 per cent of the population emigrated. The islands with the next highest emigration figures for that period were Dominica, 13.3 per cent, and Anguilla, 13 per cent – well under half the proportion of the exodus from Montserrat.

The poet E. A. Markham is from Harris. He, too, left Montserrat – not to flee share-cropping, but to continue his education. In 1956, aged seventeen, he left for England, went to university, taught in London, and then spent many years in France, Papua New Guinea and Ulster. Now head of creative writing at Sheffield Hallam University, he explains how his sense of survival – as 'the resourceful traveller' – is partly fed by his past. He has written about how his sense of home – his grandmother's house in Harris, his childhood environment – is a recurrent theme in his work, although his grandmother is long dead and the house a ruin. His poem *The Sea*, for example, begins: 'It used to be at the bottom of the hill/ and brought white ships and news/of a far land where half my life/was scheduled to be lived.'[3]

His prose sketch entitled *Life before the Revolution* swings between Montserrat and England, with recollections and dreams of home. The title is explained in the first sentence: 'That was what we used to call it, Life Before the Revolution, and we used, in the early days, to draw improbable parallels between us and the victims of real revolutions who had to flee abroad, leaving their possessions behind.'[4]

Perhaps the parallels are no longer improbable. While earlier generations of Montserratians went to new lands as quintessential economic migrants, this time Montserratians have had to flee a force as potent as revolution: urgent change, no return to a familiar past, an unknown future; all impelled by the volcano.

So there was a different quality to this exodus. First, there had been no time to prepare for exile. Second, no one had wanted to go. These were reluctant migrants. The sense that they might not have a home to return to was acute. Earlier migrants could always hold the idea of 'home' in their hearts, even if it was only a place to be buried in. As Christian Aid put it: 'Exile [in the past] has been tolerable because [migrants] have had a home – a house in Montserrat that is their own in a country that is their own.'[5] This time there was no such guarantee.

So the volcano crisis forced Montserratians down another phase of migration, one whose route was unknown. They started leaving soon after 18 July 1995. At that stage, they had hoped it would not be for long. Governor Savage said that those feeling 'uncomfortable' should consider leaving. Those who most feared the volcano were among the first to go; their fears reached out to others. 'I recognised that it was better for some people to leave. Those who didn't face their fears, it was better that they went away, to take a break and then come back,' said Pastor Joan Meade. But for the most part, people left for practical reasons. They had lost their jobs, they had nowhere to live, there was no sixth form for teenage education. While those who left for exile represented all sectors of the community, the largest numbers were of women and children, in contrast to the largely male migrations of earlier times.

The numbers leaving ebbed and flowed, but in the first year of the crisis, some 3000 people had left. By the end of March 1998, with the height of the exodus over, approximately 7500 islanders, two thirds of the population, had gone. Of these,

46.7 per cent went to the UK; 38.7 per cent to Antigua; 13.3 per cent to other Caribbean countries and 1.3 per cent to North America.[6] After that, the exodus slowed but did not stop. A further 246 islanders, for example, left between April and October 1998 and the exodus trickled on into 1999.

At first, there were no official procedures for Montserratians wanting to leave. The islanders made their own arrangements, paid their own fares or were helped by voluntary organisations, such as the Antiguan-based Citizens and Friends of Montserrat, or relatives abroad. Until 1997, said Mary Maxwell, the acting British High Commissioner in St John's, Antigua, the British government had not decided how to deal with the situation and 'we didn't have handouts'. Then, nine months after the start of the crisis, in the wake of the third and final evacuation of Plymouth, the British government announced its first initiative. On 23 April 1996, the Home Office said that Montserratians, who up to that moment had had no automatic right to live in the UK, would now have 'exceptional leave to remain' for up to two years (this was extended to indefinite residence on 21 May 1998). They would also have full access to the UK benefits system, but they would pay their own fare and have to find a British sponsor to accommodate them. Sixteen months later, on 21 August 1997, in response to the deteriorating situation, it was announced that air fares would be paid to the UK and the need to have a sponsor would be relaxed. Under this 'assisted passage scheme' 2733 people left Montserrat. (At the same time a 'voluntary regional relocation package' for those choosing to stay in the Caribbean region was announced.)

Pam and Percy Arthurton of Carib World Travel watched the evacuees as they arrived in Antigua at the gateway of their journey. The Arthurtons, who had moved their business to Antigua, had been contracted by the UK to handle the ticketing and to look after Montserratians during their stop-over in Antigua. As Montserratians, they knew what the evacuees were experiencing and did their utmost to ease the trauma. 'The people were coming off the ferry and they didn't know what to expect. They were disoriented,' said Pam Arthurton. She recalled images of bewilderment and distress, painful memories for her. 'Many had relatives in the US but they couldn't go there. People got separated. Children didn't want to go. There were children with no passports. People were under pressure, some were made to feel like traitors for leaving, but the shelters were full. Some didn't know where they were going to go in the UK. Some had no money.'

Montserratians had become 'no-where-ians', according to a Montserratian woman as she looked out to sea from the ferry terminal in Antigua. Simon Maty, the accountant from Broderick's, was one of those. He had lost his job because of the volcano, and then had tried a small business venture growing hydroponic vegetables. The vegetables had failed because of the ash. He had no more savings. Eventually his options closed down. 'I came empty handed. You have nothing to cling to any longer so you give yourself up to any eventuality,' he said.

In May 1996 Christian Aid had reported that 'remarkably little information is available in Montserrat to those who might wish to go to Britain'. It urged the British government to prepare an information pack ('the decision . . . to go to Britain is difficult and personal: it should not be taken in ignorance'[7]) but until August 1997, little material was available. Even then, it was perfunctory. Printed on two sides of A4 paper, the advice was along the lines of 'Take some warm clothing if you have any' and 'Your televisions and VCRs will not work in the UK – please do not take them.' It was not until November 1997 that a reasonable survival guide was published. Entitled *Moving to Britain: Your Questions Answered*, it contained clear factual information, but it could not convey the complexities of a life in Britain in thrall to the social security system.

Danny Daley is a retired manager with London Transport. A Montserratian who has lived in England for many years, he became involved in the plight of the evacuees through his membership of the Montserrat Overseas People's Progressive Alliance (MOPPA), one of the two key Montserratian organisations in the UK. 'If you send a man to climb a mountain,' he said, 'you have to tell him there is ice up there.' There were rumours coming from Montserrat that 'houses would be waiting for them in London'. Although many of the evacuees had been to the UK before, many had not. Some believed that 'Birmingham is only up the road from London'. As Daisy Aymer, another Montserratian long established in the UK, said: 'It is a frightening experience, [after] what they have been through in Montserrat, to come here, and they are still frightened – a strange country where they have not been before, strange surroundings.'[8]

BWIA 900 flies into Heathrow Terminal 4 from Antigua every Thursday. One morning in August 1998, twenty Montserratians were among the passengers. To receive them were two members of Travel Care, the Heathrow-based social work charity, which had co-ordinated the reception of Montserratian refugees at Heathrow (and later at Gatwick) since late August 1997. Danny Daley also regularly assisted Travel Care with the new arrivals. The evacuees were met at immigration. In the baggage hall, the suitcases came off the carousels: enormous ones, small ones, bulging cardboard boxes smothered in heavy-duty tape, plastic bags, colourful children's backpacks. Bob Mennear, the service co-ordinator of Travel Care, said: 'Luggage has been the defining moment of this job – either mountains of luggage or just two plastic bags.'

The new arrivals looked like most people who have spent the night on a transatlantic flight in economy class. Travel Care offered everyone coffee and fruit juice, and seats were found in the bustle of the arrivals' hall. There was nowhere else to go.

It had not been government policy to provide a reception centre for the Montserratians. Those with experience of the Ugandan Asian refugees, who had been housed at West Malling RAF camp in 1972, said that although such a camp would nowadays be viewed with horror, it had possibly prepared people for their new lives, providing them with breathing space. More recently, Bosnian refugees had been welcomed to specially adapted residential centres and provided with health checks and 'orientation support'. Sandy Buchan, director of Refugee Action, had proposed this procedure for the Montserratians, but there had been 'no particular clamour' for it to go ahead. The British government had taken note of the prevailing view among Montserrat community leaders that the evacuees should be offered proper accommodation immediately because so many had come straight from shelters. So, for most Montserratians, it was off the plane and on to a coach or a train to a new home in a new country.

That August morning there were three single men in the group of arrivals. One was an ex-policeman, who knew the UK and had somewhere to go. An electrician, who had been living in Antigua, was now off to relatives in Nottingham. He bought his own coach ticket out of the £40 that he had brought with him. Travel Care gave him £30. A young man from Harris in a baseball singlet and shorts was met by his sister who had evacuated early on in the crisis. Travel Care paid their taxi to Clapton in east London.

While Danny Daley looked after some of the families, Bob Mennear used a mobile phone to call housing departments and arrange transport. It had been a long morning and one family remained in the arrivals' hall. Matilda and her four children, the eldest aged fourteen and the youngest only six months, wanted to go to Chorley in Lancashire where Matilda had a sister. Travel Care rang Chorley, but the housing department said that no emergency housing was available for that night. Matilda and her children dozed in exhaustion while Travel Care tried to sort out the next twenty-four hours of their lives. A local hotel was rung: it would cost Travel Care £100 for the family for the night, and more for food. Chorley rang back to say that the family could be accommodated the next night, a Friday, and if the family could arrive early someone would be able to show Matilda around. Travel Care promised to see what it could do, but feared that transport would be complicated.

The only direct coach arrived at 9.45 p.m.; alternatively there was a coach involving a change at Preston and then a taxi. Or perhaps a taxi, all the way for £210, would be for the best? In the meantime the family were taken to their hotel and bought cheeseburgers. Mennear and his colleague, Dana Lancaster, were anxious to get the family to their destination: 'How could you leave these people to fend for themselves?'

Apart from Travel Care and a telephone advisory line, there was no officially funded support system for the Montserratian evacuees to the UK until the Montserrat Project opened in January 1998. As a result, the care and support of the Montserratians who left to go to the UK became as much an issue of concern as did the quality of life of those who stayed. The lack of official support was to cause much distress and, in some cases, destitution. As the International Development Committee pointed out: 'There was no official reception committee or liaison officer established within Whitehall to act as an adviser and troubleshooter for Montserratians.'[9] The problems should have been anticipated, said Sandy Buchan of Refugee Action, but due to short-term thinking and a lack of 'joined up government in Whitehall', Montserratians had to a great extent to rely on families, friends and the wider community to aid them.

Daisy Aymer, one of many Montserratians who supported relatives, described her experiences to the Committee: 'It was the families who had to take the responsibility. Even when the assisted passage was introduced, even then, nothing was set up.' Aymer and her disabled husband had supported five members of her family – a couple in their eighties, a young woman and two children – for three months, until finally, their housing and benefits were sorted out. 'When the family first arrived, we were giving them accommodation, food, bed and clothing and whatever. After a time it became difficult and we did not have the finance to give them, so I myself had to start to borrow to give them until their benefit was sorted out and then I was able to pay back.'[10]

Every evacuee had a different experience. This is the story of Loretta and her two teenage children, Lenroy and Verlene (all names have been changed), who arrive at Heathrow one June morning in 1998. They do not have friends or family connections in the UK. The family request accommodation in London. They are put in a taxi and arrive at their new address: a 'duplex' in an elegant Georgian street near King's Cross. The landlord, a local housing association, says it is temporary accommodation. It has three bedrooms upstairs and a bathroom, and downstairs a front room with two large windows, a lavatory and a kitchen. It has basic furniture: three mattresses, a black three-piece suite, round table, three chairs and fitted carpets. There is a stove and fridge in the kitchen. There is no bed linen and no kitchen equipment.

However, it is light and clean and modern and looks out on to the edge of a tree-filled square. Around the corner are buses, a newsagent, smart coffee shops and wine bars, and slightly further away, towards the poorer end of the neighbourhood, a couple of Asian-run groceries and a Halal butcher. There are no Montserratians in the neighbourhood, and very few Afro-Caribbeans. Loretta does not mind this. She likes to keep to herself. The family arrives at the flat on a Thursday, with their clothes, a large television – it does not work in the UK – and video and Lenroy's bike. The electricity has been cut off.

In many ways the *laissez-faire* approach to those arriving from Montserrat aggravated their situation. They were not classified as 'refugees', as were the Vietnamese or Bosnians, for example, although many argued that their trauma was similar. Instead, they were to be treated like British citizens (although they were not). This had a particular effect, said Janice Panton, co-ordinator of the Montserrat community organisation MAC89, which played a key role in lobbying for official support for the evacuees. 'They were treated as homeless people,' she said, 'and were put on the housing list in the same way as anyone else.' Some were given priority treatment (families, the elderly); some were not (single men). Their 'points' were added up, like any

British citizen seeking housing. A memorandum from Baroness Symons, under-secretary of state at the Foreign and Common-wealth Office in February 1998, made this quite clear. She said that the reason for the government being unable to offer statistics as to the 'types of relocated Montserratians' claiming benefits was that 'Montserratian claims to benefits are processed in the same way as claims from other people'.[11] While this was the official line, the reality was that they were not like any other British citizen. As Bob Mennear noted: 'It was a political decision that Montserratians should be treated like UK citizens – therefore there was no need to do anything, no need to plan. My view is that people who are displaced as the result of a disaster are different.'

Lazelle Howes, manager of the Montserrat Project, believed that Montserratians should have been offered some sort of grant to help their settlement here. 'We argued for that with the Home Office and the Benefits Agency but they were not prepared to consider it,' she said. Bernie Grant told the House of Commons in a debate on Montserrat: 'The Government should have said to them, "Here you are; here is a package – perhaps a bundle of warm clothes plus x pounds – so that you can settle yourselves down . . ." This has not happened, and there is grave concern about it.'[12]

A minority of Montserratian leaders in the UK argued that to create a special structure would label Montserratians as refugees and create an 'outsider' status. 'The easy way for the British to think of you as an outsider is if you make the structure con-tainable,' said Jennette Arnold, a Labour councillor for the London borough of Islington, born in Long Ground, Mont-serrat, but brought up in Birmingham. This, she knew, was a tough position to take, but her argument was that she was looking at the long-term position of Montserratians. However, the majority view was to lobby for a special liaison facility, an organisation to look after the interests of evacuees in the UK. As Janice Panton put it in her letter to the chair of the International Development Committee in October 1997: 'This diaspora . . .

needs to be dealt with before irreparable damage is done to an already damaged community.'[13]

Eventually, the sought-after liaison facility, the Montserrat Project, opened its doors, taking over from the voluntary work done by MOPPA, MAC89 and the Red Cross. In its first year, the Montserrat Project was managed by Refugee Action and supported by Montserratian community associations. Based in London and Birmingham, with advice centres in several other cities, and with funding of £800,000 and a staff of twenty for its first year, it concentrated its efforts on helping evacuees to sort out their immediate needs. During that time 1600 evacuee households had been in contact with the Project. In its second year, with a greatly reduced budget, the Project began to concentrate on longer-term community development.

Inevitably the Montserrat Project attracted criticism. The staff, for example, were largely non-Montserratian; initially, manager Lazelle Howes was the only member who had been born in Montserrat. This alienated some evacuees who felt that the staff 'were not of the culture'. There was also resentment that Montserratian volunteers, who had worked hard in the early years of the crisis to support the evacuees, did not get jobs with the Project. The appointment of Howes, a former minister in the Reuben Meade administration and herself an evacuee, was also questioned. Despite such difficulties and what was seen as an unwillingness to devolve power to local community groups, the Montserrat Project provided long-awaited help and resources.

Loretta has been in the flat for the weekend without electricity. The long summer evenings reduce the urgency for light, but without electricity she can not use the fridge or heat water. She has been told by the housing association to ring the electricity board. She has bought a £10 phonecard but finds out that it doesn't work in the nearby phone boxes. So she uses coins to telephone the electricity board. The woman begins to explain what Loretta has to do. The coins run out. When she rings again the woman explains that an 'operative' had gone to the house on Friday, but no one was there. Please can someone visit again, Loretta asks. The woman says that the housing association must make 'a call order' to the electricity board. Loretta rings the housing association and speaks to Miss G who says that she will have to pay £37.50 for reconnection because the housing association will only pay for one reconnection visit. Loretta runs out of coins again. Miss G kindly says that if Loretta stays in the phone box she will ring the electricity board and then phone her back. She does. Loretta will still have to pay but can do so gradually. Miss G has arranged for the reconnection to be made between Tuesday at 5.30 p.m. and Wednesday at 5.30 p.m. Someone must be there all the time to answer the door. The electricity is reconnected.

One of the key difficulties faced by Montserratians, some of whom arrived virtually penniless in the UK, was the long delay before receiving benefits. The waiting time, as estimated by the Revd Gualter de Mello of the Co-Ordinating Committee for the Welfare of Evacuees from Montserrat was between four weeks and four months in Hackney.[14] Compounding this distress was the endless encounters with bureaucracy – letters from and visits to benefit offices, employment offices and housing departments, waiting in queues to claim this and that. 'The amount of hassles you get. They tell you, you have to go find work, ask different questions, tell you to go to different places,' said John Robinson, formerly of Farm, whose parents died in the pyroclastic flows of 25 June. Such procedures were unfamiliar to Montserratians, who had never before been a claimant in an overpressed welfare state.

Miss G of the housing association says that Loretta must go immediately to Camden Town Hall to sort out her income support, otherwise her first week's rent may not be paid. She walks the half mile or so to the town hall but it is the afternoon and the office is closed from 1.30 p.m. Loretta must return tomorrow.

She gets a letter from the housing department. They need her

National Insurance (NI) number. Loretta gets a letter from the benefits office. They need her NI number. Loretta doesn't have an NI number. She goes to the benefits office to try and sort out her problems. The guy behind the window says his father comes from Dominica and that the man on the switchboard comes from Montserrat. He goes away and asks for the processing to be done as quickly as possible. He says that he has put her papers on the top of the pile. If she doesn't get her money by the middle of next week, she should telephone.

Loretta has been in the UK for just over three weeks and now has no money left. A worker from the Montserrat Project visits and gives her £20. Someone from the local social security office has also been to visit and asked her questions about employment. Loretta gets a letter from the housing department, asking her in which housing estate/area in the borough or outside it she might want to live when her short-life tenancy in the Georgian duplex ends. Not surprisingly, she has no idea how to fill in the form. She doesn't know any part of London except the immediate area around her flat where she goes to buy her food and make her phone calls. She gets a letter from the housing assessor at Camden to say that unless she brings in her income support book, she may have to be evicted. She has no income support book. She has yet to be allocated an NI number.

The delays in receiving benefits were attributed in many cases to the vexed problem of a National Insurance number. De Mello drew attention to this in his memorandum to the International Development Committee. He wrote: 'Hackney Benefits Agency are reluctant to give out temporary National Insurance (NI) numbers for fear of fraud. No NI number means no benefits, no grants or loans, no assistance for school or college, and makes taking above-board employment impossible.'[15]

While Hackney came under particular scrutiny from the Committee, it was clear from the work put in by the voluntary community associations that many local benefit offices appeared to have ignored or been ignorant of the Home Office circulars which explained the rights of Montserratians. Vincent Browne, a social worker, who settled in east London, said: 'The benefits office either didn't know or didn't care. We were not British but they used the same criteria. We were not asking for special status but we were in a crisis situation.' His sister, Rosamund, added: 'They claim they have never heard of Montserrat and as a result it's a long process.' Anecdotal information from many evacuees all pointed to similar experiences. MAC89 spent much time faxing government circulars to benefits offices to tell them about the special situation of Montserratians.

Apart from access to benefits, accommodation was the main concern for evacuees. Many wanted to go to areas where they had family and friends. The Montserratian communities – built around those who migrated in the 1950s and 1960s – are concentrated in London, with smaller pockets in Birmingham, Preston and Leicester; Manchester and Nottingham have even tinier numbers. In London the key Montserratian areas are in some of the poorest areas of the capital, in particular Stoke Newington, Hackney and Finsbury Park. Montserratians 'back home' know of these parts of London, and Ridley Road market has long been famous as a Montserratian heartland. The requests to move close to established communities put an extra burden on the already overstretched local authorities charged with providing accommodation at short notice. 'Very soon the availability of properties dried up so that temporary accommodation and bed and breakfast was all that was left,' said Mennear.

The UK government had tried to warn evacuees of the pressure on accommodation in its pamphlet entitled *Moving to the UK*. Those who had come from spacious villas were now confined to small terraced houses; those who had lived in villages surrounded by fruit trees were now in high-rise estates where no one else wanted to live. Sometimes it was hard to accept the housing that was on offer, even if you were desperate. Nurse Sharmen Thompson, who arrived in London with her blind mother and daughter, was allocated a flat in Hackney; there was fungus on the walls and the wallpaper had been torn off.

'The windows didn't lock, it had one bed and a stove. The whole place was falling apart. It was really horrible,' she said.

Another problem was that the evacuees had little money left for furnishing their new accommodation. MOPPA wrote to the Benefits Agency to draw attention to the problems of evacuees without funds finding themselves in unfurnished flats. It recommended that evacuees be offered a grant from the Social Fund rather than a crisis loan. Having at first been turned down for a grant, Sharmen Thompson appealed and was eventually awarded £700. 'This was the first time I had rented. I had to have some funds,' she said. Some were never successful. John Robinson, for example, got his Hackney flat in October 1997. 'Everything was empty. I asked for a grant twice but they turn it down. You have to lie down on the floor. I have to cry in the night. I used to lie down on the floor as a child. Now, I see I have to go back to the floor.' Gradually, friends found him furniture, bed, chairs, carpet. But the comparisons with home remind him of what he has lost. 'At home, I used to live decent,' he said.

Bernie Grant and Dianne Abbott, both black Labour MPs for poor London constituencies, also drew attention to the evacuees' problems. Both addressed meetings of Montserratians, helped evacuees in their surgeries, witnessed their problems and spoke in the House of Commons on the subject. From their position, it was clear that there had been poor co-ordination and little effort to ease the trauma of the islanders. As Abbott, whose constituency includes Hackney, said in February 1998: 'The problem is that we have Government documents and soothing words from Ministers, but on the ground, the experience of Montserratian evacuees is very different.'[16]

Once benefits and accommodation had been sorted out, the evacuees were then anxious to find employment. But this was a problem, even for skilled workers, and in particular for men. As Lazelle Howes of the Montserrat Project explained: 'The majority of the men who came up were in building construction, plasterers, carpenters and so on. In Montserrat they had

no need for certificates, but here they need recognised qualifications.' However skilled and experienced a worker, the lack
of an NVQ certificate for construction work meant no job. Even
those with formal qualifications gained in the Caribbean, in
social work and teaching, for example, were in no better a
position. They are not recognised in the United Kingdom
'People don't know what level you have achieved and don't
know your skills,' said Vincent Browne.

Some of those who suffered most were those who had had
responsible jobs. The accountant Simon Maty arrived in England in September 1997. He was allocated one room in a multi-
occupied house in north London. He could not open a bank
account because he could not show a bill in his name. He wrote
for 300 jobs in accounting. 'They all mentioned my age or said
I have no UK experience. I registered at the job centre, but they
say, if you're not on the phone, forget it. It's a hostile environment and it goes on and on and on.' With no job in sight,
Maty decided to return to education, and he was accepted at
the University of North London for an MA in business administration. 'I didn't want to waste my time here so the obvious
thing was to go back to school,' he said. (Montserratian students
had to pay overseas' students fees until October 1997 when grant
fees of £4400 and living expenses of £3500 were awarded.)

Glenn Lewis and his family arrived in England in October
1997, leaving their spacious home in Richmond Hill outside
Plymouth. He and his wife, three teenage children and disabled
mother-in-law found a terraced house to rent in east London.
An electrical engineer and photographer, Lewis had hoped to
get a job. He signed on at a job centre, but without success.
'No one would employ me because I did not have references
and my qualifications, my certificates from the 1970s, are not
recognised here . . . Not being able to work, it cripples you,'
he said. Eventually, he went to St Kitts, where he could work,
leaving the rest of the family temporarily in England where the
children were at school and university.

For less skilled, older people, employment seemed an ever

more remote possibility. John Robinson felt that, at fifty, he was too old to get a job. He went to ask about a job as a forklift truck driver. 'First thing he asked me how old you be. It's terrible. I'd love to do something. I used to live decent, but I can't make the money up here.'

Education and retraining became key aspects of the resettlement agenda for many Montserratians. One of the main reasons for leaving had been the decline in the educational service and, from time to time, its non-existence. Education is prized and Montserratians have always been proud of their educational standards. Gertrude Shotte, the former headteacher of Kinsale Primary School who had herself been displaced, became a postgraduate student at London University's Institute of Education, working on the educational experiences of relocated Montserratians in the UK.

Shotte interviewed students, parents and teachers in twenty-one schools in seven English cities to see how Montserratian children were adapting to their new school environment.[17] Among the positive aspects, the students told Shotte, were encouraging and supportive teachers, the cafeteria system, access to computers, a wide subject choice, work experience and career guidance. The unfavourable impressions of English schools included absence of assemblies, not enough homework, lack of respect for teachers, racist bullying and smoking. The overall approach to discipline in English schools puzzled children instilled with a more traditional respect for those in authority. 'The children always talk back to the teachers,' one Montserratian student told Shotte. 'The teachers are afraid of them. It is useless to complain when you are pushed around.' One group of students reported that some Montserratian boys were harassed by other Afro-Caribbean students and called 'soft' and 'weak'. Others said that Montserratians were teased about their refugee 'status' and about wearing jumpers on a 'hot' day. 'Boys, more so than the girls, tended to be victims of racist bullying,' said Shotte, who later discovered an increasing number of boy evacuees being excluded from school.

The Montserratians felt that they were academically more advanced than English children. Shotte herself firmly believes that the Caribbean education system is superior to the British, with CXC, the examination equivalent to the GCSE, 'head and shoulders above'. Ixchel Brade, aged twelve, is now living in Leicester. She said that school in England is one year behind Montserrat. 'We're just going over the same things.' She would also like a more disciplined atmosphere at her new school. 'Then we would work harder,' she said.

Shotte looked closely at some of the factors influencing the ability of the children to make a smooth transition to life in England. Apart from family and community support, she concluded that schools, the 'third ring of security', generally had 'the support services that refugee students need'. Shotte found that while 75 per cent of teachers acknowledged the 'traumatic experiences of Montserrat students before their arrival in the UK', they had only a superficial grasp of what had happened. However, once the teachers were made more aware of the situation, most seemed 'willing to employ any additional strategy' to ease the transition of their students. Apart from support from family and teachers, it was the students' 'personal commitment to succeed and the desire to contribute to rebuilding Montserrat' that had been 'positive influences in the adjustment process,' said Shotte's report.

Verlene and Lenroy need to go to school. Loretta wants them to go to the same one: there are two mixed secondary schools in the borough. One of the schools says that it has no room; the other says it has a waiting list for Lenroy, but could take Verlene immediately.

The school invites Loretta and the children for an interview. At the school Loretta explains the situation about the volcano. The teacher asks Verlene what language she speaks at home. Verlene says English. The teacher explains that a lot of the children at the school do not have English as a first language. The lively school prospectus says that the students can study Bengali. Verlene wants to know whether she can do computers. The children are asked what they like doing outside school. Verlene says she likes music, netball and reading. Lenroy says he likes cricket (they do not play cricket at that school). The teacher, who is friendly and welcoming, says that Verlene can start the next day and that she will see what she can do to find a place for Lenroy. She tells Verlene to bring trainers (she doesn't have any), leggings (she doesn't have those either) and a T-shirt. The family is shown round the school. They like the classrooms and the equipment.

Verlene starts school. Soon, Lenroy hears he can start at the same school in September. Verlene is doing work experience at a day nursery. Lenroy's bike, which he had left outside the house, chained to the railings, has been stolen.

Loretta's benefits gradually seem to be in hand so she can relax a little. 'I know everything will be all right. Praise the Lord,' she says. She and the children join the library. Lenroy has been to a holiday steel band course. Loretta found out about it in the local newspaper. Verlene stays at home, but hopes to find a holiday job next year. The family has bought plants for the flat, and a second-hand computer. The children use it; so does Loretta, who is going to free computer classes at the children's school on Saturday mornings.

Financial problems, poor accommodation and lack of employment were key constraints to settling in the United Kingdom. There were other, less tangible, aspects to adjustment. Besides racism, there were cultural differences. 'We thought the UK was a God-fearing place, respectable and dignified,' said Sharmen Thompson, who eventually got a nursing job at Homerton Hospital, Hackney. 'It was a big shock. When I moved to Hackney, I thought I had come to the ghetto – it's so shabby and rundown. People in England are so disrespectful.' A middle-aged farmer from Lee's had little good to say about life in England. 'It's the worst place I've ever come to in my life. They are just like wild beasts, they don't say good morning.' His sad-eyed wife used to sell vegetables in Plymouth market. She finds it lonely here. Hackney is a long way from the once gentle foothills of the Soufrière volcano, and Ridley Road market, even though it is a familiar meeting place for Montserratians, does not match up, she said, to the one at home.

A few weeks after her arrival, Loretta goes to Ridley Road one Saturday morning. She says she will know people there. She sees plantain, breadfruit, yam, christophene. 'Nice yam. Nice this, nice that.' She meets a lanky fellow in a singlet and greets him. 'Since when you been here?' She meets two men, one older, one younger. The older one wears a felt hat, which he doffs to Loretta. He has one tooth and a sweet smile: he was in the same shelter as Loretta. He has just arrived to be with his son, a former policeman from Plymouth. A young man in shiny trousers and a round face greets her. He is from Gages and used to go to the same church as Loretta. A smart woman passes in a hat. 'Montserrat?' inquires Loretta. The woman nods and smiles. Two other women pass; they look back and stare at Loretta, but don't acknowledge her. 'They're ungodly street people,' according to Loretta. She finishes her visit to Ridley Road by buying beans, watermelon, banana; she looks at shoes and underwear and gives money to a begging woman and baby.

While many evacuees clustered in areas with established Montserratian communities, one group found themselves particularly isolated. In November 1997 a charter flight flew into Newcastle-upon-Tyne airport, in the north-east of England. On board were thirty-five special needs cases, each accompanied by a relative. The plan had been devised in the wake of Sir Kenneth Calman's visit to Montserrat to relieve its hard-pressed health service. Newcastle-upon-Tyne had been chosen because it was thought to have the most appropriate health care, but at the last minute Durham became the temporary base for the evacuee group. Many of them wanted to go to London. Alternative accommodation was to be found within two weeks of their arrival. In the event, it took a year before the last person was eventually housed elsewhere. At one stage, said Lazelle Howes of the Montserrat Project, 'bags and bags of West Indian food' were being sent to Durham to provide the evacuees with a familiar diet.

While many were initially grateful for the support offered by the established Montserratian groups, differences began to emerge. There was an unspoken perception by some of the established community in England that compared with Montserratians who arrived in the 1950s and 1960s, the evacuees 'have it laid on a plate, whether or not it's a plate they would like'. For their part, the evacuees began to feel that the community organisations could not provide for their needs. 'Many wanted to have a voice in the organisation, they didn't just want to be on the receiving end of help,' said Lazelle Howes. Bearing this out, some of the new arrivals set up the Montserratians and Friends Organisation of Birmingham in September 1998. Its chairman, William B. Riley, said that this group aimed 'to give help around education, health, laws and spiritual aspects of life' as well as to provide cultural and social events. For Riley, after the frustrations of the early days in the UK, saw that there were important opportunities for evacuees here. 'There are plusses here for men and women to get themselves better equipped, to go to school and college. They are now able to get a grip of themselves and enjoy life here,' he said.

Jane O'Brien of Cork Hill expressed a similarly realistic point of view at a luncheon club for Montserratians run by Daisy Aymer and other established islanders. 'I miss home. Montserrat is the best place in the world. Here, every place is so far away, you get lost,' she said. 'But we have to settle down here.' Lucinda Hogan, a social worker specialising in domestic violence and child abuse, said she thought settling down was harder for the men. 'Women have the responsibility for the home. The men get bored very easily, and going out for them is problematic – the distances, the sense of insecurity, the unknown culture of pubs.' Jennette Arnold, co-ordinator of a Montserrat women's group, believed that the women had taken charge. 'Many professional women here are determined to work together and help each other and looking to see how the children can benefit,' she said.

Even so, everyone felt a sense of physical containment. As Lucinda Hogan said: 'I miss my yard, my trees. Here I am confined to my flat.' The lack of space was a real deprivation – space to hang the washing out, for people 'to get the air', to sit on the veranda, to live in a large rather than a small home. 'There I could go out and cut a banana . . . there is nothing here,' said John Robinson in his 1950s, red-brick Hackney council flat where the walkways echo with footsteps and the staircases curve endlessly between one floor and another. But even for Robinson, time offered some hope. 'Now, slowly things are turning around. Now I sometimes go different places. I get a bus pass, or go to dominoes in the evening.'

Eventually – at the end of July, six weeks after her arrival – all Loretta's benefits are sorted out. Loretta is finding her way around London. She tells the children to 'mark' the buildings and the names of the streets. She has become familiar with the buses and the tube. She and the children have been to the Houses of Parliament – Verlene took some photographs – and walked down Whitehall. They have been to a barbecue organised by the nearby homeless persons unit, which has a community centre in the nearby square. They also went on a day trip by coach to the seaside, to Brighton, organised by the unit.

Loretta says that being in England is 'like being like a baby again, you have to learn how to do things all over again for the first time'. But she is not planning to return to Montserrat for some time. She thinks the children will never return.

For those who chose to stay in the Caribbean region, the ways of doing things were more familiar and the culture was closer to home. But it was not home, and many of the problems, such as housing and employment, echoed those experienced by evacuees to the UK. Like them, the evacuees who went elsewhere left Montserrat with no official assistance, financial or otherwise, until 21 August 1997. (As one woman put it: 'The British have us like feathers in a bag. They just open the bag and scatter us everywhere.'[18]) At that point the 'assisted regional voluntary relocation' scheme was announced. On 5 September 1997, a further announcement was made: those who had left their home between 18 July 1995 – when the volcano crisis began – and 16 August 1997 would also be eligible for the grant, but for those in employment the grant would be means-tested.

The relocation grant (see chapter 5) was paid out over six months. For the earliest beneficiaries, their money had been fully paid by mid-1998. There was no official financial support thereafter. The British government said that it was 'not prepared to fund from the aid programme a permanent system of benefits for Montserratians in the Caribbean region'. It did, however, announce in April 1998 what it called 'a community empowerment project' to encourage financial independence, while a charitable fund was also introduced for the old and disabled. In addition, a £1 million loan scheme for Montserratians to set up small businesses was put in place in Antigua.

Tricia Bridge was manager of the Department for International Development's office in Antigua during the regional relocation programme. From the beginning, there had been concern that the money was not enough and that it did not take individual circumstances into account. 'I think that London thinks that moving from one Caribbean island to another is like moving from one English county to another,' she said. The International Development Committee also made adverse criticism, less regarding the amount of the grant than the means-testing. It described this restriction as 'unnecessary and unfair' and 'crude'. It was to cause considerable hardship.

A total of 2372 Montserratians registered for the Caribbean regional relocation grant scheme, but many more went to the region on their own accord. Perhaps 3000 (the exact figures are unknown) went to Antigua. Some also went to Anguilla, St Kitts-Nevis, Dominica, Barbados; nearly every Caribbean island received at least a few evacuees. Antigua is the island that has the most familiar links with Montserrat. Some had family and friends there, the legacy of earlier migrations. Even so, there were differences and difficulties. Candia Williams, then co-ordinator of the Montserrat Information Office (set up by Montserratians in Antigua at the end of June 1997), said: 'For some people it's a new and strange country. All the familiar things have gone. In Montserrat people dropped by, and here you're a stranger.' Marcell Ryan, who had lived in a tent at Gerald's, had eventually moved to Antigua with her mother and two sisters. She noticed the differences: 'In Antigua, no one says good morning, I'm accustomed to saying that. But here everyone minds their own business.' Perhaps it was not so different from the UK after all.

The cost of living was also higher than at home. In Antigua, nearly two thirds of Montserratians rented accommodation; the rest lived with family or friends. According to a social survey of Montserratians living in Antigua, rented accommodation ranged from EC$275 per month for two rooms without amenities to EC$1000 per month for an unfurnished two-bedroom house with all facilities. When Marcell Ryan first went to Antigua, she and her family lived with a brother. Then they got their own two-bedroom house, but the rent was high. 'You can't save because the house rent is dragging everything,' said Ryan. Many Montserratians no longer had any savings. The social survey reported that there was widespread poverty, unemployment and distress among the evacuees. It recommended a housing and public assistance programme. Housing became a priority, said Candia Williams. 'Montserratians would like to get land to build their own homes,' she continued, emphasising that the problem of long-term needs rather than short-term hand-outs had to be addressed.

Jobs were hard to come by although there was some employment for men as taxi drivers or in the construction business. While Montserratians were offered access to the education and health care services, both were inferior – and costlier – than at home. Unlike Montserrat, there is only private pre-school education in Antigua, while the public health system (which the rich eschew) covers chronic illness but not such ailments as hypertension or diabetes. Montserratians discovered that everyday standards were lower in Antigua. 'We're a very small society in Montserrat, but we are accustomed to very high standards. But here the development is very superficial,' said Pam Arthurton of Carib World Travel.

Myrle Roach first went to Antigua in December 1996 when she lost her job in Montserrat as secretary to the dean of the American University of the Caribbean (the university closed soon after the onset of the crisis). She got a job as secretary to the manager of the Halcyon Rex Hotel. She was not eligible for the relocation grant because she came early and found a job. Her mother, however, was eligible. Despite the fact that she was working, Roach said it was 'tough starting from scratch. I've never paid rent before, I am paying for everything in the home.' But she had never dreamed of going to the UK – 'I like the freedom here,' she added.

For the government of Antigua and Barbuda, the arrival of perhaps 3000 people, adding to a total population of 65,000, posed significant difficulties. Antigua's none too developed services felt the strain. On 25 August 1997 Prime Minister Lester Bird made a radio broadcast to the nation. First of all, he congratulated Antiguans for welcoming Montserratians. He went on to point out, however, that 'there is now a serious burden on our social services'. Bird demanded that the UK shoulder its responsibilities. 'Montserrat is a British colony and the people of Montserrat are British subjects. It is the British government which has the primary responsibility for the welfare of the Montserratian people,' he said. Toughening up his message, he said that unless Britain produced 'very firm proposals backed up by resources' Antigua and Barbuda could only offer itself 'as a haven' for any more Montserratians on a 'short-term basis'. Bird's High Commissioner in London, Ronald Sanders, was charged with 'opening a dialogue' with the UK government about its obligations to Montserratians in Antigua. Sanders later said that the British government tended to talk of Montserratians moving to other countries in the Caribbean 'as if those Monsterratians had a right to do so, and the Caribbean had an obligation to accept them'. The British responded with a £3 million grant for health and education projects and a three-year waiver of a £3 million loan.

Other Caribbean governments also asked for assistance. Anguilla, another British colony, had received a considerable number of Montserratians. Its chief minister, Hubert Hughes, pointing to the numbers of Montserratians who were not able to earn a living in Anguilla, asked the UK 'to meet these financial obligations'.[19] He said that he would accept 250 Montserratians in addition to the 200 already on Anguilla, provided that the United Kingdom paid the cost. St Kitts-Nevis also requested support. Some evacuees to St Kitts reported that they had not been able to access the social security system, while others were alarmed by the comparatively high crime rate. The British government rejected the requests for help from Anguilla and St Kitts-Nevis, arguing that the burden for islands other than Antigua and Barbuda was 'of a much lower order of magnitude'.

Some of those who had first gone to Antigua or one of the other islands eventually chose to go to the UK, paying for their passage out of the last pay-out from the relocation grant. Making it in the Caribbean with no job and no welfare state had proved impossible. Maybe the UK would offer more security.

Shanell O'Garro, a pupil at Kinsale Primary School, wrote the following poem, called *Evacuation Time*.

> When the volcano was rumbling
> All the people started mumbling
> Now it was time for evacuation
> We needed plenty transportation
> Some people went off island
> Some people went to North

> Some had lots of fun off island
> And some did not
> Some went to America
> Some went to Antigua
> Some came back
> But some did not[20]

And so it was. Despite the difficulties, the longer Montserratians stayed away, the more adjustments they would make to a new life in a new country. For the young, in particular, the emotional ties would loosen more quickly, city lights and the opportunities, in particular in education and training, would keep them away from their island. 'There is a saying that Montserrat's best export is its people,' said Janice Panton, the government of Montserrat's information officer in the UK. 'We do well abroad, but always need to go home. We fete our politicians who come here, not just because they are dignitaries but because we want to know what is happening at home, what we can do to help.'

So the new diaspora, forged by the faraway volcano, would continue that tradition. But if the volcano had driven Montserrations from their homes, it also seemed to have reinforced them – even those with only remote connections to the island – with a new sense of themselves as they campaigned for their homeland and redrew their picture of themselves as Montserratians in exile.

8

....

Seeds for Change

The inquest into the deaths of 25 June 1997 took place in the makeshift coroner's court, in the new annexe to Salem Primary School, in the last months of 1998. In charge was coroner Rhys Burriss, a British lawyer under a one-year contract as senior magistrate and coroner. Over the seven weeks of the inquest Burriss took evidence from fifty-two witnesses, including three chief ministers, former governor Frank Savage and relatives of the dead. Long statements were submitted by many of the witnesses as well as given in oral evidence. Chief Minister David Brandt, in typically florid language, described 25 June as 'like the days of tribulation and desolation in the Bible'.

Montserrat's Coroner's Act of 1950 allows for considerable scope (more so than in current English law) for jury intervention. Burriss decided that he would widen the scope of the inquest by asking not just what happened on the day but by looking at why the victims were where they were when they died. He thought it appropriate to look at the wider picture. Although there was no legal requirement to have a jury, Burriss felt that given the widespread concern, he wanted one. The commissioner of police appointed a jury of five, four men and one woman.

The inquest raised many of the points discussed by the International Development Committee. It also revealed interesting aspects of the emergency not significantly touched on by the Committee, in particular the continued operation of the airport and the plight of the farmers. 'That farm was my livelihood. There is nothing else in place that I could support my family or make payments to the banks,' said Harry Lewis, whose wife Isolyn died. Crop farmers like Lewis were selling to the Emergency Operations Centre and to the Glendon Hospital, as well as donating food to the shelters. They were seen as 'essential workers'; they were allowed through the checkpoints. Then there were livestock farmers, like Lenroy Daley, who survived the flows. He told the inquest that his animals were still in the exclusion zone on 25 June. He would return to feed and check on them; he was getting complaints that they were damaging crops and he had wanted to move them, but there was no other land available. The farmers had no organisation to represent their interests, no compensation, no crop insurance scheme.

Should the farmers have been allowed to risk their lives to feed the people? It was their choice, but it was a narrow moral line for the authorities to take no responsibility for the deaths when the farmers were contracted to sell their crops, not just on the street, but, through the Ministry of Agriculture to the Emergency Operations Centre, whose boss was the British governor. To keep the islanders who were living in shelters supplied with fresh vegetables, other islanders chose to risk their lives.

The jury's verdict on the nineteen who died was that 'death was by natural catastrophe of volcanic eruption/pyroclastic flow'. The physical cause of injury was 'neurogenic shock resulting from total body burns'. However, in fourteen of the cases the jury decided that there was a contributory cause of death. In nine cases, it was the failure of the British and Montserratian governments to provide lands for displaced farmers, in four cases, the continued operation of the airport, and, in one case, the 'deplorable' conditions in the public shelters.

The jury also added two general riders to its verdicts. One focused on the shelters. It criticised the UK government for not acting 'in a more positive manner to relieve this distressing situation' and urged it to respond to the housing problem 'with imagination and generosity'. The second rider was addressed to the government of Montserrat: 'The process of public information could have been more comprehensive and therefore more effective in counteracting the extremely strong motives people had to enter or remain in the evacuated areas.' This could have been done through greater use of 'posters, radio jingles, printed messages on T-shirts, broadsheet advertising and television'.

The coroner, in his own statement, pointed out that one of the functions of an inquest is to make recommendations in order to prevent jeopardising the safety or health of the people in the future. Burriss's forthright remarks emphasised the pressing need for land in the north to be made available for housing. In describing the British government's response as 'unimaginative, grudging and tardy', he urged Prime Minister Tony Blair to take 'personal charge' and provide enough funds for land to be bought and 'adequate and decent housing' to be built. In a letter to Burriss, Blair described the coroner's statements as 'surprising and inaccurate'. Burriss's comments were also dismissed by George Foulkes in the House of Commons. But in Montserrat, Burriss briefly became something of a hero. Despite his wish to continue in his job, his contract was not renewed. He was told that the government of Montserrat was looking for a replacement from the Caribbean.

The verdicts drew some sort of line under the deaths of 25 June but they also reaffirmed the complexities of the crisis. The jury had had to digest and interpret immense amounts of material and unravel processes worthy of the complexities of the volcano itself. And like everything else that had happened during the volcano years, the events of 25 June were more complicated than they had first appeared to be. The future would be just as complex.

'Montserrat will never be the same again. Old Plymouth is gone, what is not buried will go. And everyone has changed.

Montserratians who have stayed have changed and so have those who left.' This was the painful but realistic opinion of Candia Williams, who had worked through the crisis assisting her fellow Montserratians in Antigua. With such dramatic changes in the physical and mental landscape of Montserrat, what would a new Montserrat look like? Had the volcano turned the clock back to a Montserrat both psychologically and economically dependent on the 'Mother Country'? Or would the volcano experience offer positive opportunities to Montserrat to rethink its destiny – and, ultimately, to empower it?

For the moment those answers lie out of reach. But what the crisis had certainly revealed were the discomfiting ingredients of a colonial syndrome. As has been shown throughout this book, a once great imperial power had sought to address a natural disaster in one of its remaining thirteen tiny colonies and had come badly unstuck. The crisis had also reminded Montserratians that while in 'normal' times they could perhaps play at being independent, this was essentially an illusion. There was no real self-determination and the colonial model was not and could not be democratic.

Montserratians were not really 'free to make our own failures', as Bennette Roach of the *Montserrat Reporter* put it.

What then were the options for the future? The possibility of independence had surely receded. In any case there had never been much enthusiasm for it. (That was also true for the other British Caribbean dependencies as well as for the French and Dutch territories.) Ted Rowlands, a former Minister of State at the Foreign Office, remembered when the UN's decolonisation committee went to Montserrat in 1975 and said: ' "We have come to rescue you from the nasty British colonial yoke." The local ministers said: "Don't talk like that. We do not see the British in those terms. We have got them rather nicely where we want them. We are quite happy in our relationship with the British government." '[1] The conservative argument was that it was more beneficial to remain a British colony and so easier to attract outside investors and expatriates.

Gordon Lewis, in his classic book *The Growth of the Modern West Indies*, talked of a Montserrat in the 1960s drained of its talent by migration and characterised by 'a corroding self-doubt'.[2] Two decades later, Howard Fergus, Montserrat's historian and poet, wrote: 'A poor developing country must, perforce, induce and placate outsiders, but national maturity and self-determination will always elude a people if critical decisions have to be based on what outsiders think.'[3] Fergus, writing before the volcano crisis, believed that constitutional independence could not be put off 'forever' but that it required an educational programme on independence which would harness the population's resources for the completion of that 'journey from slavery to emancipation'.

While the crisis postponed discussions about independence, it also became an important catalyst. It prompted the UK to review its relationship not just with Montserrat, but with all of its Overseas Territories. It concentrated the Whitehall mind. The result was the White Paper of March 1999 on the UK's Overseas Territories. The White Paper offered British citizenship, protection and support to achieve sustainable development and the right to self-determination to the 160,000 people of its Overseas Territories. In return, the UK demanded good governance, in particular with regard to financial regulation and human rights. The White Paper stated that in line with its international obligations, in particular to the European Union, the UK expected the Overseas Territories to enact the necessary reforms themselves but that 'in the absence of local action, legislation could be imposed on the Caribbean Territories by Orders in Council'.

For Montserrat, the human rights issue centred on its legislation forbidding the practice of homosexuality between two consenting adults in private (judicial corporal punishment and capital punishment were abolished in 1991, the latter by Order in Council). Most Montserratians are generally conservative about, if not hostile to, gay rights and the British demand for legislative change was seen as further interference in the distinctive Montserratian 'way of life'; Montserrat was not, it was said, like London or Amsterdam where 'the curse of Sodom' flourished. The issue illustrated how, despite the British claims for a new and modern partnership, the political landscape remained fraught. The view of Chief Minister David Brandt, speaking at the Dependent Territories Association conference in February 1998, was that 'no amendment should be made to any Overseas Territory constitution without the direct and active involvement with the people concerned'.

The White Paper offered the peoples of the Overseas Territories a closer bond with Britain. For the first time, Britain offered citizenship but, in return, they demanded they become, as it were, 'more like us'. However, it in no way addressed the constitutional problem of dividing responsibility and power that had so concerned the International Development Committee. Britain had also rejected radical change. It had, for example, eschewed the French model of France *d'outre-mer*. In the French Caribbean territories of Guadeloupe and Martinique, for example, the people elect deputies to the French Assembly, have French passports, obey the same laws as those in Metropolitan France and thereby enjoy a far higher standard of living than their independent neighbours. Such integrationist policies remain acceptable to most French Antilleans, who prefer to 'stay safely tucked up inside the body of the great French beast, rather than wander alone in the outside world'.[4]

While to be tucked up inside the body of the great British beast was not an option for Montserrat, neither was the likelihood of closer political links with the rest of the Caribbean. This was a pity since Montserrat – more so than the other British Caribbean dependencies – had a history of participation in a cluster of regional institutions. However, the Caribbean's laggardly – and unsuccessful – attempts at integration meant that Montserrat could not look realistically to its neighbours for a political solution or an economic future. Antiguan Tim Hector, opposition politician and radical, had suggested to the British that Montserrat could be brought into some sort of relationship with Antigua and Barbuda. Hector's party failed, however, to win power in the elections of 1999. His vision for a wider and deeper Caribbean would not be realised.

So Montserrat would remain inside Robin Cook's new 'partnership for progress and prosperity'. Yet over and above the political relationship, there was an ambivalence about the less tangible links between the UK and Montserrat. On the one hand, there was the concept of the beneficent 'Mother Country', of the child in need, seeking the care and protection of its mother. This link would now bring a further range of financial, educational and freedom-to-travel benefits. On the other hand, the 'maternal' links with Britain were not close. They had never been nurtured. 'We never felt that Montserrat was looked upon as an important part of the UK,' said Myrle Roach, the secretary who settled in Antigua. 'It was always a hassle to go up there,' she said. 'When you wrote British on a form, they looked at you and crossed it out.' That attitude was something that Robin Cook had recognised: 'The residents of the Overseas Territories are proud of their connection with Britain but often puzzled that Britain appears not to be proud to have them as British citizens.' There were few on-island institutional ties to the UK other than the Queen's Birthday celebrations. At the same time, the influence of the United States had grown. Montserrat was no different from anywhere else in the Caribbean in its vulnerability to 'cultural penetration'. There were also many American expatriates on the island. In its imperious way, the United States watched over the Caribbean – it was 'back yard' after all; in contrast, the UK had not paid much attention to the region, largely indifferent even to its own territories.

However, the political system had always been thoroughly British. But the loss of population and the loss of land on Montserrat had prompted a rethink of at least one aspect of the system. With only two whole constituencies (Northwestern and Northern) remaining out of seven, an Elections Commission was set up in 1999 to examine options for future elections. There was consultation with Montserratians both on and off island. Ideas were put forward about the possibility of breaking with the Westminster model. Some people felt that the political party was a divisive instrument in such a small society and that the new Montserrat should emphasise unity and not division. In fact, the recommendations included a proposal to replace the multi-constituency, first-past-the-post electoral system with a single constituency electoral system. The commission also recommended that nominated membership of the Legislative Council should be abolished and that the elected membership of the council be increased from seven to nine.

This then was Montserrat's political framework as it emerged from the volcano crisis – a further retreat from independence, closer ties with the UK, an offer of British citizenship, a possible change in the electoral system. But what of the island's economic framework? The Country Policy Plan for the three years up to 2001 indicated that the economy would be driven by infrastructural development. That was vital. However, as Christian Aid noted, quoting a local businessman: 'Infrastructure is not enough: by itself infrastructure creates nothing.'[5] There would be jobs in the construction industry and support for small businesses. The economic strategy also seemed, to a great extent, to be returning to a reliance on tourism – seducing the expatriate market back to their villas – and the import business. That model is common in the Caribbean. 'Are we going to become anything more than a haven for the very rich and the people who service them?' asked one leading Montserratian.

Whatever the economic model, it would need the continued support of the UK for many years to come. While the British government noted at the end of 1998 that government revenue was improving and that the private sector would 'meet a higher proportion of future investment needs', it also acknowledged that it was premature to speculate on when Britain could gracefully withdraw its financial assistance. The £75 million, allocated until 2001, would soon be used up.

And what size of society would it be? Would such a dependency-based economy attract home well-educated, emancipated young Montserratians? 'I can see the sun rise and the sun set here – but the next generation won't come back,' said one islander who had returned from England in the middle of the crisis to farm in the north. Those in the UK with children of school-going age, those improving their qualifications and settling down to a new life might not return for some time. Those who felt that they had nothing to go back to might never do so. Even the announcement that all return fares home from the UK would be paid from 1 June 1999 did not trigger a wave of returnees. Not that people did not want to go home; they were being cautious. And in any case, as David Brandt told a meeting of Montserratians in London: 'You cannot come home now, we do not have anywhere to put you.'[6]

There would also be new social dynamics, such as the impact of living in unfamiliar places or on a 'housing estate'. Most of the old village communities had gone. And, of course, there were the distinctions now between those who left and those who stayed: each would bring a different set of experiences to the task of rebuilding. There was a need for the Montserratian government to rise above its insecurities and create a vision for a future Montserrat. 'Until the people who are in Montserrat decide in their own terms what sort of society they wish to live in, they will continue to inhabit economic and political institutions that they do not own,'[7] said the Christian Aid report in May 1996, in the middle of the crisis. That was no less true for the post-volcano situation.

The future also depended on the size of the viable part of the island. There were optimistic signs. The 'north' had begun to creep south with the reopening of Salem and the area north of the Belham River. Then in April 1999 unrestricted access to Isles Bay, just south of the mouth of the Belham River, was announced. The next step would be reoccupation of this villa area, and then, perhaps, Cork Hill, Fox's Bay and Richmond Hill, north of Plymouth, if the level of ash in the air was ruled to be low enough for habitation. There was even unofficial talk of reopening Harris, that key community in the east that had endured the trauma of 25 June 1997. The physical retreat from the volcano was probably, but not certainly, over.

This was important because, for most Montserratians, it was the hijacking of the land by the volcano that had inflicted some of the most painful wounds. How long would it take for those ominous grey slopes to grow green again? Thirty-six years after the eruption at the ultimate catastrophe of Krakatoa, a visiting botanist noticed continuous grass cover and small pockets of trees; a decade later, the trees had formed continuous forest.[8] At the end of 1902, nearly seven months after the volcanic eruption on St Vincent, Daniel Morris of Kew Gardens reported 'seeing crops growing up through layers of ash'.[9] One year after the destruction of St Pierre, Angelo Heilprin wrote that 'little colonies of ants and other insects were inhabiting the ruins and the land-snail had come to live with them'; creepers and other plants, he said, 'hung about the battered masonry'.[10] As in all volcanic situations, the land would recover, but it would take time.

In Montserrat, the process of rebirth was only just beginning in 1999. Georg Waldmann, a biologist specialising in the interaction between plants, animals and volcanoes, explained the chronology: 'The first invaders will be grasses, then herbaceous plants, shrubs and finally trees.' Waldmann had already noticed areas of new grass – but it had been a false dawn. 'The grass looks green and lovely, but it is not convincing,' he said. 'It is growing on areas where the ash has been washed away. It has shallow roots and it is not a stabiliser.' It would not survive. Coconut and almond seedlings had also been seen in ashy deposits at the airport, but without water and shelter these would also die. However, eventually, the dead matter would build up, contribute to a new layer of soil and provide enough goodness for seedlings to take root. There were already established seedlings in damp little gullies full of wind-blown leaves on the mudflow deposits of the Belham River valley. These were good signs. So too were the ground lizards nesting in the warm pyroclastic flows, and the bees, spiders and beetles present on the margins of the deposits. Nature would slowly change grey to green. Waldmann was also working with the Ministry of Agriculture on a plan for a National Volcanic Park and for a replanting programme of indigenous plant species.

The coral reefs had suffered as had island animal life. Montserrat's two endemic species – the mountain chicken (a species of frog) and the golden oriole, the island's national bird – had lost their Soufrière Hills habitat. The ash, lack of tree cover and changes in insect life had threatened the survival of the mountain chicken, which had retreated to the Centre Hills. So, too, had the Montserrat oriole, and its survival depended on its successful breeding in a restricted habitat. As Gerard Grey of the Ministry of Agriculture said poignantly: 'The oriole is our national bird and we don't want to lose it. Many people have left the island but the orioles and other wildlife have nowhere else to go.'[11]

With so many Montserratians in the diaspora, the search for identity – a key concern of the post-colonial Caribbean – had again become a focus of discussion. Unlike a manmade disaster there had been no 'enemy'; the Soufrière Hills had never been interpreted in that way. What the volcano had done was to sharpen the sense of 'home' even if for many Montserratians their land and homes had disappeared for ever. This, in itself, would force a reflection of what it was to be Montserratian. As the surgeon Lowell Lewis put it: 'This is the only place that my soul is at rest . . . Montserrat is the place where you matter. It is an important thing to be able to matter. Regardless of how much good work I do anywhere else, I know Montserrat is where I can make a difference.'[12]

Like other ravished cities and landscapes, Montserrat would reinvent itself. As in other disasters, those moments of destruction would become both pivotal and incidental. In his great novel *Texaco* the Martinican writer Patrick Chamoiseau uses the eruption of Mont Pelée as the point of change in the story of his people's history, from the Age of Straw to the Age of Crate Wood: 'Whoever came from Saint-Pierre had nothing to remember or even to explain.'[13] The English writer Patrick Leigh Fermor, who was also inspired by the Martinican disaster, based his novel *The Violins of Saint-Jacques* on the destruction of St Pierre. At the end the whole island disappears into the sea. The one survivor speaks of her loneliness in holding such unimaginable memories:

> The eruption shrank to the size of an insane and wicked interruption, an unnatural accident which had inflicted a cruel and undeserved death on all the people I loved, and broken and drowned the world we had lived in. The disaster seemed as wanton as the blows and tramplings of some immense and muscular idiot. For a long time, a very long time afterwards, Saint-Jacques and its inhabitants were the only real things for me, and the outside world a shadowy limbo. I felt as a solitary surviving inhabitant of Atlantis might have felt when his foothold had vanished under the waves.[14]

The Soufrière Hills volcano inspired Montserrat's own voices in music, prose and poetry, even as the crisis was unfolding. There were the songs of Arrow, Montserrat's world-famous calpysonian, including 'One Day at a Time' and 'Montserrat Still Nice'; and there was Randy Greenaway's gentle album *Seismic Glow* with its defiant lyrics, as in 'Montserratians Won't Say Die'. Among the poets was Howard Fergus. One of his poems, called *Class*, written early on in the emergency, has each verse deliberating on a different rage of nature: hurricane, flood, heat, earthquake – and volcano:

> But volcano is boss man, only one in its class, man
> It spouts fire and water from the same fountain
> to blister and cool us. Hot mud on a spree
> embracing all in its orbit from mountain to sea
> turned emerald brown closed the town down
> and to be frank has locked up the key
> from the Governor-in-Chief compelling
> lesser powers that be to beg for relief
> That is classic, that is class.[15]

The generation of children who saw and heard the volcano 'tumble and rumble' will be the ones to tell their volcano stories to their children. They will also be the ones to chart the survival of a post-volcano Montserratian society and culture. The science, the politics, the changed lives will be woven into the chronicles of the disaster. Whatever that myth – and that history – will become is for the people of Montserrat to decide. Montserrat's identity will be forever entwined with its volcano days.

Glossary

Ash cloud Eruption cloud containing volcanic ash.

Crater Bowl-shaped depression, often the vent for the volcanic material.

Dome collapse Occurs when a steep-sided, growing lava dome becomes unstable. Sections of the dome may break away to form a pyroclastic flow. Sudden gravitational collapses can also trigger explosive eruptions – when lava fragments are hurled out from the dome – by relieving pressure on the dome's interior.

Eruption column Generated by a pyroclastic flow or explosion and composed of ash-sized rock particles that move high into the atmosphere, creating a potential danger for aircraft.

Fountain collapse Explosively discharged mixture of ash, pumice and gas which collapses under gravity to form pyroclastic flows.

Lava Magma (molten rock) which has reached the earth's surface.

Lava dome A steep-sided growth of viscous lava, squeezed out like toothpaste from a vent.

Magma A mixture of liquid, crystals and volcanic gases that erupts from a volcano.

Magma chamber Underground reservoir of magma in the earth's crust.

Phreatic eruption Emission of ash and steam from a vent.

Pumice Light, porous volcanic rock.

Pyroclastic flow Fast-moving mass of hot rock fragments formed from the material ejected in a volcanic eruption. The material, generated by a dome or fountain collapse, also forms plumes of fine ash and hot air that rise above the flow. Also known as 'nuée ardente', French for 'glowing cloud'.

Pyroclastic surge Hot mixture of turbulent gas and volcanic ash; less constrained by topography than a pyroclastic flow.

Seismograph Instrument that registers and records the features of earthquakes.

Seismology The science of earthquakes.

Seismometer Instrument that measures ground vibrations.

Soufrière Vent which emits sulphurous gases. Name of volcanic centres in Montserrat, Guadeloupe and St Vincent and of villages in St Lucia and Dominica.

Vent Opening in the earth's crust through which volcanic materials pass.

Notes

References to sums of money are in the currency cited by the official authority or individual concerned. At the time of writing, £1 (UK sterling) = EC$4.25 (Eastern Caribbean dollars; US$1 = EC$2.70).

All quotes are from interviews with the author unless otherwise reflected in the notes.

Chapter 1 · The Day of Death

1. Montserrat Volcano Observatory (MVO), transcripts of interviews between scientists and those involved in the eruption of 25 June 1997, 1997–8 (unpublished).
2. David Lea, *The Price of Paradise*, vol. 4 (video), 1997.
3. MVO, op. cit.
4. Ibid.
5. Ibid.
6. Ibid.
7. Ibid.
8. *The Price of Paradise*, op. cit.
9. *Montserrat Reporter*, 4 July 1997.
10. Transcript of inquest, 1998 (unpublished).
11. MVO, op. cit.
12. Howard Fergus, *Volcano Song: Poems of an Island in Agony* (Macmillan Caribbean, forthcoming).

Chapter 2 · A Fateful Arc

1. Fred Olsen, *The Last of the Arawaks* (University of Oklahoma Press, 1973), p. 93.
2. R. T. Hill, Report on the volcanic disturbances in the West Indies, *National Geographic Magazine*, vol. 13, 1902.
3. Angelo Heilprin, *Mount Pelée and the Tragedy of Martinique* (J. B. Lippincott, 1903), p. 65.
4. Frank M. Bullard, *Volcanoes of the Earth* (University of Texas Press, 1976), p. 124.
5. Ibid., p. 127.
6. John B. Shepherd and William P. Aspinall, *Earthquake and Volcanic Hazard Assessment and Monitoring in the Commonwealth Caribbean: Current Status and Needs for the Future*, paper given at meeting of experts on hazard mapping in the Caribbean, 1987.
7. Frank Perret, *Volcano-Seismic Crisis at Montserrat, 1933–37* (Carnegie Institution of Washington, 1939), p. 6.
8. C. Harford, 'The Volcanic Evolution of Montserrat using 40AR/39AR Geochronology', *Journal of Volcanology and Geothermal Research*, special issue, forthcoming.
9. P. E. Baker, 'Volcanic Hazards of St Kitts and Montserrat', *Journal of the Geological Society*, vol. 142, 1985, pp. 279–95.
10. Ibid.
11. G. Wadge and M. C. Isaacs, 'Mapping the Volcanic Hazards from Soufrière Hills Volcano, Montserrat, West Indies using an Image Processor', *Journal of the Geological Society*, vol. 145, 1988, pp. 541–51.
12. Nicholas Nugent, 'An Account of "The Sulphur" or "Souffrière" of the Island of Montserrat', *Transactions of the Geological Society*, 1811, pp. 1185–1790.
13. Henry Coleridge, *Six Months in the West Indies* (John Murray, 1826), p. 163.
14. John Davy, *The West Indies before and since Emancipation* (Frank Cass, 1854), p. 429.
15. Howard Fergus, *Montserrat: History of a Caribbean Colony* (Macmillan Caribbean, 1994), p. 5.
16. *Montserrat Herald*, quoted in Perret, op. cit., p. 64.
17. Howard Fergus, ed., *Eruption: Montserrat versus Volcano* (University

of the West Indies, School of Continuing Studies, Montserrat, 1996), p. 21.

18. *Keep Montserrat Alive Magazine*, vol. 1, no. 1–4, 1997, p. 12.
19. Perret, op. cit., p. 62.
20. Ibid., p. vii.
21. Sir Gerald Lenox-Conyngham, 'Montserrat and the West Indian Volcanoes', *Nature*, vol. 139, May 29 1937, p. 907.
22. Fergus, 1996, p. 119.
23. George Abbott, 'The Collapse of the Sea Island Cotton Industry in the West Indies', *Social and Economic Studies*, vol. 13, 1964, pp. 157–87.
24. J. A. George Irish, *Alliouagana in Agony* (J. A. G. Irish, Plymouth, 1974).
25. Shepherd and Aspinall, op. cit.
26. G. Wadge and M. C. Isaacs, *Volcanic Hazards from Soufrière Hills Volcano, Montserrat West Indies: A Report to the Government of Montserrat and the Caribbean Disaster Preparedness and Prevention Project*, 1986.
27. Baker, op. cit., p. 294.
28. International Development Committee, *Montserrat. First Report* (The Stationery Office, 1997), p. 103.
29. Wadge and Isaacs, 1988, p. 551.
30. Wadge and Isaacs, 1986.
31. Ibid., p. 551.
32. Wadge and Isaacs, 1986.
33. Perret, op. cit., p. 2.
34. International Development Committee, op. cit., p. 102.
35. Ibid., p. 128.
36. Development Plan, Government of Montserrat, 1989.
37. J. Panton and R. Archer, *Waiting on the Volcano: A Visit to Montserrat* (Christian Aid and Montserrat Action Committee, 1996), p. 16.

Chapter 3 · Collapsing Domes and Dangerous Uncertainties

1. Cathy Buffonge, *Volcano! A Chronicle of Montserrat's Volcanic Experience, 1995–96* (published privately, 1996).
2. Richard Fiske, 'Volcanologists, Journalists and the Concerned

Local Public: A Tale of Two Crises in the Eastern Caribbean' in *Explosive Volcanism: Inception, Evolution and Hazards* (National Academy Press, 1984), pp. 170–76.

3. International Development Committee, *Montserrat. First Report* (The Stationery Office, 1997), p. 101.
4. Howard Fergus, ed., *Eruption: Montserrat versus Volcano* (University of the West Indies, School of Continuing Studies, Montserrat, 1996), p. 11.
5. Christopher Kilburn, 'Playing with Fire', *The Guardian*, 24 August 1995.
6. B. Voight, 'The Management of Volcano Emergencies: Nevado del Ruiz', in R. Scarpa and R. A. Tilling, eds, *Monitoring and Mitigation of Volcano Hazards* (Springer, 1996), pp. 719–69.
7. J. Panton and R. Archer, *Waiting on the Volcano: A Visit to Montserrat* (Christian Aid and Montserrat Action Committee, 1996), p. 29.
8. International Development Committee, op. cit., p. 180.
9. Buffonge, op. cit., p. 17.
10. International Development Committee, op. cit., p. 127.
11. Montserrat Volcano Observatory, *Assessment of the Status of the Soufrière Hills Volcano, Montserrat and its Hazards*, December 1997.
12. Electronic Evergreen, Internet news group, September 1996.
13. Panton and Archer, op. cit., p. 2.
14. Susan Edgecombe, *Tradewinds Newsletter*, April–May 1997.
15. P. Baxter *et al.*, *Preliminary Assessment of Volcanic Risk on Montserrat* (Montserrat Volcano Observatory, December 1997).
16. International Development Committee, op. cit., p. 114.
17. Ibid., p. 118.
18. Susan Edgecombe, *Tradewinds Newsletter*, September–October 1997.
19. Sir Robert May, *Note by Chief Scientific Adviser* (Montserrat Volcano Observatory, December 1997).
20. Susan Edgecombe, *Tradewinds Newsletter*, March–April 1998.
21. Angelo Heilprin, *Mount Pelée and the Tragedy of Martinique* (J. B. Lippincott, 1903), p. 25.
22. *Montserrat Reporter*, 23 October 1998.
23. Montserrat Volcano Observatory Team, 'The Ongoing Eruption in Montserrat', *Science*, vol. 276, 18 April 1997, pp. 371–2.
24. International Development Committee, op. cit., p. 101.

25. Montserrat Volcano Observatory Team, op. cit.
26. International Development Committee, op. cit., p. 127.
27. B. Voight, 'Volcanologists' Efforts on Montserrat Praiseworthy', *Bulletin Of Volcanology*, vol. 60, 1998, pp. 318–19.

Chapter 4 · 'Refugee in me own Country'

1. Zunky N'Dem, *Seismic Glow*, P.O. Box 9, Plymouth, Montserrat (Arrow Music Ltd, 1996).
2. International Development Committee, *Montserrat. First Report* (The Stationery Office, 1997), p. 80.
3. Ibid., p. 78.
4. Ibid., p. 80.
5. P. Fletcher and R. Groves, 'Natural Disaster', *Inside Housing*, 29 May 1998.
6. J. Panton and R. Archer, *Waiting on the Volcano: A Visit to Montserrat* (Christian Aid and Montserrat Action Committee, 1996), p. 6.
7. *Daily Mirror*, 30 August 1997.
8. International Development Committee, op. cit., p. 45.
9. Don Romeo, *Volcano – People's View* (private video, 1995).
10. Tracey Skelton, *A Place Called Home: Montserratian Senses of Place/ Senses of Self* (unpublished draft paper, 1998).
11. *Appeal to the United Nations High Commission for Refugees by Citizens and Friends of Montserrat* (unpublished, 1997).
12. Sir Kenneth Calman, *Report into the Health & Health Service Implications of the Montserrat Crisis*, London, 1997.
13. International Development Committee, op. cit., p. 201.
14. Ibid., p. 184.

Chapter 5 · From Golden Elephants to White Elephants

1 International Development Committee, *Montserrat. First Report* (The Stationery Office, 1997), p. xv.
2. *The Times*, 26 August 1997.
3. *The Observer*, 24 August 1997.
4. *Caribbean Insight*, September 1997.

5. *The Times*, 26 August 1997.
6. *The Independent*, 25 August 1997.
7. International Development Committee, op. cit., p. 171.
8. Ibid., p. xii.
9. Cathy Buffonge, *Volcano! Book Three. Events in Montserrat during 1997* (published privately, 1997), p. 97.
10. Montserrat Social Survey, Department of Statistics, Ministry of Finance and Economic Development, Montserrat, November 1997.
11. International Development Committee, *Montserrat – Further Developments, Sixth Report* (The Stationery Office, 1998), p. 26.
12. International Development Committee, op. cit., 1997, p. 98.
13. Personal communication.
14. International Development Committee, op. cit., 1998, p. viii.
15. *Montserrat Reporter*, 11 September 1998.
16. *The Times*, 27 August 1997.
17. *Montserrat Reporter*, 4 December 1998.

Chapter 6 · What Went Wrong

1. J. Panton and R. Archer, *Waiting on the Volcano: A Visit to Montserrat* (Christian Aid and Montserrat Action Committee, 1996), p. 32.
2. International Development Committee, *Montserrat. First Report* (The Stationery Office, 1997), p. xxiii.
3. Ibid., p. 11.
4. Foreign Affairs Committee, *Third Special Report* (The Stationery Office, 1998), appendix.
5. International Development Committee, op. cit., p. 96.
6. Ibid., p. 98.
7. *Keep Montserrat Alive Magazine*, 1996, 8 November.
8. *Montserrat Reporter*, 16 July 1997.
9. International Development Committee, op. cit., p. 2.
10. International Development Committee, op. cit., p. xviii.
11. Panton and Archer, op. cit., p. 24.
12. International Development Committee, op. cit., p. 26.
13. Ibid., p. 25.
14. Ibid., p. 22.

15. Ibid., p. 19.
16. *Montserrat Reporter*, 9 October 1998.
17. International Development Committee, op. cit., p. xxx.

Chapter 7 · *The New Diaspora*

1. Stuart Philpott, *West Indian Migration: The Montserrat Case* (The Athlone Press, 1973), p. 20.
2. Ibid., p. 35.
3. E. A. Markham, ed., *Hinterland: Caribbean Poetry from the West Indies & Britain* (Bloodaxe Books, 1989), p. 199.
4. E. A. Markham, *Misapprehensions* (Anvil Press, 1995), p. 53.
5. J. Panton and R. Archer, *Waiting on the Volcano: A Visit to Montserrat* (Christian Aid and Montserrat Action Committee, 1996), p. 8.
6. Government of Montserrat, Department of Statistics, 1998.
7. Panton and Archer, op. cit., p. 10.
8. International Development Committee, *Montserrat. First Report* (The Stationery Office, 1997), p. 136.
9. Ibid., p. xxviii.
10. Ibid., p. 136.
11. International Development Committee, *Montserrat – Further Developments. Sixth Report* (The Stationery Office, 1998), p. 3.
12. House of Commons debate on Montserrat, 18 February 1998, *Hansard*, p. 1008.
13. International Development Committee, op. cit., 1997, p. 203.
14. Ibid., p. 131.
15. Ibid.
16. House of Commons debate on Montserrat, op. cit., p. 1016.
17. Gertrude Shotte, *The Educational Experiences of Relocated Montserratian Students in the UK: From 1995 to Present* (unpublished MA thesis, University of London, 1998).
18. *Appeal to the United Nations High Commission for Refugees by Citizens and Friends of Montserrat* (unpublished, 1997), p. 27.
19. Caribbean News Agency, 22 August 1997.
20. *Out of the Mouths of Babes*, poems edited by Gertrude Shotte (Kinsale Primary School, Montserrat, 1996).

Chapter 8 · Seeds for Change

1. George Drower, *Britain's Dependent Territories* (Dartmouth Publishing, 1992), p. 44.
2. Gordon Lewis, *The Growth of the Modern West Indies* (Monthly Review Press, 1969), p. 137.
3. Howard Fergus, *Montserrat: History of a Caribbean Colony* (Macmillan Caribbean, 1994), p. 213.
4. Helen Hintjens, 'Governance Options in Europe's Caribbean Dependencies', *Round Table*, vol. 344, 1997, pp. 533–47.
5. J. Panton and R. Archer, *Waiting on the Volcano: A Visit to Montserrat* (Christian Aid and Montserrat Action Committee, 1996), p. 18.
6. *Montserrat Reporter*, 7 May 1999.
7. Ibid.
8. Richard Fisher *et al.*, *Volcanoes: Crucibles of Change* (Princeton University Press, 1998), p. 243.
9. Bonham Richardson, *Economy and Environment in the Caribbean* (The Press, University of the West Indies, 1997), p. 204.
10. Angelo Heilprin, *The Tower of Pelée* (J. B. Lippincott, 1904), p. 11.
11. Press Association, 30 November 1996.
12. Interview on ZJB radio, 29 April 1998.
13. Patrick Chamoiseau, *Texaco* (Granta, 1997), p. 164.
14. Patrick Leigh Fermor, *The Violins of Saint-Jacques* (John Murray, 1953), p. 131.
15. Howard Fergus, *Eruption: Montserrat versus Volcano* (University of the West Indies, School of Continuing Studies, Montserrat, 1996), p. 121.

Bibliography

BOOKS

Buffonge, Cathy, *Volcano! A Chronicle of Montserrat's Volcanic Experience, 1995–96* (published privately, 1996)

Buffonge, Cathy, *Volcano! Book Two. Into the Second Year* (published privately, 1997)

Buffonge, Cathy, *Volcano! Book Three. Events in Montserrat during 1997* (published privately, 1997)

Bullard, Frank M., *Volcanoes of the Earth* (University of Texas Press, 1976)

Caribbean Islands Handbook (Trade and Travel Publications, 1995)

Chamoiseau, Patrick, *Texaco* (Granta, 1997)

Coleridge, Henry, *Six Months in the West Indies* (John Murray, 1826)

Crewe, Quentin, *Touch the Happy Isles* (Michael Joseph, 1987)

Davy, John, *The West Indies before and since Emancipation* (Frank Cass, 1854)

Decker, Robert and Decker, Barbara, *Volcanoes* (W. H. Freeman & Co., 1979)

Drower, George, *Britain's Dependent Territories* (Dartmouth Publishing, 1992)

Fergus, Howard, *William H. Bramble: His Life and Times* (University Centre, University of the West Indies, Montserrat, 1983)

Fergus, Howard, *Montserrat, Emerald Isle of the Caribbean* (Macmillan Caribbean, 1983)

Fergus, Howard, *Montserrat: History of a Caribbean Colony* (Macmillan Caribbean, 1994)

Fergus, Howard, ed., *Eruption: Montserrat versus Volcano* (University of the West Indies, School of Continuing Studies, Montserrat, 1996)

Fergus, Howard, *Gallery Montserrat* (Canoe Press, 1996)

Fergus, Howard, *Volcano Song: Poems of an Island in Agony* (Macmillan Caribbean, May 2000)

Fermor, Patrick Leigh, *The Violins of Saint-Jacques* (John Murray, 1953)

Fisher, Richard *et al.*, *Volcanoes: Crucibles of Change* (Princeton University Press, 1998)

Fiske, Richard, 'Volcanologists, Journalists and the Concerned Local Public: A Tale of Two Crises in the Eastern Caribbean', in *Explosive Volcanism: Inception, Evolution and Hazards* (National Academy Press, 1984), pp. 170–76

Heilprin, Angelo, *Mount Pelée and the Tragedy of Martinique* (J. B. Lippincott, 1903)

Heilprin, Angelo, *The Tower of Pelée* (J. B. Lippincott, 1904)

Irish, J. A. George, *Alliouagana in Agony* (J. A. G. Irish, Plymouth, 1974)

Markham, E. A., ed., *Hinterland: Caribbean Poetry from the West Indies & Britain* (Bloodaxe Books, 1989)

Markham, E. A., *Misapprehensions* (Anvil Press, 1995)

Olsen, Fred, *The Last of the Arawaks* (University of Oklahoma Press, 1973)

Perret, Frank, *The Eruption of Mt Pelée 1929–32* (Carnegie Institution of Washington, 1935)

Perret, Frank, *Volcano-Seismic Crisis at Montserrat, 1933–37* (Carnegie Institution of Washington, 1939)

Philpott, Stuart, *West Indian Migration: The Montserrat Case* (The Athlone Press, 1973)

Richardson, Bonham, *Economy and Environment in the Caribbean* (The Press, University of the West Indies, 1997)

Scarpa, R. and Tilling, R. A., eds, *Monitoring and Mitigation of Volcano Hazards* (Springer, 1996)

Wheeler, Marion M., *Montserrat West Indies: A Chronological History* (Montserrat National Trust, 1988)

Bibliography

ARTICLES, PAPERS AND REPORTS

Abbott, George, 'The Collapse of the Sea Island Cotton Industry in the West Indies', *Social and Economic Studies*, vol. 13, 1964, pp. 157–87

Appeal to the United Nations High Commission for Refugees by Citizens and Friends of Montserrat (unpublished, 1997)

Baker, P. E., 'Volcanic Hazards on St Kitts and Montserrat', *Journal of the Geological Society*, vol. 142, 1985, pp. 279–95

Baxter, P. et al., *Preliminary Assessment of Volcanic Risk on Montserrat* (Montserrat Volcano Observatory, December 1997)

Calman, Sir Kenneth, *Report into the Health & Health Service Implications of the Montserrat Crisis*, London, 1997

Foreign Affairs Committee, *Third Special Report* (The Stationery Office, 1998)

Harford, C., 'The Evolution of Montserrat using 40AR/39AR Geochronology', *Journal of Volcanology and Geothermal Research*, special issue, forthcoming

Hill, R. T., 'Report on the Volcanic Disturbances in the West Indies', *National Geographic Magazine*, vol. 13, 1902

Hintjens, Helen, 'Governance Options in Europe's Caribbean Dependencies', *Round Table*, vol. 344, 1997, pp. 533–47

International Development Committee, *Montserrat. First Report* (The Stationery Office, 1997)

International Development Committee, *First Special Report, Government Response to the First Report from the Committee, Session 1997–98, Montserrat* (The Stationery Office, 1998)

International Development Committee, *Montserrat – Further Developments. Sixth Report* (The Stationery Office, 1998)

Kilburn, Christopher, 'Playing with Fire', *The Guardian*, 24 August 1995

Lenox-Conyngham, Sir Gerald, 'Montserrat and the West Indian Volcanoes', *Nature*, vol. 139, 1937

May, Sir Robert, *Note by Chief Scientific Adviser* (Montserrat Volcano Observatory, December 1997)

McElroy, Jerome and de Albuquerque, Klaus, 'The Economic Impact of Retirement Tourism in Montserrat: Some Provisional Evidence', *Social and Economic Studies*, vol. 41, 1992, pp. 127–52

[207]

Montserrat Social Survey, Department of Statistics, Ministry of Finance and Economic Development, Montserrat, November 1997

Montserrat Volcano Observatory, daily reports, 1995–9

Montserrat Volcano Observatory Team, 'The Ongoing Eruption in Montserrat', *Science*, vol. 276, 18 April 1997, pp. 371–2

Montserrat Volcano Observatory, Government of Montserrat, *Pyroclastic Flow Activity on June 25 1997* (MVO Special Report 3, 1997)

Montserrat Volcano Observatory, Government of Montserrat, *Daily Reports, June 1997* (MVO Open File Report 97/6, 1997)

Montserrat Volcano Observatory, *Assessment of the Status of the Soufrière Hills Volcano, Montserrat and its Hazards*, December 1997

Montserrat Volcano Observatory, Government of Montserrat, *Dome-building Eruptions* (MVO Open File Report 98/15, 1998)

Nanton, Philip, *Montserrat Replacement Airport Study*, London, 1998

Nugent, Nicholas, 'An Account of "The Sulphur" or "Souffrière" of the Island of Montserrat', *Transactions of the Geological Society*, 1811, pp. 1185–1790

Panton, J. and Archer, R., *Waiting on the Volcano: A Visit to Montserrat* (Christian Aid and Montserrat Action Committee, 1996)

Partnership for Progress and Prosperity (Foreign and Commonwealth Office, 1999)

Physical Development Plan for North Montserrat (Physical Planning Unit, Montserrat, 1997)

Shepherd, John B. and Aspinall, William P., *Earthquake and Volcanic Hazard Assessment and Monitoring in the Commonwealth Caribbean: Current Status and Needs for the Future*, paper given at meeting of experts on hazard mapping in the Caribbean, 1987

Shotte, Gertrude, *The Educational Experiences of Relocated Montserratian Students in the UK: From 1995 to Present* (unpublished MA thesis, University of London, 1998)

Skelton, Tracey, *A Place Called Home: Montserratian Senses of Place/Senses of Self* (unpublished draft paper, 1998)

Skinner, Jonathan, 'The Eruption of Chances Peak, Montserrat, and the Narrative Containment of Risk', in *Risk Revisited*, ed. Pat Caplan (Pluto Press, 1999)

Sustainable Development Plan, 1998

Thorndike, Tony, *No End to Empire* (Staffordshire Polytechnic, 1988)

Voight, B., 'The Management of Volcano Emergencies: Nevado del

Bibliography

Ruiz', in Scarpa, R. and Tilling, R. A., eds, *Monitoring and Mitigation of Volcano Hazards* (Springer, 1996)

Voight, B., 'Volcanologists' Efforts on Montserrat Praiseworthy', *Bulletin of Volcanology*, vol. 60, 1998, pp. 318–19

Wadge, G. and Isaacs, M. C., 'Mapping the Volcanic Hazards from Soufrière Hills Volcano, Montserrat, West Indies using an Image Processor', *Journal of the Geological Society*, vol. 145, 1988, pp. 541–51

Wadge, G. and Isaacs, M. C., *Volcanic Hazards from Soufrière Hills Volcano, Montserrat West Indies: A Report to the Government of Montserrat and the Caribbean Disaster Preparedness and Prevention Project*, 1986

NEWSPAPERS AND PERIODICALS

Caribbean Insight
Caribbean News Agency
Daily Mirror
Daily Telegraph
The Guardian
Hansard
The Independent
Inside Housing
Keep Montserrat Alive Magazine (KMAM)
Montserrat Newsletter
Montserrat Reporter
Nature
Outlet Newspaper, Antigua
Press Association
Science
SeismiCity News, Montserrat
The Times
Tradewinds Newsletter

VIDEOS

Romeo, Don, *Volcano – People's View* (private video, 1995)
Lea, David, *The Price of Paradise*, vols 1–6, 1995–1999

Index